DATE DUE

JAN 0 3 1991	
ILL 4-24-91	
ILL 7-3-91	
NOV 1 2 1991	
DEC 2 1991	
DEC 1 8 1991	
SEP 2 5 1992	
ILL 01-04-93	
ILL 7-12-93	
ILL 12-01-93	
SEP. 2 7 1994	
APR 1 9 1995	

America B.C.

AMERICA
B.C.

Ancient Settlers
in the New World

BARRY FELL

Newly Revised and Updated Edition

POCKET BOOKS

New York   London   Toronto   Sydney   Tokyo

Newly Revised and Updated Edition

FRONTISPIECE
Venus of the snows, the mother goddess of the American Celts, lying as we found her, on a pine-clad slope of the Green Mountains. Inscriptions on the ruins of nearby temples give her Celtic name as Byanu: circa 500 B.C. See page 244.
Joseph D. Germano

POCKET BOOKS, a division of Simon & Schuster, Inc.
1230 Avenue of the Americas, New York, N.Y. 10020

Published by arrangement with Quadrangle/
The New York Times Book Co.
Library of Congress Catalog Card Number: 75-36269

ISBN: 0-671-67974-0

Pocket Books trade paperback printing January, 1986

10 9 8 7 6 5 4 3

POCKET and colophon are registered trademarks
of Simon & Schuster, Inc.

Printed in the U.S.A.

Contents

PRECOLUMBIAN VOYAGES AND SETTLEMENTS, 5500 B.C.–A.D. 225

5500–5000 B.C.

Earliest of the inferred trans-Atlantic crossings, achieved by the Maritime Archaic Red-Paint Cultures of western Scandinavia and northwest Europe. The archeological remains of these people, carbon-dated in Norway to 5500 B.C., are very similar to those of the Maritime Archaic Red-Paint people of Labrador and New England, carbon-dated back to 5000 B.C. On both sides of the North Atlantic these peoples operated sea-going wooden vessels and used similar fishing devices for hunting swordfish and marine mammals.

4500 B.C.

Oldest known dated examples of dolmens appear in Europe, including Ireland.

3200–1000 B.C.

Cup-and-ring petroglyphs are cut in rocks of Europe, notably in Britain and in North America; also elsewhere. Although the American examples have not yet been dated, they appear to be the work of the same sea-going peoples.

3000–1000 B.C.

Megalith builders active in western Europe, including Iberia and Britain, erecting dolmens, stone chambers, men-a-tol, solstice stones, and related monuments. Some American examples may date from this era. Gadelic Ogam inscriptions occur and show that Celtic language and religion had already reached both sides of the North Atlantic.

2000 B.C.

Sumerian political power wanes and is extinguished in Mesopotamia, under the assault of Semitic invaders. In South America Sumerian colonists appear, perhaps as refugees from their Mediterranean homeland, to establish animal husbandry and plant cultivation among the native Andean peoples of the Altiplano.

2000 B.C. on

The Old Copper Culture of north Michigan and Lake Superior region, carbon-dated to this era, with some 5,000 copper mines in operation on and near the Copper Peninsula. Millions of pounds of copper extracted and apparently exported abroad, as inferred by researches of mining engineers.

1700 B.C.

Nordic navigator-traders arrive in Ontario from Scandinavia, bringing woven textiles as barter material for Canadian copper ingots, shipped back to Scandinavia. At Peterborough site in Ontario they leave a pictorial record, annotated in Tifinag script, an early Norse language, reporting their religious, astronomical, calendric, and trading interests, in their contacts with the Algonquians. Ogam and Celtic elements also present. In Ireland, the Beaker People invade and bring Celtic speech (See MacAlister, 1977).

1500 B.C. on

Iberian, Celtic, and Egyptian contacts with Indian nations of the northeast. Much of the extant Algonquian vocabulary related to law, medicine, and navigation is derived from these contacts, and overseas scripts, notably the Basque syllabary and Egyptian hieroglyphs, probably acquired from this time onward.

300–100 B.C.

Traders from Carthage visit North America and Caribbean, bringing coinage of the issues of Punic Sicily and North Africa, the work of Greek artists, modeled on the issues of Syracuse, later bringing also low-value bronze coins of other Mediterranean states. Similar coins, often perforated with a hole for use as an ornament, likewise carried to the noncivilized Balearic Islands.

250 B.C.

Celtiberian and Ogam inscriptions on bone and stone artifacts buried with skeletons of both Amerind and Europoid types at sites in eastern Tennessee, and radio-carbon-dated to this era, = Early Woodland Indian.

A.D. 1–200

Carthaginian civil calendar, lettered in degenerate late Punic script, interred with Mayan and other inscribed ceramic objects in Mayan temple and pyramid structures at Comalcalco, Mexico.

A.D. 225–625

Hebrew-inscribed stone at Bat Creek, Tennessee, buried with skeletons and wooden artifacts, now radio-carbon-dated to this era, having previously been considered to be Cherokee and modern by Smithsonian excavators. Ancient Hebrew coins also found at other sites in southeastern states.

PRECOLUMBIAN VOYAGES AND SETTLEMENTS, A.D. 225–A.D. 1450

A.D. ca. 225

Roman shipwreck of Cunabara Bay, near Rio de Janeiro, marked by two sets of tumbled heaps of amphorae of this date lying on the sea floor. Specialists in ancient Roman ceramics point to the port of Zilis, Morocco, as the place of origin of the shipment. A similar find of amphorae also on the seabed off Honduras.

A.D. 375

Roman ship wrecked off Beverly, Massachusetts, the purser's chest containing then current coinage of the reigns of four emperors who ruled in the mid–late fourth century; these coins are now being cast ashore by wave action.

A.D. ca. 500

Inscribed ceramic tablet bearing Christian image and Libyan script, buried in Mayan temple at Comalcalco, Mexico, with numerous other Mayan inscriptions.

A.D. 500

Christian Celtic traders and monks from Ireland and Hebridean islands reach North America and leave Ogam religious and other texts cut in rock faces and in caves, in various states, notably West Virginia.

A.D. 800–1200

Moslem Arab voyages both trans-Pacific and trans-Atlantic, evidenced by Kufi Moslem rock-cut texts, especially in western desert states of North America. Also Arabic nautical, legal, and religious vocabulary acquired by Amerind languages.

A.D. 982

Viking discovery of Greenland; exploration and settlement begins.

A.D. 1000

Viking discovery, exploration, and settlement of Labrador and Newfoundland (Vinland settlements).

A.D. 1050 on

Vikings introduce cattle and other farm animals into Greenland, which, at this era, was partly free from ice. Churches erected at various places and parishes.

A.D. 1124

Pope Callixtus II raises Greenland to the ecclesiastical status of Bishopric, with a cathedral at Gardar. Viking church tower at Newport, Rhode Island, built about this time.

A.D. 1250

Christian Viking settlers in Greenland number about 4,000 souls.

A.D. 1250

West African voyagers present in Caribbean. In earth carbon-dated to this epoch, Smithsonian investigators have found two male African skeletons in the Virgin Islands. African-related artifacts found in Mexico probably date to about this time.

A.D. 1206 on

Letters addressed to the Archbishop of Nidaros, Norway, by various Popes, regarding the status of the Greenland Christians and their tithes. Among the extant correspondence in the Vatican Library are letters from Popes Innocent III (A.D. 1206), John XXI (dated 1276), Nicholas III (dated 1279), Martin IV (dated 1282).

A.D. 1310–11

Abubakiri, King of Mali, leads two fleets, totaling 400 vessels, to explore the Atlantic, and none returns to Africa.

A.D. 1362

Thirty Norse explorers in Minnesota attacked by Indians. A record of the event recorded in Middle Norwegian runes on the so-called Kensington runestone (now determined to be genuine after exhaustive research since 1986).

A.D. 1396

Prince Henry Sinclair, Earl of Orkney, leads the last Norse-Celtic Atlantic Expedition, landing in New England. Two years later, in 1398, a member of the expedition, Sir John Gunn, dies at Westford, Massachusetts, where his rock-cut memorial and coat of arms may still be seen.

A.D. 1448

Pope Nicholas V, in a letter addressed to the Church leaders in Norway, gives expression to his concern at reports that the Christians of Greenland had been attacked by a fleet "from the Neighboring shores of the Pagans" (i.e., Labrador), and their homes and churches devastated by fire and sword, leaving only nine parish churches intact.

A.D. 1450

Basque fishing fleets at about this time active on the North American coast and bringing back to Europe specimens of the tusks of the narwhal for the royal natural history cabinets.

A.D. 1492

First voyage of Columbus, with Basque pilots.

Acknowledgments

To my language teachers of forty years ago, Mairi and Anna ni Asgail, Alec mac Coinneach and members of Clan Macleod in Assynt, where the cadence of the Gaelic lent enchantment to summer days and winter nights; to fellow students at Edinburgh University who introduced me to the megalithic monuments; to army comrades who added Welsh wit and Irish oaths to further enliven a manner of life at times too lively for comfort; to my predecessor of a century ago, Professor Walter J. Fewkes of the Museum of Comparative Zoology who (curiously) passed from the study of seastars to establish the archeology of the Pueblo peoples; to Professor A. W. Crompton and my colleagues at Harvard who sanctioned a repetition of the Fewkes experiment; to Professor Norman Totten, who aided and abetted these studies; to Peter Garfall, who leavened photography with other talents, in the field and in the laboratory; to Joseph Germano who prepared some black and white photographs and color slides, and who with Haris Lessios, photographed Aegean scripts for me; to John Williams, who accompanied me on unnumbered journeys, covered some 11,000 miles by road, and a further 800 miles on foot over the mountains, to become expert at finding buried inscriptions in remote places, and a good-humored partner in discovery, both in the field and among the dusty books and manuscripts of Harvard College Library; to James P. Whittall, II, whose unrivalled knowledge of the megalithic archeology of Portugal and Spain brought new insights to the American scene; to the Portuguese archeologists whose knowledge and personal kindnesses to Jim Whittall during his 1975 expedition illuminated our New England findings, in particular to Dr. Fernando Lanhas, Director of Archeology at the Museum of Ethnology, Porto; to Dr. Philine Kalb, Director of the Instituto Arqueologico Alemao, Lisbon; to Dr. Maria Maia of the Belem Museum; to Dr. Castro Nunes of Coimbra; to Jorge Pinho and Mario Varela Gomez of the Belem Museum, Lisbon; for access to the data gained on his own researches in Spain and Portugal, as well as in New England, I am doubly indebted to James P. Whittall, as also for numerous discussions of shared problems and for his day-to-day cooperation, in the course of which I came to respect him as a world authority on megalithic architecture; to my fellow linguists Professor Linus Brunner of Sankt Gallen, Marge Landsberg of Haifa, Dr. Reuel Lochore of Auckland, and Erik Reinert of Oslo and Harvard; to Ruth K. Hanner of Kauai, generous sponsor of the Epigraphic Society and indefatigable investigator of Pacific epigraphy; to Professor George Carter of Texas, who alerted us to a whole forgotten literature on American inscriptions, and who led us to Gloria Farley, whose epigraphic discoveries are unparalleled for their importance in understanding the ancient voyagers who ascended the Mississippi and its branches; to Malcolm Pearson who, with William Goodwin, first began the photographic study of New England's megalithic chambers and rock inscriptions; to Robert E. Stone, director of the megalithic site at Mystery Hill, New Hampshire, who placed every relevant piece of data at my disposal, and who has lived on the site these twenty years; to Osborn Stone, and to Dorothy Stone who has been a thoughtful hostess throughout busy days; to Midge Chandler, Betty Sincerbeaux, Professor Thomas Lee, Andrew Rothovius, Dr. Clyde Keeler, Donald Buchanan, Gertrude Johnson and Arlene St. Laurent, all of whom aided us in various ways; to Byron E. Dix, megalithic astronomer, whose contributions to solving the "root-cellar" problem have been of major importance; to Professor Ch. Chhabra, epigrapher and Sanskritist, who brought fresh insights to our understanding of the Celtic fertility cult; to Gerhard Kraus, who put us in touch with Spanish archeologists and encouraged our studies from afar; to Dr. Antonio Beltran Martinez and the authorities of the Museo Canario, for copies of Libyan and other early inscriptions found at the Canary Islands; to Salvatore Trento for data on incised pottery he is excavating in Majorca; to Carol Hunt of the Putnam Museum, Davenport, Iowa, for photographs of the ancient steles in that museum; to Bernard Leman and David Oedel, who aided me in ransacking the libraries for obscure vocabularies and dictionaries of half-forgotten tongues; to Sentiel Rommel, who recreates ancient astronomical instruments from my decipherments, and who was my host and companion on a tour of the Long Island Sound antiquities; to Dr. Elizabeth Giddings and Mrs. Millicent House of the Haffenreffer Museum of Anthropology, Brown University, who aided our work in Rhode Island; to Mr. and Mrs. W. J. Cowell, our guides in Connecticut; to the librarians of the Widener Library, Harvard College and the Robbins Library, Arlington, Massachusetts, for many aids; to Harold S. Gladwin, that far-seeing archeologist whose weekly telephone calls and letters of wise advice and encouragement were to us both an honor and a joy; to Lydia Wunsch and Gerald Heslinga who brought artists' skills to our reports; to Dr. Clifford Kaye, who aided us with information on glacial and sea-level problems; to the kind landowners of Vermont who permitted us to study the monuments on their properties—and who, until the antiquities are safely protected, cannot at this time be named; and especially to my two advisors in writing this book, Edward Gruson, who is an inspiring editor, and my wife Rene, who creates the environment in which books are apt to be written.

To these good friends and others who contributed their knowledge and time I offer my grateful thanks.

After the text of the book had already gone to press a number of important new finds came to my attention, in some cases through correspondents who had seen press reports on the New England inscriptions. Additional illustrations and brief captions have been incorporated, but fuller details will be given in the *Occasional Publications* of the Epigraphic Society. I wish to thank the following colleagues through whose efforts the material was collected and photographed in time for inclusion here: Gloria Farley, Dr. Edward J. Pullman, Gertrude Johnson, James P. Whittall, Dr. Clyde Keeler, Weldon W. Stout, and Malcolm Pearson. To Ruth K. Hanner, who materially supported the field program of the Epigraphic Society, the gratitude of all epigraphers is due.

Museum of Comparative Zoology
Harvard University
November 1975

Foreword

America B.C. was originally written to commemorate the Bicentennial, in 1976. Over the intervening years many new discoveries have been made. Now we are approaching the Quincentennial of Columbus' first voyage, and the time is ripe for an updated version of the book. I wish to thank all those who have contributed information and photographs, and especially the Epigraphic Society in whose *Occasional Publications* fuller details can be found.

Harvard University and
  The Epigraphic Society
6625 Bamburgh Drive
San Diego, CA 92117
January 1989

America B.C.

1

An American Enigma and Its Solution

TWO centuries of independence, two hundred years of national awareness, these are the underlying themes of countless festivities now in progress or planned throughout fifty American states. The world at large pauses a moment to reflect upon the prodigy that grew from the thirteen rebellious colonies when George III lost his American domains.

But wait a bit. There is more to America's past than appears upon the surface. A strange unrest is apparent among many of the younger historians and archeologists of the colleges and universities, a sense that somehow a very large slice of America's past has mysteriously vanished from our public records. For how else can we explain the ever-swelling tally of puzzling ancient inscriptions now being reported from nearly all parts of the United States, Canada, and Latin America?

The inscriptions are written in various European and Mediterranean languages in alphabets that date from 2,500 years ago, and they speak not only of visits by ancient ships, but also of permanent colonies of Celts, Basques, Libyans, and even Egyptians. They occur on buried temples, on tablets and on gravestones and on cliff faces. From some of them we infer that the colonists intermarried with the Amerindians, and so their descendants still live here today.

There was once a time when such finds were attributed to the misguided folly of uprooted colonists from Europe, to forgers or cranks fabricating tradition for a society that has none. But skepticism changed to bewilderment when it was discovered that American inscriptions, some of them known for a century or more, turn out to have been written in

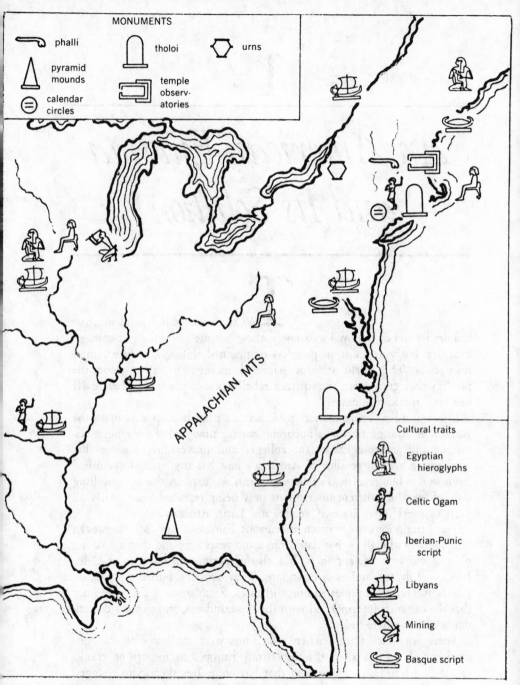

MONUMENTS

phalli	tholoi	urns
pyramid mounds	temple observatories	
calendar circles		

APPALACHIAN MTS

Cultural traits

Egyptian hieroglyphs

Celtic Ogam

Iberian-Punic script

Libyans

Mining

Basque script

European and North African cultural interfaces and colonies, circa 800 B.C. For sailing routes, see map on pages 106–107.

ancient scripts of a type only recently deciphered in Europe or North Africa. Thus the truth has slowly come to light, ancient history is inscribed upon the bedrock and buried stone buildings of America, and the only hands that could have inscribed it were those of ancient people. America, as we now realize, is a treasure house of records of man's achievement upon the high seas in bygone ages. Even more so are our inscribed rocks and tablets a heritage from a forgotten era of colonization. They tell us of settlers who came from the Old World and who remained to become founding fathers of some of the Amerindian nations.

These ancient writings can easily be classified into some half dozen styles, each now known to be associated with one or other of several ancient peoples whose languages have been in part recovered. New inscriptions are being discovered almost every day, from localities thousands of miles apart, usually under circumstances that preclude any possibility of fraud.

This book gives the plain facts about the inscribed stones together with an explanation of how the messages are being deciphered, and what they tell us about the people who wrote them and how they came to be in America some two thousand to three thousand years ago. But it is also my hope that something more than just the plain facts of the research may find its way into these pages. Something of the simple joys of shared discoveries (for what use is there in finding something new if there is no one to tell about it?); something of the good companionship of the men and women who contribute so much of their time and knowledge to exploring our back-country hills or searching the cliffs of offshore islets for long-forgotten carvings made by ancient mariners; and something, too, of our occasional disappointments, for it has not been an easy road all the way and sometimes it has demanded more than the usual modicum of good humor to temper patience with tenacity.

These remarkable facts began to come to light in 1975 in the course of an archeological survey of New Hampshire and Vermont. Numerous inscriptions among the ruins attest the vitality of a Celtic civilization in pagan times and tell a wonderful story of how European traders lived during the Bronze and Iron Ages. Our first season's work yielded only hints of the fate of the Celtic settlements here, but this book relates what we have been able to find out of the first thousand years or so of their presence in North America.

About three thousand years ago bands of roving Celtic mariners crossed the North Atlantic to discover, and then to colonize, North America. They came from Spain and Portugal, by way of the Canary Islands, sailing the trade winds as Columbus also was to do long afterward. The advantage of this route is that the winds favor a crossing from east to

Two generations ago Edward Read was plowing his property near White River, Vermont, when the earth gave way beneath him, and he discovered an underground passage leading into this chamber. Here John Williams examines the interior. Deeply inscribed letters on a buried lintel later disclosed that the chamber is a small temple dedicated to the sun god Bel. *Peter J. Garfall*

west, but for Celts accustomed to a temperate climate it had the one drawback that it led them to the tropical West Indies, no place for northerners. So although their landfall lay in the Caribbean, it was on the rocky coasts and mountainous hinterlands of New England that most of these wanderers finally landed, there to establish a new European kingdom which they called *Iargalon,* "Land Beyond the Sunset." They built villages and temples, raised Druids' circles and buried their dead in marked graves. They were still there in the time of Julius Caesar, as is attested by an inscribed monolith on which the date of celebration of the great Celtic festival of Beltane (Mayday) is given in Roman numerals appropriate to the reformed Julian calendar introduced in 46 B.C.

In the wake of the Celtic pioneers came the Phoenician traders of Spain, men from Cadiz who spoke the Punic tongue, but wrote it in the peculiar style of lettering known as Iberian script. Although some of these traders seem to have settled only on the coast, and then only temporarily, leaving a few engraved stones to mark their visits or record their claims of territorial annexation, other Phoenicians remained here and, together with Egyptian miners, became part of the Wabanaki tribe of New England. Further south, Basque sailors came to Pennsylvania and established a temporary settlement there, leaving however no substantial monuments other than grave markers bearing their names. Further south still, Libyan and Egyptian mariners entered the Mississippi from the Gulf of Mexico, penetrating inland to Iowa and the Dakotas, and westward along the Arkansas and Cimarron Rivers, to leave behind inscribed records of their presence. Norse and Basque visitors reached the Gulf of St. Lawrence, introducing various mariners' terms into the language of the northern Algonquian Indians. Descendants of these visitors are also to be found apparently among the Amerindian tribes, several of which employ dialects derived in part from the ancient tongues of Phoenicia and North Africa.

The Celts seem first to have settled near the mouths of rivers of New England, as at North Salem on a branch of the Merrimac River in southern New Hampshire. At some time they ascended the Connecticut River, sailing as far north as Quechee, Vermont, where a western branch of the river joins the main stream through a precipitous gorge. Attracted doubtless by the seclusion of the uplands beyond the gorge, the Celts turned westward and colonized the hanging valleys of the Green Mountains. Quechee, incidentally, perpetuates the ancient Gaulish pronunciation of the Celtic word *quithe,* meaning chasm or pit, and the river that flows through the gorge, the Ottauquechee, similarly is an Amerindian rendering of the Celtic name meaning Waters-of-the-Chasm.

In the secluded valleys and on the hilltops, the priests (or Druids) erected the temples and circles of standing stones required by their religious beliefs, using, like their European cousins, the great stone boulders left upon the land by the retreating glaciers at the end of the ice age. On these stones they cut their inscriptions, using the ancient Celtic alphabet called *Ogam.*

In Europe the Celts doubtless did the same, but when Christianity came to the Celts the priests caused all the ancient pagan inscriptions to be erased, replaced by Christian Ogam, or left blank, while all the offending fertility paraphernalia were totally destroyed.

Not so in America. Here Christianity never came to the Celts, their old pagan inscriptions remain intact, and a host of giant stone phalluses char-

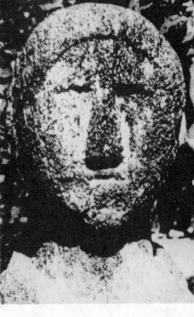

acterize the places of worship. Here we may yet see and read the ancient inscriptions of the rite of initiation to manhood, and see the sites of ritual worship of the powers of fertility in nature. In short, we have preserved in North America the oldest phases of religious thought and action of European man, of which only the merest traces have survived in Europe itself.

The consequences of these discoveries for archeology and history are, of course, immeasurable. As one historian, Professor Norman Totten, has pointed out, it means that 2,500 years of American prehistory must now be transferred to history; for history begins when writing begins, and we now have the oldest written documents of our nation, and the names of the men who wrote them. For archeology a whole new view is called for. During the past hundred years the belief that no European settled America before Leif Eriksson or Columbus has grown from an hypothesis into a firmly rooted dogma.

For European archeology, where more liberal views as to the antiquity of the Celts have been developing in recent years, the new discoveries in America may be expected to bring a flow of information on such topics as the dates of construction of megalithic buildings, as well as on the purposes for which they were used, and the gods whose rites were once performed within their precincts. For in as much as no Christian priests came to expunge the pagan inscriptions from the megalithic monuments of New England, America's surviving records may well supply the key to discovering who built the corresponding structures in Europe, where no trace remains of inscriptions made before the coming of Christianity.

When we reflect upon the events of the past two centuries of America's nationhood, we perceive that the course of British and American history is shaped like the letter Y. The lower upright of the Y represents the common stream of Europe's cultural heritage, reading upward until we reach the fork of the Y, which represents 1776. Thereafter America and Britain part company, each to pursue a separate path toward whatever destiny may lie in store.

Now it is an indisputable fact that not only has the history of the two

Early colonists in eastern America, as they saw themselves. Above, right, a Celtic portrait from Stark County, Ohio. This sculpture represents Bel, the sun god, and his Afro hairstyle symbolizes radiant energy. Right, a maritime Celt as depicted by a sculptor of ancient time; this stolid portrait still stands in the open air in Vannes, Brittany, and a similar head, excavated in New England, is now in the Peabody Museum, Salem, Mass. Left, an olive-skinned Libyan, as seen by a mosaic artist of Roman Tunisia. The Libyans were the ancient world's most brilliant navigators and explorers. The Zuni people of the southwest descend in part from ancient Libyan sailors, whose language they have preserved in a modified form to this day. **Dr. Clyde Keeler, Joseph D. Germano**

English-speaking nations bifurcated like the arms of the Y, but also the *teaching of history* in the schools and colleges of the two nations has followed a similar divergence. British children continue to learn the history of Britain from the remotest stone-age era, through the Celts, the Roman invaders, the Saxon invasions, the Norman invasion, and so on through the middle ages into the present era. American children, on the other hand, use history books which (to judge by the examples that teachers have given me) begin with an account of the benighted state of Europe in 1492 and lead directly, as you turn the first page, to a portrait of Christopher Columbus, followed by an account of his daring exploits and discoveries.

Here you have in a nutshell the difference in approach to history as presented in the schools that most people attend on either side of the Atlantic. For the European, history begins in vague, remote, and romantic mists of antiquity and slowly emerges into the brighter illumination of more recent time. For the American, history begins with the crash of cymbals as great and famous men stride onto the stage, fully documented or so nearly so that one might be pardoned for thinking that their birth certificates and social security cards are stored in the national archives in Washington. Two English humorists, in the book *1066 and All That,* suggested some years ago that there are only two dates in history that British people can remember—55 B.C., when Julius Caesar landed in Britain, and 1066, when William the Conqueror conquered. It is their mock-serious thesis that since the common man in Britain remembers no other event well enough to date it, no other events exist in British history! I suspect that an analogous satire on American history would have discovered essentially the same thing, except that the two dates every American remembers are 1492 and 1776. Hence there can be no American history prior to 1492, *quod erat demonstrandum.*

Of course the argument is false, but it does contrive to point out, in a blundering way, the nature of certain profound differences in the view of history as seen from the two sides of the Atlantic. Now let me restate the matter, this time with chapter and verse, and this time in earnest.

The year is 1712. Queen Anne rules in England, by remote control also in New England. Learned savants of the kingdom are at work studying ancient monuments and reporting their finds to the Royal Society in London. From Ireland a famous Welsh antiquary named Edward Lhyd (pronounced Lloyd) reports to the Society that he has just discovered a previously unknown kind of writing engraved on a stone at Trabeg, near Dingle, in County Kerry. Lhyd has no idea as to what the inscription might mean, or what language it is written in, but he takes care to make a copy of it to send to the Royal Society. Hopefully, he reasons, sometime someone may discover a key to the writing system, and then perhaps the Trabeg inscription may turn out to be important. Here, for the time being, action ceases on this particular problem.

Meantime, across the seas in New England, a Puritan clergyman named John Danforth in 1680 has discovered some strange writing on a rock at Dighton, Massachusetts. Both he and a fellow minister, Cotton Mather, write to inform the Royal Society, and the Society duly records the matter in the *Philosophical Transactions* for 1712.

No further advance in epigraphy was made for two generations, during which time span America became a separate nation, with her own learned societies publishing their own records of research and philosophical inquiry. One unfortunate result was that whereas Lhyd's inscription in Ireland continued to exercise the minds of savants in Britain, Cotton Mather's report from New England now ceased to have any direct interest for British investigators and (since it was recorded in a British journal) it was simply forgotten in America. This was the parting of the ways of British and American antiquaries, as is well illustrated by the subsequent fate of the two reports that had been made in 1712. In contrast to the oblivion that now enveloped Cotton Mather's letter, the corresponding letter from Lhyd was to generate both a controversy and eventual enlightenment.

More than seventy years later, on June 24, 1784, a letter was received by the Society of Antiquaries in London from a certain Colonel Charles Vallancey, in Ireland, informing the Society that he had discovered an ancient Irish tombstone on Mount Callan, County Clare. He had been able to decipher the writing on it, so he reported, and found that it marked the grave of an ancient Irish chieftain named Conan Colgac. This startling information was accompanied by an explanation of how the decipherment had been carried out, and how he had recognized the writing as a script called Ogam, identical with the unknown script that Lhyd had reported three generations earlier.

In a later chapter you will find the explanation of Charles Vallancey's brilliant achievement. He was the first of a long line of linguists who have been responsible for virtually every major decipherment in archeology. Most of them have not been professional linguists teaching in a university department of languages, but rather men whose occupation requires them to deal with mathematical probability theory, or algebra, or some other activity involving the solution of mutually dependent variables.

My own interest in languages stems from high-school days, when I first began to collect miscellaneous Etruscan words quoted by Latin authors whose works we read. Later I followed the work of Michael Ventris, a London architect who solved the writing called Linear B found on ancient tablets of Crete. Like others at that time, I rejoiced in his final success but mourned when his last paper arrived accompanied by a letter from the Hellenic Society reporting his death in a street accident. Apart from an early interest in ancient languages for their own sake, my work as a marine biologist led me to investigate ancient Libyan inscriptions found on remote islands in the Pacific, for these seemed likely to throw light on how man's dispersal across the earth may be influenced by winds and ocean currents.

But the point I wish to make as I close this chapter is that the parting of the ways of American and British savants following the revolution meant that Vallancey's discovery passed unnoticed in New England. The whole documentation of the oldest known literate Celtic society in the world—here in New England—even its very existence, was doomed to lie in limbo for two more centuries. Eight generations of American youth went to school, learned to think of the United States as a nation without historical roots in the soil of the new world, and without any traditions into the remote past save the undocumented speculations of those who looked toward the Bering Straits as the one and only portal of entry for pre-Columbian man. All Amerindian languages were classed together as supposed indigenous products of the New World, and the massive Phoenician, Libyan, and other old-world elements of their vocabularies passed undetected. Scripts that have been deciphered and well documented in Europe have, when discovered in American contexts, generally been dismissed as "marks made by plowshares or the action of the roots of trees," leading to the ridiculous inference that the same must also be true in Europe. When I surreptitiously introduced a well-authenticated Phoenician inscription from Sardinia into an exhibit of my American inscriptions and showed it at a lecture I gave in a department of archeology at a well-known university, no one seemed to notice any difference between the Susquehanna or Pennsylvania stones and the Mediterranean intruder!

Indeed, there was a time when I found it hard to get any archeology professor to examine inscribed stones, and when they did, as often as not the inscriptions were held upside down or sideways. The plain truth is that ancient languages are not usually studied by archeologists in America. So the arbiters of such research here really had little or no knowledge of the ancient scripts which they so readily dismissed as fortuitous markings made by the roots of trees or by plowshares. Happily, these obstacles to our work have now diminished, and many university teachers are now interested in this developing field.

To the matter of plowshares and the marks they make I have paid special attention, watching farmers at work in the fields around me on my expeditions, and discussing with them what happens when a plow strikes a stone. In point of fact all that results is a dent, for either the stone flies out of the ground when it is struck, or the plow itself bounces off it if the stone doesn't move. The one device that farmers use capable of cutting grooves in stones is the chain with which they drag a large stone out of the ground; but such grooves are long and curving and bear not the slightest resemblance to any script known to me. Given such facts as these, it is not surprising that the theorists who seemed to attribute the invention of writing to the plow have never explained how it is that plows in Pennsylvania usually write in Basque or Iberian Punic, whereas those of New England are apt to ascend the walls of stone buildings to write Celtic Ogam upside down on the ceiling.

Perhaps the most pressing reform needed in courses in archeology in America today is to introduce the study of epigraphy, by which is meant the art of reading ancient inscriptions engraved or otherwise imprinted on stone or other durable materials. The need for courses in epigraphy was brought home to me in no uncertain terms after the news media began to report some of these finds. Each week now brings me letters from many parts of the country enclosing photographs or drawings or rubbings of inscriptions people have found on their own properties or elsewhere, and requesting an explanation. Many of these inscriptions are the work of later Amerindians and are not writing in the strict sense; many others are more or less illiterate but genuine records cut by the modern colonists and explorers, often recording the death of a comrade on the trail or the visit of a survey party; a few are patent forgeries of which the finder becomes the innocent purveyor. But many others are genuine ancient records and hence part of the cultural heritage of America.

It is saddening to see that many cliff-cut mementos of a visit by an ancient voyager have been overlaid by the recent scrawls of thoughtless vandals or shattered by the bullets fired at them by persons who think it incumbent to destroy otherwise enduring records cut into rock, high above the normally destructive processes of flood or fire. All too often an ancient inscription has survived two thousand years in the reverent custody of Amerindian tribes only to be ruined by the ignorant sharpshooter of modern times. If we are to stop the destruction of these national archives we must make it our business to inform young people as to what these inscriptions represent. School teachers can do much in this regard, and I am sure they will respond to the appeal.

2

America's Oldest Archives

IN March 1493, the Catholic Church was presented with an unforeseen problem. Christopher Columbus had just landed in Lisbon after an eight month's voyage that was to have taken him to the Indies but, instead of so doing, had led him to discover a new world. The difficulty now confronting the prelates was that he had returned with passengers, Amerindians, who had all the appearance of being human beings. But how could their existence be accounted for? The biblical account of creation described three continents, each occupied by the seed of the three sons of Noah who survived the flood, Shem, Ham, and Japheth.

Columbus seems already to have been aware of the impending theological problem, for, in a letter dated February 15, 1493, written at the Canary Islands, he assures King Ferdinand that the people he found were no monsters, but on the contrary very well formed; neither were they negroes. And when he put ashore in Lisbon on March 6, his journal records "many people came to see the Indians, and it was a great marvel."

As the second and third and later voyages produced ever mounting evidence of large numbers of man-like creatures inhabiting the Americas, a cold wind of skepticism began to blow through the monasteries to ruffle the equanimity of those who so boldly preached the absolute truth of Genesis. For a time Rome disregarded the matter, as Pope Alexander VI, Rodrigo Borgia, was otherwise engaged, save only when he found time to draw a line of demarcation between the Spanish and Portuguese portions of the New World. But in 1512 a new pope, Giuliano della

Rovere, Julius II, summoned the Fifth Lateran Council and issued an official declaration certifying that American Indians are true descendants of Adam and Eve, and hence human beings. The failure of the Bible to account for them and their continent was made good by the inference that Amerindians are the descendants of Babylonians, expelled from the Old World on account of the sins of their ancestors.

Backed by this authority, it was now safe for speculative churchmen to ponder the route from the Garden of Eden to America. After considering the possibilities that Noah's Ark might have added an American port of call to her scheduled sailing plan, or that angels might have transported people across the ocean, "holding them by the Haire of the Head, like to the Prophet Abacuc," a Spanish thinker, José de Acosta, dismissed both propositions in favor of transportation by shipwreck and accidental tempest of weather.

The inquiry was now taken up by others, and by the seventeenth century both Protestant and Catholic churchmen were agreed that Asia must have been the original homeland of the Amerindian forefathers because "only the rude Tartars, above all nations on earth" resemble the inhabitants of America in respect to "their gross ignorance of letters, and of arts, their idolatory and above all, their *incivility*." Alas for Pocahontas; there was no Fenimore Cooper on hand to defend the six nations, no Deerslayer yet to win hearts or minds for the dwellers in the wilderness.

One dissident, Cotton Mather in Boston, in the course of a long series

Pope Julius II's theory (1512) to account for the discovery of the Amerindians, no mention having been made of these people in the Genesis record of how the sons of Noah inherited the earth.

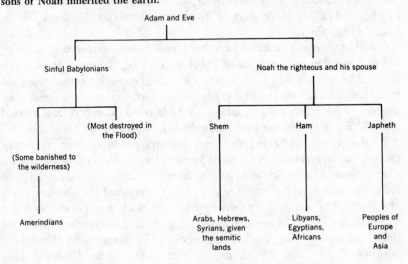

of extraordinary letters to the Royal Society of London, drew attention to the existence in Connecticut of a tribe of Indians which practiced circumcision, thereby showing, he thought, that the American Indians should be considered as the lost tribes of Israel. Voltaire, on the other hand, considered that the American Indians had arisen *de novo* in America, by whatever mechanism had similarly caused human beings to appear upon the face of the earth in other continents.

By 1811 such scientists as Humboldt recognized the similarities between some American tribes and those of the Mongol race, and postulated that the Amerindians are descended from a mingling of ancient Americans and later inwanderers from Asia. Later still most anthropologists came to agree that all American Indians are descended from ancestors that entered the Americas by way of the Bering Strait, and that no European came to America before Leif Eriksson or Columbus. In recent years one lone voice has protested such oversimplification, that of Harold Sterling Gladwin. In his various writings Gladwin has repeatedly drawn attention to cultural features and material objects, particularly pottery, that show that American tribes must have had relatively recent contacts with the Old World, especially with the Mediterranean and the Orient. The nature of the various art styles to which he drew attention is such as to point to direct voyages between the Old World and the Americas as late as classical times, about 2,000 years ago. Gladwin's views have until very recently been ruled anathema, and excluded from the college curricula. Luckily this exclusionist attitude is now considerably ameliorated. His writings, once forbidden reading, have even become prescribed texts at places such as Harvard.

For generations the archeological world has been beset by the notion that only the navigational techniques introduced in Europe in the fifteenth century made it possible for Europeans to cross the Atlantic (though some grudging acquiescence is conceded to those who point to the evidence of the sagas, showing Viking crossings by way of Greenland). So, at the time when Gladwin issued *Men out of Asia* (1947), he too felt compelled to bring the Mediterranean influence to the Americas by way of an Asian and Indonesian land-hopping route, the vectors being supposedly the ships of the fleet of Menarchus, left stranded in Asia after the death of Alexander the Great. In recent years new discoveries in the Pacific caves have begun to lend much support to this facet of Gladwin's theories, but at the same time the newer evidence also shows very clearly that the Atlantic was by no means the great barrier that earlier thinkers had supposed.

What, it is reasonable to ask, is this newer evidence? In fact, it is not new in itself, for it has lain intact for two thousand years; all that is new

Pioneer archeologists who contributed to the solution of the mystery of European settlements in northeastern United States prior to the medieval voyages. Above left, Harold Sterling Gladwin (1889–   ), who demonstrated Mediterranean influence in the classical period. Upper right, Richard Rolt Brash (1817–1876), the leading Irish Ogam scholar of his day. Left, William B. Goodwin (1868–1950), who first protected Mystery Hill from further destruction, and first perceived Celtic features in its archeology. *Harold B. Alexander, Malcolm D. Pearson*

is our ability to read the inscriptions concerned. For indeed, they *are* written and in some sense documents, carefully engraved on the bedrock of America, on temple lintels, and on the gravestones of kings and chiefs. They speak to us of a long-forgotten age of exploration and colonization, the subject of this book.

When American archeologists first began to send me inscriptions for decipherment and translation I was astonished to learn that such documents exist here. All my earlier work had been on ancient tablets and cave inscriptions of the Old World, records of the Sea Peoples of the Bronze Age and early Iron Age some 3,000–4,000 years ago. What I now began to receive from unimpeachable sources in North America were essentially the same types of document, engraved in stone, and either excavated from some archeological site, recorded from cliff faces, or photographed on massive rocks discovered by the early colonists. I had never seen such materials mentioned or illustrated in books on the archeology of the Americas and indeed was oblivious of their existence.

"How is it," I asked my friend and colleague Professor George Carter of Texas, "that you are sending me all these materials? Has no one studied them before?"

His answer was, "For twenty-five years I have been knocking on the study doors of professors of Greek and Latin, each time to be told that the objects I had in my hand look like writing, but that it is not Greek or Latin nor any script known to my consultant. So I emerged no wiser than before."

The very manner in which George Carter and I were brought together is in itself instructive, for it illustrates both the difficulties now besetting communication between men working in different disciplines and the strengths of those more liberal institutions of learning that encourage their faculty to cross the lines that divide the disciplines. Carter trained as an archeologist at the University of California at Berkeley, but he has chosen to devote much of his life to the study of the geographical distribution of man and his domesticated plants and animals. Through his researches at Johns Hopkins and later at Texas A. and M., his work became well known to biologists at Harvard, especially to botanists working on the evolution and distribution of plants cultivated by man.

I for my part, though a marine biologist, have spent much of my life studying the ancient voyages of peoples who left inscriptions on remote islands which, of course, could only have been approached by sea. As a marine biologist I felt obliged to examine this evidence, for it would have a bearing on how the dispersal of man, plants, and animals might be influenced by ocean currents and winds. So the decipherment of ancient inscriptions, the art of epigraphy, became my second specialty. It was through my fellow biologists at Harvard that Carter and I were introduced to each other's work. I learned that he had amassed a fine collection of American inscriptions in the hope that their eventual decipherment might explain or illuminate his own researches, and he for his part now found a man who claimed to recognize the languages on his tablets. We soon found that the emerging information is consistent with our other, independent investigations, and so the seal was set on a collaboration that proved most rewarding.

When word began to appear in linguistic and archeological periodicals of this joint effort, other archeologists and some linguists contacted us. A flow of information now began that soon swelled to proportions far beyond anything either George Carter or I had dreamed. The Epigraphic Society was established, and we began to publish our findings, as well as those of others, in a form readily available to other interested people, both professional and amateur. So began the busiest and most productive period in my life, an exciting journey through space and time, bringing new friendships in a score of countries.

From the information we gleaned from the first American tablets to be deciphered we gained important hints as to where more inscriptions might be expected. So I deserted my study table and the world of dictionaries for a while to spend a wonderful summer crisscrossing the hills and valleys of the New England countryside, rejoicing whenever a terrace or ridge top yielded yet another inscribed stone. My field companions and I became deeply aware of the presence all around us of traces of a vanished civilization that had once flourished there.

On these New England excursions I was most often accompanied by John Williams, a young schoolteacher from Connecticut who soon made himself expert in detecting the presence of inscribed rocks beneath the soil and later carried out many exploratory trips on his own. Between the two of us we covered some eleven thousand miles on the roads, and hundreds of miles on foot, clambering up hillsides, or more often, pushing through the woodlands that once more occupy much of the back country. We were often joined by my wife Rene, who occasionally made discoveries of her own. Another frequent companion was Peter J. Garfall, joined later by Joseph D. Germano who, whenever they could spare the time, would bring their cameras to record the finds.

When the suggestion was made at one stage in one of the newspapers that we might be forging the inscriptions it became increasingly necessary to have cameras as well as witnesses on hand to record the thick coat of lichens covering the inscriptions before they were brushed clean for making a plaster cast. Other companions from time to time were our

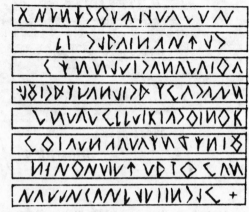

Examples of Iberian inscriptions from North America (left), and from Europe (right). The American inscription, engraved on a stone tablet, was found in 1838 at a depth of 60 feet in a large burial mound at Grave Creek, West Virginia, together with a skeleton and copper arm rings. It was at once recognized by Professor Rafn of Copenhagen as being Iberian, though that script had not at that time been deciphered. Recent studies show that the language of the tablet is Punic (Phoenician), written in the form of alphabet used in Spain during the first millennium B.C. It may be translated as follows (the writing reading from right to left):

(1)   The mound raised-on-high for Tasach
(2)   This tile
(3)   (His) queen caused-to-be-made

The alphabet of the tablet was deciphered by Spanish scholars, and published by the English epigrapher D. Diringer in 1968. The language is basic Semitic, and all words occur in standard literary Semitic dictionaries, such as that of Professor Wehr. The decipherment of the tablet is explained by Fell in *Occasional Publications*, vol. 3, issued by the Epigraphic Society.

The European inscription, with which scholars such as Rafn and Schoolcraft compared the Grave Creek inscription, and shown to the right of the Grave Creek tablet, is written in the Iberian alphabet and in the Punic language, but alternate lines read from right to left, and then from left to right (this is called *boustrophedon*, meaning "as a plowman walks"). The translation, by Fell, is as follows:

(1)   Various ways of making a prediction
(2)   The planets reveal indications of . . . (letters missing)
(3)   He who understands how, may himself obtain information about hidden truths
(4)   When the radiant gleam is seen of the myriads of the heavenly host following their courses on high
(5)   The directions of their wanderings are the signs of omens
(6)   The crescent moon, appearing below the planet Mars, is a favorable sign
(7)   When Venus makes a transit through the constellation of the Ram
(8)   She bestows upon mankind peace and mild government

The tablet, evidently only the first part of an astrological text, is deciphered in detail in the *Occasional Publications*, vol. 3, of the Epigraphic Society.

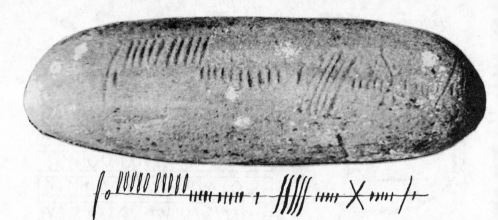

Ma-q — q -i -i -a -r -i y i m a

Ancient phallic stone at Ballintaggart, County Kerry, Ireland, apparently re-engraved in Christian times with the name of a deceased person. The first part of the inscription is a rendering of a Celtic name also known from a Cornish inscription, Maqqiiari or Magari. The last part cannot at present be interpreted. *James P. Whittall II*

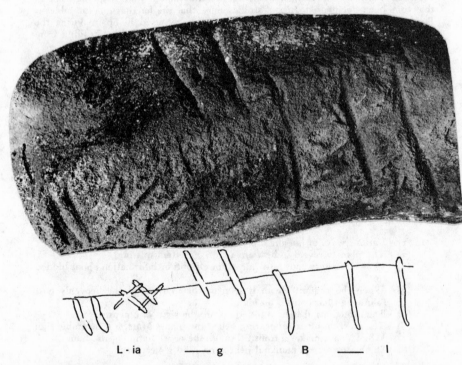

L - ia — g B — l

Iberian Ogam inscribed stone from Vermont. The American Ogam inscriptions use the Iberian form of Ogam in which vowels are omitted. These are much older than the Irish Ogam and date from the late Bronze Age, as is shown by Punic letters associated with them of dated types. The inscription here reads "Stone of Bel," but when complete it probably read "Stone of Beltane." *Joseph D. Germano*

archeologist friends and local residents who sometimes could lead us directly to a site known to them. They were long days, from dawn till near midnight, but we managed to bring back to Boston a fine series of aluminum-foil impressions from which casts could be prepared on days when the weather forbade field work.

The alphabets and languages found on American inscriptions are fully discussed later in this book, but the representative examples on pages 21–22 show how the American colonists or visitors wrote in the first millennium B.C. Note the similarity to corresponding examples from Europe.

While John Williams and I roamed the New England back country for Celtic inscriptions, another colleague was making notable finds in the midwest and southwest. This was Gloria Farley, an intrepid explorer of the cliffs and caves that border the banks of the Arkansas and Cimarron Rivers and their tributaries. Armed with camera, snakebite antivenom, rubber latex (for making impressions), and a ladder, Gloria systematically assembled a remarkable series of records of visits and settlements by European voyagers who had ascended the Mississippi, then turned west to follow the Arkansas River, eventually to reach the Cimarron along the border between Oklahoma and Colorado. Her discoveries showed that some Celts had followed this southern route and that Libyans and Punic-speaking Iberians, and even one Basque king, had ventured into the heartland of the continent centuries before Christ. Gloria Farley will be remembered for these fine contributions to our national archives, a bright example of grit and determination in the face of discouragement on the part of those who might have helped her.

On account of the skepticism, and even opposition to our work, that we experienced at first from some professional archeologists, nearly all of the inscriptions we first examined were ones that we discovered ourselves, John Williams and Gloria Farley being the leading explorers. Later, when our work became better understood, we began to receive valuable help from museum curators and some universities or other institutions where mysterious inscribed stones or tablets had been deposited by finders long since. We received no financial support from any scientific fund, but through the generosity and faith of Ruth K. Hanner, the Epigraphic Society has been able to establish its own modest fund and this, supplemented by our family budgets, has financed our travel expenses and the cost of latex and other materials needed for making copies of inscriptions cut in rock. Those who have participated in the exploration include Malcolm Pearson, a gifted photographer who has recorded inscriptions for many years, and who originally led William Goodwin to the ruins at Mystery Hill; James Whittall, architect-archeologist, a Harvard graduate and authority on the megalithic structures of Portugal, Spain, and New

England; Robert Stone, curator and present owner of the Mystery Hill site in New Hampshire, which he has protected and opened to the public, and who first demonstrated the existence of an ancient astronomical observatory among the ruins, in an American setting; Elizabeth Sincerbeaux of Vermont, who perceived the antiquity of the supposed colonial "root cellars" and encouraged a young amateur astronomer, Byron Dix, to investigate what he later discovered to be calendar sites in that state. These and others to be named in later pages were the colleagues who now became our closest collaborators, and who like us had to endure much opposition. But the work was its own reward, and all of us who took part in the research agree that we lived exciting days and loved every minute of them.

Yet these treasures are endangered!

Christopher McIntosh, an English investigator, has given an account of the ever-increasing threat of destruction of ancient sites as a result of modern highway construction and like developments. He called his 1971 report "The Race to Save Britain's Past," and it often seemed to us in Vermont that we too are racing against time, with the added threat of vandalism. As the months went by I perceived a change in the attitude of my field collaborators who seemed to become imbued with a new zest, determined to save these relics, come what may.

Coordination of different disciplines is a feature of successful fieldwork. Above left, Byron Dix uses an equatorial to determine sunrise and sunset azimuths for each day of the year for each of the sites. His demonstration that the temples have well-defined astronomical axes, matching those of the solstice and equinox stones, was a major part of the proof that these stone buildings were the work of European visitors and their descendants. John Williams, above right, with Fell taking measurements, and, below, students of Castleton College take part in the field work. *Peter J. Garfall, Harry S. Jaffe, Joseph D. Germano*

3

How Irish Ogam Was Deciphered

URING the past three thousand years the shores of America were visited by mariners, sometimes by colonists, from several different civilizations that once flourished on the other side of the Atlantic. This means, of course, that the inscriptions they left behind are engraved in several languages, and sometimes inscriptions of different periods occur on the same rock or cliff face. If I were to report the decipherments in the order in which they were carried out the result could not be other than confusing. Therefore I have tried to bring out the main profiles of our work by concentrating on what appears to be the central theme, namely the Celtic decipherments, even though these were the last to be completed. The Celts have been a lifelong interest for me, at least ever since my college days. When Celtic inscriptions stared back at me from American bedrock it seemed like the end of a long, tortuous trail that started so many years ago when I was a student at the University of Edinburgh, in Scotland. If I have exaggerated the importance of the Celtic role in history or in the colonization of America in ancient times it is perhaps because I was better equipped to recognize faint trails if their scent was Celtic. Others, perhaps, may be more successful in smelling out other ancient voyagers, guided by signs that I never learned to notice. So without further excuses I return to Irish themes and the story of Charles Vallancey.

The problem confronting Vallancey was different in nature from that we encountered in American inscriptions. Whereas he did not have to convince anyone that Celts had once lived in Ireland, this very advantage also did him a disservice. For the ancient Irish scribes had no doubts that their Celtic alphabet could be understood in a Celtic land, and so they never once felt obliged to compose bilingual inscriptions in dual alphabets. So the methods we used in North America, as outlined in chapter 5, were not available to Vallancey. Old Irish monks, however, had composed books about Ogam, and it was through one of these that he learned of the nature of this ancient script.

In his recent lecture series and book *Civilisation* Lord Kenneth Clark has depicted the monks of Ireland in the dark ages as the repository of learning while Europe lay shattered by the barbarian invaders. In their stone cells and remote islet hermitages these devoted servants of God somehow contrived to keep the oil burning in the few fragile lamps that survived the collapse of the western Roman Empire. For four centuries they alone preserved the learning of the ancients. Later, as petty kingdoms were replaced by more stable institutions of government, the monks emerged to establish more splendid houses of the Church, until by the ninth century and the onset of the middle ages a steady stream of manuscripts was generated to fill the libraries of those bishops who cared for learning or had the wealth to commission fair copies of ancient works for their own delight. Not all of the manuscripts can be classified as works of art, but some of the more commonplace in execution contain information that is priceless. One such is the volume known to us as the *Book of Ballymote.*

This celebrated book is thought to have been assembled about eight hundred years ago from a collection of miscellaneous manuscripts. The last manuscript included in the book is known as the Ogam Tract, because it deals with about seventy varieties of ancient Celtic script called collectively by the name Ogam, meaning "grooved writing." It is thought that this name may be derived from an ancient Greek word *ogme,* meaning "groove," though some Celtic tradition attributes the script to a god called Ogmios.

The principle of Ogam writing, as set out in the Ogam Tract, is simple enough. It is, in fact, an alphabet, comprising fifteen consonants and five vowels, together with a few other signs representing double letters such as the sound ng, and diphthongs. The letters are constructed from single parallel strokes placed in sets of one to five, in positions above, across, or below a guide line. A portion of the first page of the Ogam Tract is illustrated on page 28 to let you see what the script looks like when written on a vellum manuscript. Further on I will explain it in more detail, but first I want to consider another topic by posing a question which, perhaps, may already have occurred to you.

The question is this: "If Lhyd had taken the trouble to consult the Ogam Tract in 1707 when he first discovered the Trabeg inscription, would he not have been able to decipher his find?"

And the answer, of course, is Yes indeed, provided that he knew of the

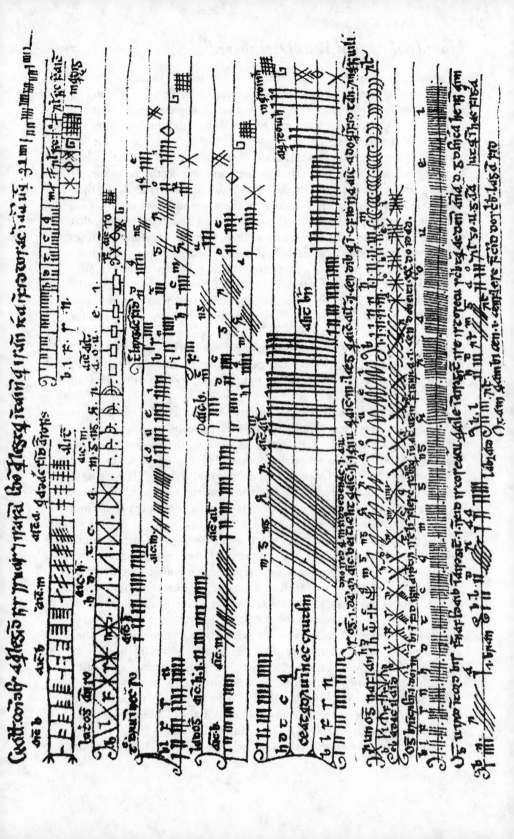

existence of the *Book of Ballymote* and where it was kept, and provided
he could also read Gaelic (for that is the language of the Tract). However, Lhyd seems to have known none of these things.

How then did it happen that Colonel Charles Vallancey was able to do
what Lhyd could not, when Lhyd (as his name shows) was a Celt,
whereas Vallancey was an Englishman? Here the answer is twofold. For
one thing Vallancey, as we learn from contemporary records, was one of
those English settlers in Ireland who fell entirely under the Celtic spell.
He became more Irish than the Irish (there have been many such); and
secondly, he was an archeologist in the strictest and original sense of the
word. Now this may surprise you, but in the eighteenth century archeology had a markedly different connotation from what it commonly carries
today, especially in America.

According to the great Oxford English Dictionary, the word was originally spelled *archaiology,* and it made its debut in the English language
in the year 1607, when the meaning it was to carry for the next two centuries was given as "Ancient history generally." As late as 1879 the word
was still defined (in the Encyclopedic Dictionary) as "The science which
treats of antiquity, which it investigates by studying oral traditions, monuments of all kinds, and written manuscripts." Earlier, the journal
Archaeologia was employing the word in the following manner: "The
contents of the Archaiology of Wales are derived from old manuscripts"
(OED vol. A, page 431).

These passages give us the clue to Vallancey's success. He did indeed
pursue the study of the archeology of Ireland by tracking down and teaching himself to read the medieval Romanesque* script of the monks and
by diligently making use of Gaelic dictionaries to acquaint himself with
the words he found in these ancient documents. There was no other way
in which the subject could be learned; no college or university courses
were offered in Celtic, and certainly none at all in any language employing the Ogam script.

Modern archeology, relying mainly on discoveries made by excavating
the ruins of former human habitations and other traces left by ancient
peoples, grew out of the groundwork of these early students of ancient

---

* The sans-serif gothic letters still used in modern Irish Gaelic.

A portion of the first page of the Ogam Tract in the *Book of Ballymote* showing a
number of different alphabets known to the medieval author of the Tract, even
though in Ireland these varieties are not at present known from inscriptions on
stone (lapidary inscriptions). The variety shown in the second line, called "Hinge
Ogam," is one that occurs in North America, the vowels however being omitted
from the American version.

manuscripts. Before ever the first Celtic towns and forts were excavated in Britain, archeologists had already made an exhaustive study of the documentation left by the Celts and their Greek and Roman visitors. So they *already* were in possession of the means of reading ancient Celtic inscriptions in both Latin and Ogam writing, and they judged the meaning of their finds by the inscriptions they uncovered or, more precisely, by the decipherments made by epigraphers to whom they sent copies of these inscriptions. Only when this framework had been established did archeologists dare to make excavations into progressively older sites, where no writing could be discovered. With extreme caution they gradually extended their work back through the older levels and into the Stone Age. Even today most excavations in Britain are concerned with periods for which a writing system is known and understood, and the most spectacular sites are generally those of the classical age, when Romans and Celts lived together in considerable opulence, as their buried cities attest. As most inscriptions are in Latin, that is naturally the language with which the British archeologist must acquaint himself. For the older periods, before the Romans came, the written monuments, some four hundred in number, use the Ogam script. Transitional phases are represented by monuments engraved in both Ogam and Latin texts.

This, then, is the background against which we have to view Vallancey's researches, and it explains in large measure why he was successful and why his successors went on to much greater things.

Here now is the story of Vallancey's deductions, as pieced together from the contemporary archeological journals which reported his work.

True to the archeological principles of his era, he began his investigations by examining and translating such ancient Irish manuscripts as he was able to locate in the libraries of Ireland and others that he obtained by purchase. One of the manuscripts he obtained was a copy of an early Irish poem entitled The Battle of Gabhra, dealing with an event said to have occurred in the year 283 A.D. and forming part of the epic of Celtic legends known as the *Ossianic cycle*. The particular passage in the poem that aroused Vallancey's antiquarian curiosity was one that is lacking from most of the copies of the work. According to O'Kearney, who edited the work for the Ossianic Society, the critical section is to be translated as follows:

> The ferocious warrior Conan
> Was not at Gabhra in the mighty strife;
> For on Beltane [i.e., May first] of the previous year
> At an assembly convened to worship the sun,
> The bold hero was slain treacherously
> By the Fenians of Fionn.

On the dark mountain of Callan
His grave was made on the northwest slope;
Sadly plaintive was his dirge,
And his name in Ogam is on a dressed stone.

The lines here italicized were those that caught Vallancey's attention, for he was acquainted with a mountain called Sliabh Calainn* in County Clare, and he learned that on the mountain was an ancient Celtic structure called a *cromlech* (a table-like giant stone monument of which American examples are noted in Chapter 8). This cromlech, known to the local villagers by the Early Irish name of *Altoir-na-Greine* (altar-of-the-sun), he suspected might be the grave of the warrior Conan. The critical question now became: Does this monument carry an Ogam inscription, and if so, is the inscription a funeral dedication to a person called Conan?

It so happened that Colonel Vallancey knew of a young man of antiquarian tastes who lived in the neighborhood of the mountain, endowed by his parents with the enchanting name Theophilus O'Flannagan. He wrote to Theophilus in 1784 asking him if he would undertake a search for the *Altoir-na-Greine* or any other hewn stone that might fit the description given in the poem, and ascertain if there were Ogam characters inscribed upon it.

It is now known that Theophilus O'Flannagan had in fact already visited the site in 1780 (as he afterwards was to record). He omitted to mention his earlier visit, however, in his reply to Vallancey, and his letter dated April 20, 1784, reads as follows:

I went in search of the monument of antiquity so particularly pointed out by you in company with a young man who had been my school-fellow. We proceeded to Mountain Callan (or Altoir-na-Greine) about eight miles westward of the town of Ennis, and soon found a large altar, about twelve feet by four, extending from east to west; it lies on the south side of the mountain, about half a mile distant from the highroad leading from Ennis to Ibrican. . . . After searching for the inscription I was much disappointed, no characters whatever appearing thereon, wherefore I returned to the peasant's cottage . . . and was informed by the peasant that he had observed another monument on the other side of the mountain, about a mile northwest of the altar, which resembled a tombstone, and that it had strokes engraved on it very unlike letters.

Fully confident that this must be the monument we sought for, he guided us to the spot; and there we found a large hewn stone of the same kind as those in the altar above mentioned; the length of the stone is between seven

* *Sliabh Calainn* (pronounced Sleeav Calin) means Mountain-of-the-Cromlech.

and eight feet, and from three to four in breadth, placed upon a kind of tumulus [burial mound], with an inscription of which the following is a facsimile representation

Imagine the trepidation with which Vallancey awaited the reply, and his excitement upon receiving it! He wasted no time in passing on to the Society of Antiquaries word of the discovery, and his letter announcing it, dated June 24, 1784, was published in Volume 7 of *Archaeologia,* the Society's journal.

O'Flannagan's facsimile of the inscription was inaccurate, and therefore Vallancey's first decipherment was similarly defective. However, the most important fact emerging from the investigation was that the predicted name Conan was identified on the stone. O'Flannagan's version, transliterated from the Old Gaelic into Roman letters, is:

FAN LI DAF ICA CONAN COLGAC COS OBMDA

From this cryptic sequence Vallancey and O'Flannagan satisfied themselves that the tumulus had contained the body of a chieftain named Conan Colgac.

Unfortunately for Vallancey and O'Flannagan the discovery was greeted with general incredulity. A Dr. O'Connor reasoned that the monument could not possibly be antique, because punctuation points occurred in the Ogam text (a completely fallacious argument, as events were to prove). Ledwich, an Irish historian, ridiculed the whole alleged find on the grounds that it is not possible for any Celtic monument to have withstood 1,500 years of exposure in a wild, unsheltered situation. A Dr. O'Donovan claimed that the whole inscription was a forgery perpetrated by a certain John Lloyd, and that the verses of *The Battle of Gabhra* were also the forgery of O'Flannagan himself, to suit the wording on the stone. Later O'Flannagan was also charged with having forged the inscription too.

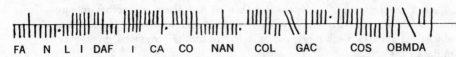

FA   N   L I DAF   I CA CO NAN   COL GAC   COS OBMDA

One of several readings of the Callin Mountain Ogam inscription inferred by O'Flannagan and Vallancey. Although the ancient Celtic could not be translated, they inferred that the monument is a memorial to a chief called Conan Colgac. Later study disclosed that the name Conan should be read as Cosaf. Although this decipherment contained errors it is a landmark in epigraphy, for it was the first ancient unknown script to be deciphered.

All these charges were eventually shown to be baseless, for as others joined in the search for Ogam monuments, a torrent of reports on new finds began to pour in from many quarters. Some of the new discoveries proved to be in a much better state of preservation, and thus the art of deciphering the Ogam inscriptions became more refined, though many of the more eroded examples have baffled translation. With the improvement in understanding how the Ogam is to be read there came a curious aftermath to Vallancey's pioneer effort. It now appeared that the letters that had been read as CONAN are in reality not that hero's name but COSAF! A possible explanation is that the unknown poet who so precisely indicated the place of burial of his Conan may have himself misread the name on the monument, and composed his lines to fit what he thought he read.

Nothing, however, can take from Vallancey the honor of having discovered how the hitherto mysterious notched stones of the Celtic lands are to be read, and his pioneer work eventually resulted in nearly 400 such Ogam monuments coming to light in various parts of the British Isles.

But Vallancey's researches have a wider implication. They showed that the key to deciphering an unknown script in an unknown language lies in researching all possible avenues of information with a view to discovering a bilingual example, where the unknown script occurs alongside one which is already known. This key Vallancey recognized in the Ogam Tract of the *Book of Ballymote*. What had been supposed to be a monkish code system was found in reality to be a key to the ancient inscriptions of the Irish, indeed of the whole Gaelic-speaking section of the Celtic peoples, in which the Ogam symbols are placed side by side with the Romanesque (or Gothic) alphabet used by the Christian monks.

From this point on, all would-be decipherers knew that they must always look for an inscription in which a known writing system is found in juxtaposition with a parallel version in the unknown system. The next great decipherment was to be Champollion's pioneer solutions of the Egyptian hieroglyphs occurring side by side with a Greek text on a Ptolemaic document now known as the Rosetta Stone. Champollion's work illustrates a special trick that decipherers have found valuable when searching for clues as to how a decipherment is to begin.

The Rosetta Stone is actually a bilingual Egyptian-Greek copy of an edict issued by the General Council of the Egyptian Priesthood assembled in Memphis to celebrate the coronation of the Pharaoh Ptolemy V. The Council met in 196 B.C., and it was not the coronation itself they celebrated, but the ninth anniversary of it. The stone was found by Napoleon's army in Egypt in July 1799. Napoleon himself was fascinated by the find, and ordered copies of the inscription to be circulated to the learned societies of Europe in the hope that someone could decipher the Egyptian writing with the aid of what appeared to be a parallel Greek text. His hopes were realized by the French scholar Jean François Champollion (1790–1832).

The method used by Champollion was to identify certain proper names (of the Pharaoh Ptolemy, for example) in the Greek text, and then to locate what appeared to be the corresponding sections of the Egyptian text, distinguished by a special mark used for royal names called the cartouche. Then by comparing the various names he was able to isolate hieroglyphs that evidently stand for the same sound in different names. As he identified each sound symbol he was gradually able to extend his reading to other words by inserting the sounds he had deduced for the symbols in those words. He then made the startling discovery that these words were the same, or nearly the same, as certain words in the Coptic language still used in the native Christian church of Egypt. So he was able to prove that the Coptic tongue is descended from Ancient Egyptian, and at the same time to employ Coptic as his guide to reconstituting the Ancient Egyptian tongue.

A variation of Champollion's method consists in finding ancient coins struck with inscriptions in two languages, one of which is known. This method has been used with great success in reconstituting the lost languages of the Far East, for during and after Alexander the Great's campaigns into Asia numerous coins were struck by Greek rulers who had established themselves in various states of India and the lands between Greece and India. In this way the ancient alphabets of India were recovered along with many other, lesser-known Asian tongues.

Yet another variant is possible in some ancient cemeteries where the names and biographical data on the deceased person may be given in the local language and in a widely spoken language such as Latin or Greek. I used this means of ingress into the hitherto unsolved language of Libya, and by following Champollion's rule of beginning with the proper names and then substituting the inferred sounds into other words, I learned to my surprise that the unknown Libyan language is in fact almost the same as the Ancient Egyptian language, the chief difference being that the Libyans used an alphabet derived from that of Carthage whereas the Egyptians used the very complicated and cumbrous system of hieroglyphs, most of which have a sound value made up of several letters. Another peculiarity was that Libyan proved to make much greater use of words derived from Greek and the Anatolian tongues.

In this book several different languages, each using a special writing system, are reported from various American inscriptions. One of them happens to be Libyan and another is the old Celtic language called

Goidelic, written in a special variety of Ogam script that originated in Spain and Portugal. Yet another is the Tartessian language of the city of Tarshish in southwest Spain; and there are others. Every one of these writing systems has been deciphered by the methods explained in this chapter. In some cases (Iberian, for example) the alphabet has been deciphered by European colleagues (from bilingual texts including proper names or from coins) while the language has sometimes been identified or deciphered by me, using related known languages as the guide. In other cases (Punic, for example) the entire decipherment has been carried out on Mediterranean inscriptions by European researchers, and all that is then required for an American example is to make use of the dictionary supplied by the European researchers. A point I want to stress is that the methods used in deciphering American inscriptions are identical to those used elsewhere.

In the previous paragraph I have stressed the difference between an *alphabet* and a *language* because, strangely enough, nearly everyone seems to confuse them. I think the cause of the confusion is that in some cases we use the same word to describe both the alphabet and the language of an inscription, while in other cases two different words are used. Let me try to clarify the matter here. An alphabet, of course, is a set of letters, each having a special sound value. A language, on the other hand, is a means of communication used by a particular people or group of speakers. But if an alphabet is used by only one particular language we often describe both the alphabet and the language by the same word; an example is Libyan, for the Libyan language uses the Libyan script. It is quite possible, of course, for a language to use the alphabet of another language. For example, the Pali language of India has no special Pali alphabet at all; it can be written correctly in the Devanagari alphabet of the Sanskrit language or in the Roman alphabet that we use, or in any of several other Eastern alphabets. Another example is the dialect of Punic (the Semitic tongue of Carthage) used in Spain; some ancient scribes wrote this Iberian Punic in special Iberian letters probably derived from the Basque people while others wrote it in the old alphabet of the Greeks of Italy. The Etruscans wrote Etruscan in a mirror-image version of the alphabet of the Greeks of Italy. English, French, and Samoan are three different languages, yet all three use the Roman alphabet.

At this distance in time from Vallancey and O'Flannagan it is easy enough for us, with the aid of aftersight, to see that these investigators used the appropriate methods and that they achieved a reasonably close approximation to the truth. It is equally easy for us to conclude that any similar investigation in America—or anywhere else for that matter— should follow along lines similar to those explored by Vallancey and

Champollion. So it would be natural enough to pass straight from the material reviewed in this chapter to the corresponding materials from the New World.

But that would be to overlook the subsequent turn of events in Ireland and in Britain as a whole, for the path of Vallancey's successors was by no means smooth. In fact, little further progress was achieved by Vallancey himself, and in the latter part of his life he was content to discover and record Ogam inscriptions without going beyond the point of claiming that they were the work of ancient Irish Celts. Much opposition existed even to that simple claim, and as for the inferred readings of the Ogam, these continued to provoke skepticism and opposition. The severest and most obtuse opposition came from Vallancey's Irish colleagues. However, as the saying has it, the darkest hour is just before the dawn. And so events were soon to prove.

4

The Celtic Revival

WHILE controversy still raged over the validity of Vallancey's daring equation of the supposed secret writing of the medieval monks with the hitherto unexplained grooved and notched stones of Ireland, the learned men of England viewed with some surprise the storm in the Irish literary circles. What significance for Britain, not to mention Europe, could there be in this crude thing called Ogam? Everyone knew that the Irish had never been any other than ignorant peasants, and as for the Scots, Samuel Johnson had given expression to the Englishman's disdain for those kilted savages. The Welsh in their secluded mountains had all but ceased their cattle rustling and, adopting the nonconformist faith of the Methodist preachers, had finally learned their lesson and ceased to trouble the serious world of the English country gentleman. English disdain for Celtic peasantry was sufficiently expressed by the Irish themselves, and when O'Connor, Ledwich, and O'Donovan launched their literary attacks on Vallancey and O'Flannagan, the English reaction was to leave the Irish to themselves.

"The Irish are a fair people," Johnson had written to the Bishop of Killaloe, "they never speak well of themselves." And, as if prescient of the scorn in store for Vallancey, Johnson had already written to the Scottish Ossianic translator, James Macpherson, in 1775: "In lapidary inscriptions a man is not upon oath."

For the grieving Irish scholars and their few English defenders never had the prospect seemed more bleak. Soon famine was to add to the miseries of the peasants. So the era of the young Victoria came to Britain.

Then suddenly and unexpectedly the tide turned. Two scholars of impeccable learning and duly certificated by the leading universities now turned up new evidence. One was the Right Reverend Dr. Graves, Bishop of Limerick and hence a pillar of the Anglo-Irish Church, the other Sir

Samuel Fergusson, distinguished lawyer and Queen's Counsel. The Bishop began to amass a collection of paper molds of the Irish inscriptions on stone, and soon was able to demonstrate that a sequence of Ogam letters spelling M-A-Q-Q-I is nearly always to be found in the middle part of an inscription, preceded and followed by two other sequences that could sometimes be matched with known personal names of the ancient Irish. Thus the funerary formula was demonstrated, a deceased man being designated by his own name, then the word *maqq* (meaning "son of," modern *mac,* the final "i" being the sign of the old Celtic possessive case) following his father's personal name. This finding made a deep impression on English scholars, for it now appeared that ancient Irish used case inflections. The parallel to Latin was much too striking and too attractive to dismiss lightly.

"Could it be," the literati now began to ask themselves, "that this old Irish language is actually related to Latin?" Now, in the days we are speaking of, a knowledge of the Latin language was widespread among all the educated people of the world. It was thought of as the most sophisticated and precise means of communication ever contrived by man, and the notion that ancient Irish might be connected in some way with the speech of the ancient Romans proved to be a much more effective advocate for Vallancey than anything else that occurred up to that time.

To this intriguing notion Dr. Samuel Fergusson, later Sir Samuel, now added new discoveries, namely that Ogam inscriptions found on the lintels of peculiar cellar-like buildings (called *raths* in Gaelic) antedate the buildings themselves, for parts of the inscriptions are concealed within the mass of the masonry. As certain raths are mentioned in Irish manuscripts as being built in pagan times, the antiquity of the Ogam on their lintels must have been even greater.

The final and most telling blow now came, of all places, from England itself. Bilingual lapidary inscriptions were discovered on which the name of the dead person appeared both in Ogam script and in Latin letters! The timing could not have been better, for under the influence of Prince Albert and the Queen, England was now turning to the nostalgic contemplation of Gothic art and printing, Tennyson was soon to sing the "Idylls of the King" to put all England under the spell of the Arthurian romances of Cornwall, Wales, and Brittany. Now, to pile Pelion on Ossa, came the incontrovertible evidence of the stone monuments that the ancient Celtic language had been contemporary with the Roman occupation of Britain.

Soon from the monasteries of Ireland and the dusty shelves of Trinity College, Dublin, came forth a stream of hitherto almost unknown manuscripts and books, decorated in a lavish and most beautiful Romanesque variant of the so-called Gothic lettering, inlaid with jewels, bound in gold, the most beautiful books the world had ever seen—and all of them composed in either the Old Irish or the Latin tongue or both. Scholars and dilettanti came from far-away places to gaze upon the discoveries, and linguists now took up the study of ancient Celtic writings.

Stunned by the turn of events, the erstwhile critics recanted or slunk away never to be heard from again, and Ireland emerged into the world of European scholarship as the savior of civilization during the darkest age of the barbarian invasions. A century of unremitting scholarly research ensued. Celtic students in all the Celtic lands took renewed heart as the historic universities of England, Wales, and Scotland now took steps to follow Ireland's lead, appointing learned men to fill the newly created chairs of Celtic studies.

While this extraordinary turn of events swept all before it in Britain, far away in New England a thrill of pride passed through the various communities of exiled Celts whose parents had fled the Highland clearances, or who had themselves crossed the waters to escape the horrors of the Irish potato famine.

How little these exiles knew of what lay all around them in those verdant New England valleys, so like the Ireland they had left behind. Far more like Ireland than they could dream, for how were they to know that the mysterious stone "root cellars" they had found on their properties were essentially replicas of the same stone structures that Sir Samuel Fergusson had shown to be ancient Celtic monuments from a forgotten age? The art of recognizing and reading Ogam was confined to a few scholars in Britain, so how were these New England Scotsmen and Irishmen to know that the peculiar lines of cross-hatched groves they sometimes would notice on the lintels of their "root cellars" had anything to do with the discoveries now being reported from Scotland, Ireland, and England?

Another century was to roll by before their grandchildren were first to learn that ancient Celts had once crossed the Atlantic, to found far-flung settlements at the edge of the world in a land that lay behind the Irish sunset. Celtic New England remained unrecognized and unsung. Oblivious of the historic importance of the strange stone buildings that dotted their properties, some of the Scots and Irish settlers incorporated them into the cellars of the farmhouses they were constructing in the new land. Many, how many we shall never know, of the "root cellars" were torn apart to yield stones for the dry-stone walls they constructed around their fields on the model of similar walls called dikes in Scotland and Ireland. Yet others were wrecked to yield masonry for the bridges and dams required by the developing communities of New Hampshire, Maine, and Vermont. A fearful havoc was wrought upon countless ancient Celtic structures and, sad to say, much of the damage was executed by men who would never have laid hand to the work had they but realized the sacrilege. By way of comfort, it should be added that there is no doubt that vast havoc was also wrought in Ireland and Scotland during the long centuries of the middle ages. This is sufficiently attested by the fact that Ogam-inscribed stones are often to be seen in Ireland, built into the walls of churches and farmhouses, as well as in the dry-stone walls around the fields that are as characteristic of Ireland and Scotland and Wales as they are in New England.

But before tracing the ancient Celts across the Atlantic there are some other matters to discuss in the European context, as Britain during the late Victorian period reversed her former attitudes to Celtic studies and assumed the role of patron of scholarship (always provided such scholarship did not lead to any reprehensible independence movements). A consequence of the newly favorable attitudes to research into the Celtic languages was that leading linguists began the task of reconstructing the ancient tongue of the Gauls and of their Gaelic cousins, the Goidels. Every inscription was now subjected to close scrutiny to discover what evidence it might yield as to the actual vocabulary used by the ancient Celts, and also as to how the form of a word might change according to the role it plays in a sentence. From the latter information scholars expected to be in a position to determine whether the ancient language of the Celts followed rules similar to those of Latin or Greek.

One of the leading authorities on Celtic archeology who now appeared on the scene was Sir John Rhys, professor of Celtic Languages at Oxford University. Like all archeologists of his day his training was that of a linguist, and he had pursued his language studies at the Sorbonne, Heidelberg, and Göttingen. His Welsh origin particularly fitted him for the mantle he was soon to assume, for he had been steeped in the literature and traditions of Wales since his boyhood days in Cardigan and had attended school in Bangor, Wales, before going on to Jesus College, Oxford. His career was such as one no longer finds among men of science: Lecturer in Archaeology at the University of Edinburgh, 1889; President of the Anthropological Section of the British Association for the Advancement of Science, 1900; Fellow of the British Academy; Member of the Commission on Welsh Universities; Member of the Commission for a National University of Ireland; Chairman of the Commission on Welsh Antiquities; Professor of Celtic at Oxford University from 1877 to 1907; and recipient of numerous honorary degrees. Here was a man fitted to make mincemeat of any linguist or archeologist who might care to cross swords with him in matters Celtic. His numerous books and papers covered such topics as *The Ogam-inscribed Stones of Dublin, Studies in* the Arthurian Legend, Outlines of Manx Phonology, Celtic Inscriptions of France and Italy, Inscriptions and Languages of the Northern Picts, and many others.

One of the tasks Rhys set himself at the outset of his career was to determine, if he could, the relationships between the various Celtic languages. This he did by comparative linguistics, and he set out his main conclusions in a book on Welsh philology published in 1877. The accompanying tables summarize his findings and combine with them the newest information we now have as to the linguistic affinity of the Celts who settled New England during the first millennium before Christ.

Rhys's method was etymological—that is to say he tabulated side by side similar words with similar or identical meanings in all the Celtic languages for which he had any information. He soon discovered that he could group the Celtic tongues into two large divisions, which he called the Q-Celts and the P-Celts. Languages of the Q-group substitute Q, K or CH in numerous words where languages of the P-group have either P or B. It is interesting to note that Q-Celtic is analogous to Latin in this regard, whereas P-Celtic is comparable rather to the Greek. Examples of these Q/P twins are given in the accompanying table.

Another aspect of the work of Celtic scholars concerns *accidence*—that is, the way in which the terminations of words in inflecting languages change according to the grammatical case in which they are employed. This subject is too complicated to discuss in detail here, but it suffices to say that as old inscriptions were analyzed it was found that the characteristic inflexions of Latin were soon recognized by the same or similar inflections in the old Celtic tongues.

German scholars meanwhile had been investigating the interrelationships between the various languages spoken in Europe and Asia. These studies led to the recognition of the Indo-European, or Aryan, family of related languages, in which Celtic was now recognized as comprising sister tongues of the better-known branches of the family, namely Teutonic (English, Scandinavian, and German tongues); Italic (the extinct tongues of northern Italy, including dialects very close to Gaulish, and the extinct Latin of Rome with its Romance descendants, Italian, French, Spanish, Portuguese, Romanian); the Greek dialects; the Slav branch (with Russian, Bulgarian, Slovene, Czech, and others); and the various eastern branches, including the Iranian and Indian divisions, of which Old Persian and Sanskrit present close parallels to Greek, Latin, and Celtic.

In the course of these studies the German investigators discovered that during the past 2,000 years or more, certain characteristic changes in pronunciation tend to recur in member languages of the Indo-European

TABLE 1

Principal Language Groups of Celtic, with Their Ancient and Modern Representatives The table reflects the researches of Rhys, to which has been added the newly recognized Celtic tongue of the Iberian Celtic settlements in North America.

LANGUAGE GROUPS	ANCIENT REPRESENTATIVES	MODERN DESCENDANT TONGUES
Q-Celtic	Goidelic (Gadelic)	Irish Gaelic Scots Gaelic Manx
	Inferred dialects in Spain and Portugal	extinct
	Iberian dialect of New England	extinct
P-Celtic	Brythonic (Gallo-Brittonic of Britain)	Breton (of Brittany) Cornish (of Cornwall) Welsh (of Wales)
	Gaulish languages of central and eastern Europe	extinct
	Pictish (of Scotland)	extinct

TABLE 2

Equivalent Q-Celtic and P-Celtic Words, with Latin and Greek Parallels

ENGLISH	LATIN	Q-CELTIC	P-CELTIC	GREEK
five	quinque	Gaelic: coig Irish: cuig Manx: queig	Welsh: pump Cornish: pymp Breton: pemp Gaulish: pempe	pente
four	quattuor	Gaelic: ceithir	Welsh: pedwar Gaulish: petor	root lacking
horse	equus	Gaelic: each	Welsh: ebol Gaulish: epos	hippos
head, peak	caput	Gaelic: ceann	Welsh: penn Gaulish: penno	pindos

family. One of the phonetic changes observed is that an original *b* tends to be softened to the sound of *v*. This change has taken place in Gaelic, but as the original sound of *b* is often retained in certain grammatical forms of the same word, it would be inconvenient to spell the word with a *v* in some cases, and a *b* in others, when the same word is intended. To overcome this problem, the old Gaelic grammarians hit upon the expedient of inserting an *h* after the *b* whenever the *b* sound is to be replaced by the sound of *v*. Thus *bata* means "ship," but *bhata* means "of a ship" and is to be pronounced as *vata*. Similar rules apply to some other letters that undergo changes of the same kind.

One of the ancient names of Ireland is *Ibheriu*, pronounced as *Iveriu*, a fact that suggests that the word is derived from a still-earlier pronunciation, *Iberiu*. Now this is very interesting, for the Gaelic histories assert that the ancestors of the Gaels came to Ireland from Iberia, the old name of Spain. Could *Iberiu* be the same as *Iberia*, the name of the older homeland having been transferred to the younger? Many people, including some linguists, think this may well be the case.

Gaelic tradition also asserts that the ancient Gaels (or Goidels) settled in England and Wales, and were later expelled by an invasion of Gauls from France. This tradition received strong support when the Ogam monuments of England and Wales were found and studied, for it then transpired that the Ogam inscriptions on these are not in the P-Celtic tongue, but in Q-Celtic, as if they had been engraved by the Goidels of England and Wales before their expulsion by the P-Celts, who were of course the ancient Britons and ancestors of the modern Welsh and Cornish.

Putting these facts together, we now discover that apparently Ogam was used only by the Q-Celts. The P-Celts contented themselves with Greek or Latin letters, as we see in Gaulish inscriptions in France.

When I was a student at Edinburgh University during the 1930s most of these facts came to my attention and I could not help but notice that in one of my textbooks on Gaelic etymology, the table of Celtic languages known at that time included an entry opposite the Q-group which read: "Q-Group: Dialects in Spain and Gaul (?)" As I had already visited Spain briefly, this entry intrigued me, but many years went by before I was able to study the problem. As it turned out, it is a question with profound implications for American archeology (see the table on page 42), and this seems to be the right place to introduce the topic, the more so since it offers an opportunity of explaining the hitherto mysterious origin of the Celtic Ogam alphabet.

But before setting out to search for the lost Ogam records of Portugal and Spain, I want to lead you first to Dublin, for there in the capital of

Ireland are some ancient bilingual manuscripts whose significance escaped the notice of scholars until 1973.

These manuscripts will lead us not only to Spain and Portugal but also to Libya, to the Canary Islands, and ultimately across the great northern ocean to a remote savage land lying far to the west. The name of this land is given as *Iarghal,* which means Beyond-the-Sunset. The monks who compiled the Irish manuscripts in the middle ages still remembered the manner in which the *Iarghalte* ("Sundowners") wrote, even though many centuries had already lapsed since any European ships had visited that distant shore.

It is in Dublin then that I stumbled upon explanations in Gaelic of the ancient alphabets of America, as well as those of Iberia, Phoenicia, and Scandinavia. In 476 A.D. the lamps went out all over Europe as the empire of Rome collapsed and men no longer sailed the great searoads to trade with the western colonies. But the memory of America survived in the writings of Irish scribes, whose alphabets now claim our attention.

5

Alphabets Galore

*A*IBIDEAL GU-LEOR, "alpha-
bets to repletion," as the Gaelic has it, incidentally giving the English
language one of the very few adjectives that must follow the noun, in the
Celtic manner: alphabets for every occasion, for foreign embassy or secret
conspiracy, they are all here, so the scribes of old inform us in the ancient
books of Ireland.

What books, and where are they? The oldest references to the Ogam
script of the ancient Gaels occurs in a book compiled by a bishop of Kil-
dare called Finn Mac Gorman who died in 1160 A.D. His compilation
is called by scholars the *Book of Leinster,* housed in the library of the
University of Dublin, originally founded by Queen Elizabeth I in 1591
under the imposing name of College of the Holy and Undivided Trinity,
near Dublin. The library was built in 1732 and, in addition to its collection of more than a million bound volumes, is custodian of such great
national treasures as the eighth-century *Book of Kells,* the most beautiful
in the world. It is in the *Book of Leinster* that we meet with the Ogam
alphabet in the form in which it commonly occurs on the ancient stone
monuments of Britain.

A similar Ogam alphabet is recorded in the *Book of Ballymote,* where
it is listed as number 16 of a series of some seventy alphabets known to
the author of the Ogam Tract. In the book it is stated (folio 62b) that
Turlogh the Younger, Son of Hugh O'Connor, ruled Connaught at the
time when the *Book of Ballymote* was assembled from a collection of
manuscripts. This means that the book as we know it today was put
together some time between 1370 and 1390. Altogether the book comprises
502 folio vellum pages. The original owner was Tomaltach the Younger,
Son of Donogh, Lord of Corann, who lived at Ballymote in County Sligo.
The book today is housed in the library of the Irish Academy in Dublin.
In addition to the tract on Ogam at the end of the book, other component

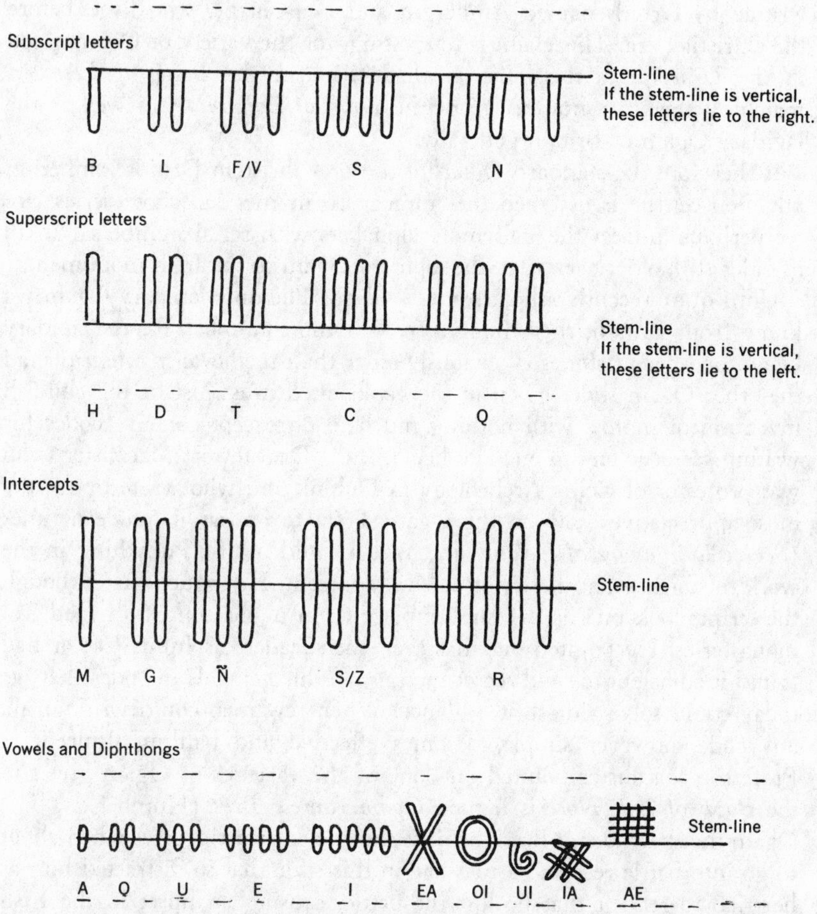

Subscript letters

Stem-line
If the stem-line is vertical,
these letters lie to the right.

B L F/V S N

Superscript letters

Stem-line
If the stem-line is vertical,
these letters lie to the left.

H D T C Q

Intercepts

Stem-line

M G Ñ S/Z R

Vowels and Diphthongs

Stem-line

A Q U E I EA OI UI IA AE

Ogam Alphabet of the *Book of Leinster*. Common variants are: (1) Vowels may be written as long vertical intercepts, in which case the consonantal intercepts are sloped. (2) Vowels may be written as mere dots. This is probably the ancient method of writing vowels, as "points," in the Semitic manner. (3) Iberian and American Ogam has fewer consonants, and omits the vowels. This is the oldest style, not found in Britain.

manuscripts deal with history and genealogy, mythology, stories about Irish saints, and the grammar of the Gaelic language.

Another ancient book in the library of the Irish Academy is called the *Book of Lecan*. This dates from 1416 and comprises 600 folio vellum pages assembled by a man named Gilla-Isa-Mor MacFirbis. It includes a grammatical treatise *Uraceipt nan-Eges* (*Primer of the Bards*), attributed to the hand of Cennfaclad the Learned, who died 677 A.D. It is further stated that Cennfaclad obtained his material from still earlier treatises written by Druids named Amhergin and Feir-ceirtne, who lived before the Christian era. This claim is interesting, for the variety of Ogam given in the *Uraceipt* is the same as that given in the *Book of Leinster*, matching therefore number 16 of the *Book of Ballymote*, as well as the lapidary Ogam of Britain generally.

If therefore the standard Ogam of the pre-Christian Druids Amhergin and Feir-ceirtne is assigned the number 16 in the Ballymote series, are we perhaps to treat the Ballymote alphabets with serial numbers 1 to 15 as older still, older even than the lapidary Ogam of the Irish monuments?

Until quite recently scholars have said no. The only lapidary Ogam we know from Britain, they thought, is Ballymote number 16. As lapidary Ogam on ancient stones is obviously older than medieval manuscripts, all the other Ogam styles given in the books cited must just be the childish invention of monks with nothing much to do except contrive codes for writing secret letters to one another. In fact, Dr. Stewart Macalister, who was professor of Celtic Archeology in Dublin, and who wrote by far the most appreciative essay on the Ogam Tract to appear in modern times (*Secret Languages of Ireland*, 1937), still could not find anything in the work to suggest that the scripts are very ancient. He argued that although the scripts look puerile, we should place them in the context of medieval monasteries. He pointed out that even such leaders as Julius Caesar had found it sufficient to send secret messages to his generals in codes that we today could solve almost at a glance. When few men could write at all, any code, however simple, becomes effective and baffling. Indeed, as Professor Macalister pointed out, one of the varieties of Ogam given in the *Book of Ballymote* is named *Ogam romesc Bres* (Number 31, The Ogam-that-bewildered-Bres) because the ancient warrior Bres when about to go into battle received a message in this style that so distracted him as he tried to read it that he lost the battle, causing an upset in the Irish World Series that year.

Incidentally, the system of *Ogam romesc Bres* is to replace each Ogam letter by the Ogam spelling of the name of the letter in Gaelic, rather as if we today were to write the name of New York "Enedouble-u wyoarkay." No wonder most European scholars dismissed the Ogam Tract as medieval nonsense!

Gwynn, an early Celtic explorer of Oklahoma, cut his autograph in two languages on a rock face on Turkey Mountain, near Tulsa, where Gloria Farley discovered it and obtained this latex mold. The upper line of Ogam script reads, from left to right, G-W-N. Gwynn, a common Celtic name, means "white," i.e., fair-haired. Below, reading from left to right, are the North Iberian letters Pa-ya-a, spelling a Punic word that also means "white," and corresponding to modern Arabic 'Byaa. The date of the inscription is perhaps around 500 B.C. *Malcolm D. Pearson*

However, these rather silly code systems are found in the latter sections of the Tract, and the straight alphabets are another matter altogether. The reason why scholars dismissed these too as of no importance was simply because *no other examples were known of such writing*. Of course, if anyone had been able to find in Ireland or Britain ancient stones with inscriptions that matched the alphabets given in the Ogam Tract, numbers 1 to 15 in particular, then the importance of the Tract would have been recognized as soon as it could be shown that the Tract yielded a successful decipherment. Indeed, even if no decipherment had resulted, the mere fact of proving that lapidary inscriptions exist using the same letters as some particular script in the Ogam Tract would have been enough to establish the credentials of the author of the Tract as one who had knowledge of ancient lapidary inscriptions.

But neither of these conditions was satisfied. Except for Ogam number 16, that is, the standard (and only) Ogam of the *Book of Leinster* and

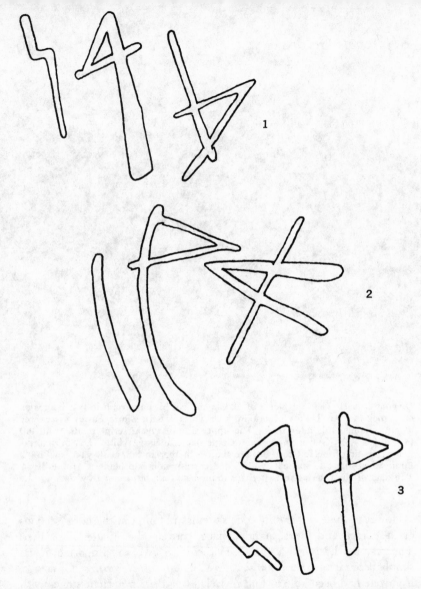

The inscriptions on the Susquehanna gravestones have until now been considered by some archeologists to be "accidental markings made by plowshares and the roots of trees." The absurdity of this is sufficiently illustrated by the fact that the same combinations of Iberian Punic letters occur repeatedly on different stones. Here are three examples of the name A-R-N (the letters to be read from right to left), spelling in the vowelless manner of ancient Iberian scribes the name Arano ("Eagle") of the Basque language. When Spanish journalists reported our finds the Epigraphic Society received letters from modern Basques who had learned that their family names are inscribed on ancient stones in America. The above examples were recorded (1) by Fell, (2) by the late William Walker Strong, original discoverer of the Susquehanna gravestones, and (3) Gertrude Johnson. Other notable Basque family names found include Galba (a family that gave Rome one Spanish emperor), and Muga (a name perpetuated also among the Shoshone Amerindians). Yet other Susquehanna gravestones carry names that also occur on an ancient Roman paymaster's list of Spanish legionnaires.

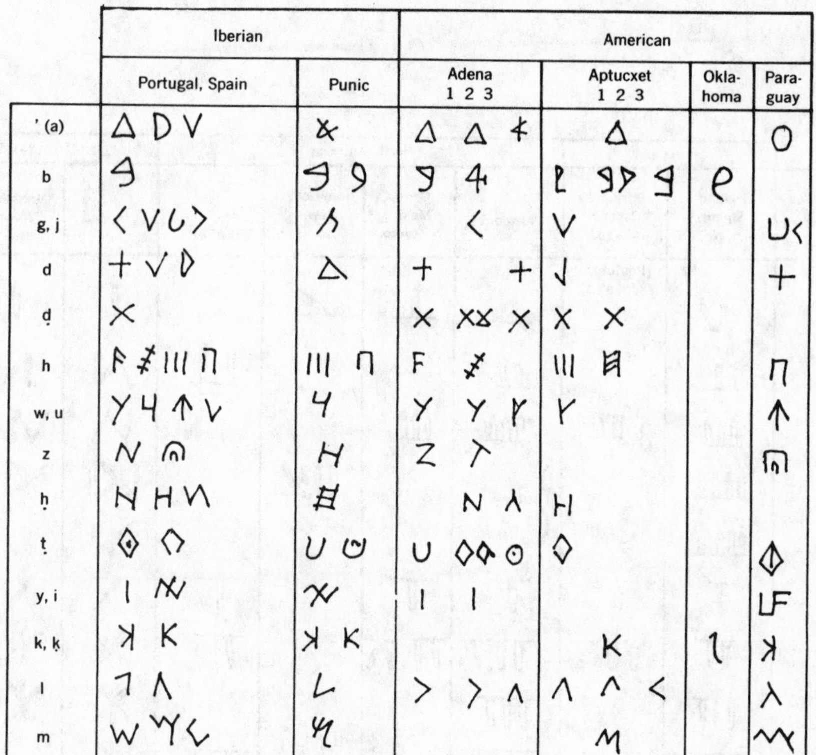
Iberian
American
Portugal, Spain
Punic
Adena
1 2 3
Aptucxet
1 2 3
Okla-homa
Para-guay
' (a)
b
g, j
d
ḍ
h
w, u
z
ḥ
ṭ
y, i
k, ķ
l
m
n
s, z
' (i)
p
f
ṣ
q
r
š
t

Examples of Iberian-Punic alphabets from Iberian and American sites, circa 800–200 B.C. Adena 1, central West Virginia, Wilson-Braxton tablet; Adena 2, Grave Creek, West Virginia; Adena 3, Susquehanna, Pennsylvania. Aptucxet 1, Komasakumkanit, Bourne, Massachusetts; Aptucxet 2, North Salem, New Hampshire; Aptucxet 3, central Vermont, temple dedications on bilingual Goidelic-Punic steles.

	Europe		North America				Ogam Tract No. 3	
Letter	Ireland Ogam Tract, No. 16	Portugal Cachão da Rapa	Vermont	Conn. Mass. N. Hamp.	Innwood, New York	Okla. Tex., Ark. Carib.	Ireland	Monhegan Maine
H		[Pontotoc, Okla. also]						
D								
T								
C			Uses G					
Q								
B								
L	UU,⋀		UU,⋀	UU,⋀				
F/V								
S								
N			uses Ñ					
M								
G								
Ñ					?			(?)
Z			lacking					
R			uses L					
Ia, Ea								
W, Ui			?			[or]		

Early Ogam alphabets of Europe and North America. The oldest styles employ only consonants, and appear to date from around 800 B.C. onwards. The fully developed Irish style, with vowels and the whole range of consonants, appears only in monuments believed to postdate the time of Christ.

Folio page of the Ogam Tract in the *Book of Ballymote*, in the library of the Irish Academy, Dublin.

The commonest variety of Ogam script in Ireland is "Edge Ogam," in which the angular edges of the stone serve as the stem-line, alternate columns being read upwards and downwards. An Irish example of edge Ogam is shown to the left (to be contrasted with the older surface Ogam of the Ballintaggart phalli, see page 22). In America examples of edge Ogam are uncommon; one from the Susquehanna valley is shown to the right, and reads from above down B B-H-L M-B la-B-G-G in the ancient vowelless style. This is apparently to be translated as "To Baal Son of Iabagug (or Habakuk)." This is from a Celtiberian community where Semitic and Basque names occur, and both Ogam and Iberian scripts are employed. *James P. Whittall II, Peter J. Garfall*

The name of the sun god Bel appears in Ogam script on the lintels of temples dedicated to sun worship. Above, B B-L (Dedicated to Bel) inscribed on a triangular plate of schist found at the winter solstice temple at Mystery Hill. Middle, the same inscription, with a solar symbol incorporated into the L, from the equinoctial temple above South Royalton, Vermont. Below, B-L inscribed on the lintel of the chamber or metonic temple at South Woodstock. *Peter J. Garfall, Joseph D. Germano*

the *Book of Lecan,* no lapidary examples turned up, despite two centuries of searching. So the modern scholars of Europe dismissed the Ogam Tract as "worthless child's play."

Now it just so happens that some of the inscriptions of North America are written in the very scripts that could not be found in Europe. They have remained unrecognized and unsolved, while over in Europe the study of Ogam was all but given up, for lack of anything new to say about the 400 inscriptions that had already been found and recorded. Never was there such a breakdown of communications among the English-speaking archeologists of the new and old worlds! While we in America could make no sense out of rock inscriptions whose solution lay clearly explained in the Ogam Tract (a fact not then known to us), our colleagues in Europe could find no such rock inscriptions and concluded that the Ogam Tract dealt with monastic fantasies, nonexistent imaginary alphabets that no one ever really used.

Nor was this the limit of the aspersions cast upon the hapless monk who wrote the Ogam Tract. In the latter part of the Tract occur a series of foreign alphabets with their Celtic gothic-letter equivalents for each letter. These too came under the scornful notice of linguists whose knowledge of epigraphy was somewhat less than adequate.

First of the foreign alphabets is one that the scribe calls Egyptian, and in this he is certainly correct, for it matches very well the tables of Egyptian Aramaic forms compiled by Professor Robert H. Pfeiffer from Egyptian papyri of the period around 400 B.C. and published in his work *Ancient Alphabets* (1947). These tables had already been completed in 1936, in which year they were exhibited as part of the special celebrations of the Tercentenary of Harvard University. Thus, as we now see from the comparative tables given in this chapter, the medieval Irish monk who wrote the Ogam Tract was already in possession of information that was only regained by modern students of Semitic epigraphy after years of excavation and research in the Egyptian desert. But all the modern students of Irish could find to say about this important correlation was

The monogram of Bel, composed of the Iberian and Phoenician letters B-L, combined with three parallel strokes to give in addition the Ogam letters B-L under a stem-line, or merely the letters B-L of either alphabet alone, occurs as engravings on flat tilelike pieces of schist, sometimes triangular in shape. These objects are found at localities where there evidently was once a temple to the sun god. The examples illustrated are: above, from Raymond, New Hampshire (where funerary stones of small module have recently been reported, built into stone walls); and below, from South Woodstock, Vermont. These stone tablets are probably votive offerings, purchased from a priest upon approaching a sacred precinct, and then left behind by the pilgrim as an offering in support of some prayer. *Peter J. Garfall*

A North American example of a lapidary inscription in the style of *Hinge Ogam* (No. 3 of the Ogam Tract), shown here as a latex mold collected on Manana Island, by Monhegan Island, about ten miles offshore from the coast of Maine. This variety of Ogam, unknown from stones in Ireland or elsewhere in Europe, was once dismissed by scholars as "worthless childsplay," supposedly the invention of medieval monks. But the American example, lacking vowels and coeval with Phoenician inscriptions, shows that this alphabet is a Bronze Age predecessor of the Irish Ogam (No. 16 of the Ogam Tract). The inscription reads from right to left (L)-NG-B-T B F-N-C C-D-H-H L-B-D, apparently to be translated as "Ships from Phoenicia, Cargo platform," the island having a flat horizontal surface of rock. This inscription is discussed in chapter 8. The occurrence of a supposedly Norse word (long-bata, i.e., longboat or ship) parallels other Norse words and personal names found on Celtiberian steles, and suggests that Norsemen were abroad long before the Viking age. *Coll. James P. Whittall II, photo by Joseph D. Germano*

that "the Egyptian alphabet, so called, is a very corrupt form of the Hebrew alphabet." Now this is rather like saying that "the Latin alphabet is a very corrupt form of the English alphabet," for it puts the cart before the horse.

After the Egyptian alphabet come two alphabets that the scribe calls African. And here, again, he is correct enough, for one of them is clearly a semicursive version of the late Numidian script in its transitional phase to becoming the Tifinag alphabet of the Berbers. I have worked with these alphabets, and recognize the affinity of the Irish manuscript variety. The other script called African by the Ballymote scribe may very well have been African at one time, though we recognize it now as a variety of the Iberian script used by Phoenician speakers in southern Spain during the first millennium B.C. On these alphabets the Irish critics have made no meaningful comment at all. What now requires to be said, and let me say it, is that modern epigraphers struggling with the intricacies of the Iberian Semitic scripts are grateful to the Ballymote scribe for having thus given us so much encouragement by confirming so many of the equivalences of shape and sound that my Spanish colleagues and I had inferred on more indirect evidence.

New world chiefs with old world names. Above, tombstone of a Vermont ruler named in the Ogam characters as Y-G-H-N or Yoghan. In modern spelling this would be rendered as Eoghan, the original form of the widespread Celtic family names Ewan and MacEwan in Scotland and Ireland; and of Evan and Efan in Wales, with derivative forms such as Bevan. This ancestor of their clan apparently ruled in New England around 500 B.C. Below, the inscribed portion of a large block of stone carrying the name in Ogam characters L-G-H M-B M-B-M, probably to be rendered as Lugh Mab Mabimo, "Lugh son of Valiant." Lew is still a name used in the old world, and Lugh probably meant a devotee of the Celtic god Lug (or Mercury, it is supposed). *Joseph D. Germano*

Yet more foreign alphabets in the Tract are attributed to the *Lachlann,* that is, the Norsemen, and they are typical of the runic series, with their numerous variations. All the Irish linguists could find to say is that they are "badly drawn!" As Johnson said, "The Irish never speak well of themselves," an assertion that in this context is by no means an over-statement.

In the tables that accompany this chapter I have taken a representative selection of the varieties of Ogam script reported in the Ogam Tract, with preference for those that appear to be old or which we have since been able to discover in actual use in lapidary inscriptions in Iberia or America. To these are added tables of the foreign scripts reported by the Ballymote scribe and matching tables compiled from the work of European epigraphers who have used data other than the Ogam Tract in deducing the sound values of the letters. Here I have also incorporated sound values determined in the course of my own researches.

Certain information given in the Ogam Tract should be mentioned here briefly, though it is discussed again when confirmatory evidence is presented in later chapters based on the newly discovered inscriptions. One of these topics is the assertion by the Ogam Tract that Ogam writing developed from finger language. This I can attest, and the evidence is given in the chapter that follows. Another point made by the author of the Tract is that Ogam can be written at will upwards or downwards or horizontally, or even along the divergent radii of a circle, and he gives examples of the same word written in these various ways. This is also well attested by the most ancient inscriptions we have detected in Portugal and Spain. In the next chapter I will show how the ancient scribes made use of this rule to contrive word pictures in rebus form, apparently intended as a means of instructing the student Druids in ac-quiring the art of writing. Although the word *rebus* is explained in a later chapter I should perhaps mention here that nearly all ancient writing systems make use of the device, for two reasons. For one thing, if you can distort letters of the alphabet just a little (without making them unread-able) you can sometimes make a word look like the object it refers to. An example of this is seen in the inscription found on many of the astronom-

When our finds of Ogam inscriptions were first announced, one professor at Yale suggested that we might be mistaking the marks made by the stonecutting drills used by colonial masons. Here (above) Dr. Sentiel Rommel demonstrates the use of a colonial drill cutting a block of stone in half. Below, Fell holds a colonial wedge to a line of "Yale Ogam" left by early colonial quarrymen in a granite outcrop near Rommel's property in Rhode Island. As is obvious, the Ogam inscrip-tions of the Celtic sites have no connection with colonial drilling. *Rommel and Fell*

ical observation pillars of the New England Celts. What looks at first
sight to be a human eye is seen on closer examination to be made up of
Ogam letters spelling the words "Observation pillar." Another reason
for using the rebus is illustrated by words that are hard to illustrate, like
"brother." If you draw a man, it will be read as *man,* and not as *brother.*
The ancient Egyptians, who used picture writing (hieroglyphs), discovered the solution. The word for brother in Egyptian is *sen.* But this
is also the same sound as the Egyptian word for a spoon. Their solution,
then, was to draw a picture of a spoon, and to draw immediately beside
it a picture of a man; this told the reader that the word *sen* is to be understood in the context of a man; that is, it had to mean brother.

6

Clues Lead to Spain and Portugal

As events were to prove, archeology was now on the brink of an exciting find that would carry the written records of the Celts much further back in time than anyone had dared to hope. Let me first recapitulate briefly the three clues that were already in our hands.

(1) Only the Gaelic Celts of Britain seem to have been acquainted with the Ogam system of writing. The Gauls of France and the P-Celts of ancient Britain employed Greek or Latin letters, as their coins attest.

(2) Gaelic tradition asserts that their ancestors came to Britain from some earlier homeland in the Iberian Peninsula.

(3) The oldest Gaelic name for Ireland is *Ibheriu,* a word that resembles *Iberia.* Migrant peoples commonly carry the name of a former homeland to the new homeland.

Putting together these three pieces of information, it became apparent to me that a search for possible Ogam inscriptions should be undertaken in Spain and Portugal. This would require research funds to cover the cost of travel. As efforts to raise a supporting grant had not been successful, however, the project had to be laid aside. Then, unexpectedly, some remarkable new data came into my hands.

Some years earlier I had made the acquaintance of the Norwegian Dr. Jan-Olaf Willums, at that time a graduate student in environmental engineering at the Massachusetts Institute of Technology. As Norwegians and Danes can understand each other's speech and I happen to speak Danish, we had occasionally chatted in these tongues. He recalled this, as well as my interest in languages, when a few years later he met another young Norwegian, a linguist named Erik Reinert also studying in Cambridge, at Harvard University. Erik had spent two years traveling in South America, where he acquired a knowledge of the Guarani and Quechua tongues in addition to about ten European languages that he had studied before coming to America. Jan now introduced Erik to me because, as I soon learned, Erik had traveled in Paraguay and brought back some pictures of rock inscriptions in an unknown script found in caves near the upper reaches of the Paraguay River. I recognized the inscriptions as Iberian, and read that they recorded a visit to Paraguay by ancient mariners from Cadiz. The writing style suggested a date around 500–300 B.C.

What was even more surprising was that some of the inscriptions were written in what I recognized as a new kind of Ogam—a variety that employed only consonants, the vowels being omitted. This habit of writing with only consonants is characteristic of the Semitic peoples and in the millennium before Christ it was especially characteristic of the Phoenicians. The Phoenicians are known to have had colonies in southern Spain; indeed, they are the founders of Cadiz, the city whose name I read in one of the inscriptions. They carried their Semitic tongue to Spain, where it was acquired by many of the native Spanish peoples, who wrote it in a variant of Phoenician script that epigraphers call Iberian.

The most curious thing about the inscriptions in Ogam is that the language contained in the Ogam writing is not a Celtic dialect, but instead a form of Phoenician. In other words, the Iberian sailors who had cut the inscriptions on the cave walls near the navigable waters of the Paraguay River had employed two different alphabets, one Ogam and the other Iberian, though the language they used in both cases was a dialect of the Phoenician tongue. Erik and I wrote a joint report on his finds that was published by the Epigraphic Society and aroused interest in Spain.

One of the consequences was that, through the kind offices of Mr. Gerard Kraus, I received from the authorities of the Museo Canario in the Canary Islands a fine series of reproductions of cave inscriptions found there by Dr. Antonio Beltrano Martinez, and with this material came a cordial invitation to attempt the decipherment of the inscriptions. I will discuss them in a later chapter, but mention them here in order to observe that some of them are in the Libyan language, *but written in Ogam letters*—consonants only, no vowels.

It was clear that we were now on the way toward finding some new evidence that could be expected to throw light on where these Spanish and Libyan Ogam-writers had obtained their knowledge of what we had always considered to be a Gaelic alphabet. It now seemed very likely that somewhere in the Iberian peninsula there must have lived during the first millennium B.C. some Celts who were related to the Gaels who later settled in Britain and Ireland.

James Whittall, whose personal knowledge of Iberian Bronze Age archeology is founded on wide-ranging travel and buttressed by a vast collection of color slides of Iberian sites and artifacts as well as an associated library of Spanish and Portuguese scientific publications in this field, now became deeply interested in our results. He had already, some years earlier, expressed the opinion that many of the supposed "root cellars" of New England are the work not of colonial farmers but of some Bronze Age people from the Mediterranean and had given further precision to his opinions in 1969 by drawing an explicit parallel between the megalithic buildings of Portugal and the similar stone structures of New England. Jim now provided me with numerous documents, books, and color slides from his collections, and it was our shared hope that somewhere in this mass of material we might find evidence on the question of whether Ogam writing was ever used in Spain and Portugal, and if it was used, what were the languages employing the Ogam alphabet. It was a fortunate chance, indeed, that brought Jim and me together at this time, for it soon became clear that his collections contained the raw data I needed to complete my epigraphic inquiries; and at the same time what I now found in his collections gave him the information he needed in order to zero in on the precise parts of the Iberian peninsula where he might expect to find archeological materials directly related to the New England sites.

Before long I was able to identify several localities in Portugal where, as I could see from the inscriptions visible in the pictures Jim had obtained, there are to be found Ogam writings, the chief of these being located on or near the Douro River, draining northern Portugal. Here, to my great satisfaction, I found bilingual and trilingual cliff and rock paintings and engravings, in which one of the languages is Celtic. More important still, the script employed is a variety of the Ogam cipher called *Aradach Finn* (Finn's Ladder) in the *Book of Ballymote*. In Professor Macalister's classification of the Ogam styles he groups together several quite diverse variants with the *Aradach Finn,* all having the common property of dissecting or eliminating the stem-line. The Iberian form now identified is closer to the common model than either of the two Irish variants that Macalister has grouped with the type example, which (significantly) is given as number 1 in the *Book of Ballymote* and which might therefore represent the oldest kind of Ogam. As was soon to become apparent, the numbering sequence of the Ogam styles in the *Book of Ballymote* is such that the oldest styles have the lowest numbers,

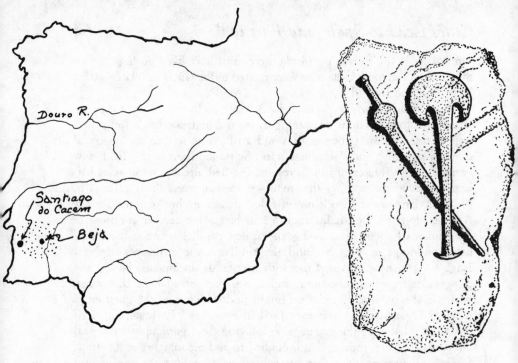

The Bronze Age Beja Culture–1. A highly characteristic development of the late Bronze Age in Portugal is a funerary culture whose monuments to chieftains are found distributed around the region of Beja, in southern Portugal. Here occur large flat slabs of schist rock, about a meter in length, cut to form the covering flagstone of a grave, and having insignia engraved of crossed weapons, in the manner of a coat of arms. Swords are sometimes incorporated in the insignia, and the variation in their form suggests dates ranging from about 800 B.C. to 500 B.C. An example from Santiago do Cacem, near the Atlantic coast south of Lisbon, is shown here. Remains found beneath Beja funerary slabs have included fragments of skeletons and pottery of Bronze Age type; some burials, however, had been looted in ancient times, and the grave site reused by later peoples. This Beja Culture, as yet little studied, may prove to be critical in determining the period and source of Celtic Iberian settlement in central Vermont, as the next illustrations show.

The Bronze Age Beja Culture–2. In 1975, by following clues yielded by my decipherment of Ogam milestones, John Williams succeeded in finding the settlement area in central Vermont which we now designate *Precincts of the Gods* (from the name given on the last milestone). On a lofty ridge above the temple area John found a partially buried and collapsed structure resembling a dolmen. What appear to be the insignia of a king of the Beja culture of southern Portugal are engraved on one end face of the large capstone.

It is probable that we have here the actual tomb of one of the early Celtic kings of New England. Excavation may disclose that the interior has been rifled in ancient times, as in the case of some of the Beja tombs of Portugal, but whether or not this proves to be so, the monument itself is a fine addition to our national treasures. Above right, tombstone with coat of arms of an early Celtic king of New England. Objects depicted are a long-handled Celtic battle-axe (or Lochaber axe), set across a palmleaf, symbolizing war and peace. Below, John Williams at the find site in Vermont. *John Williams, Joseph D. Germano*

and it is these low-numbered archaic styles that are most widely distributed outside of the British Isles.

As the illustrations show, the Iberian style of Ogam, especially as seen at the Cachão da Rapa in the Douro valley of northern Portugal, is associated with solar symbols such as the disk of the sun and the checkerboard symbol that seems to represent an early form of sundial, already well known from sites of solar cults elsewhere in Europe, as for example early Iron Age cultures of Tarentum, Naples, and other southern Italian locations. At some of these European sites the checkerboard symbol is associated with the sun-rotula, or miniature spoked wheel, a universal sun symbol. Later, in North America, we were to find the same symbols associated with evidence of sun worship and, like the Iberian examples now confronting us, accompanied by Ogam script of the Finn's Ladder variety.

Particularly important was one inscription of the Cachão da Rapa series in Portugal for here, as already noted, I was able to read the letters G-L-N, placed between a painting of the disk of the sun on the left and a sundial checkerboard on the right. In modern Gaelic *grian* is the word for sun, matching Welsh *greian* and Sanskrit *ghṛniṣ,* sunshine. It is evident that in the vowelless form of Ogam (matching the vowelless Phoenician that occurs also at Cachão da Rapa), the Ogam writer did not distinguish the letters *r* and *l*. This is a characteristic of many languages and writing systems such as Japanese. The two sounds intergrade through a series of letters, lacking from English, but carefully distinguished in some oriental languages by signs such as r, ṛ, ḷ, and l (or their equivalents in eastern scripts). In Hawaii, for example, *aloha* (love) is so spelled and pronounced. In New Zealand it is spelled and pronounced *aroha;* but in the intervening islands the European ear is bewildered and his tongue bedevilled, for there is neither an *r* nor an *l* in the word but something in between. Mariners visiting the islands, however, have never allowed this linguistic problem to interfere with international friendship.

The Ogam inscriptions of the Cachão da Rapa are painted in brilliant blues and vermilions on the face of a cliff shelter where rain seldom percolates, so they are well preserved and have in fact been known to archeologists for at least two centuries. Since such bright pigments were

Symbols of sun worship–1. Throughout all phases of the Bronze Age in Europe, worship of the sun was a conspicuous religious trait, and sites where solar worship occurred werè indicated by esoteric engraved or painted signs, especially the rotula or sun-wheel, and a checkerboard or sometimes ladderlike symbol, perhaps signifying a sundial. Examples shown here are: (a) from Serrazes, San Pedro do Sul, Portugal; (b, c) southern Italy; (d) an amulet from Tarentum, southern Italy; (e) detail from an amulet, Naples, Italy; (f) La Vaux, Brittany, engraved monoliths; (g) southern Italy. (*a, after Rodrigues; others from Dechelette*)

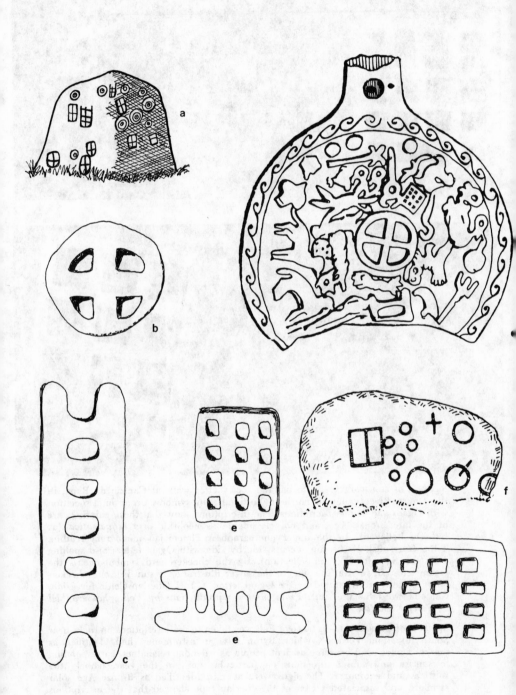

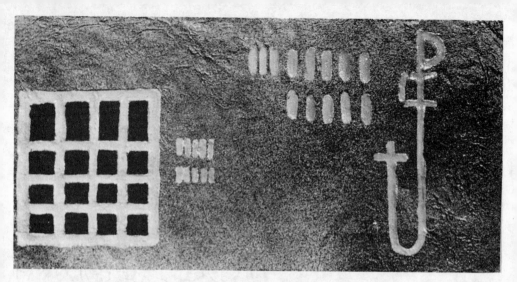

Symbols of sun worship–2. On painted rock-shelter walls at Cachão da Rapa, in the Douro River valley in northern Portugal, sun symbols occur in association with Ogam and Punic inscriptions. The inscriptions show that these paintings are of the late Bronze Age, and not classifiable as neolithic *arte esquematica* (as hitherto believed). In the upper photograph a Phoenician monogram reading T-R-S (turs, disk of the sun) occurs side by side with Ogam letters also spelling T-R (the S omitted as an inflection). By the checkerboard symbol occurs the Ogam letter R, for Ra, the sun. In the lower illustration a sun disk and checkerboard pattern are separated by the Ogam letters G-L-N (Iberian Celtic for *grian*, Goidelic word for the sun). *From plaster reproductions by Fell, photographed by Peter J. Garfall*

Symbols of sun worship–3. In 1975 Fell was taken to see inscriptions on rocks near South Royalton, Vermont, which Byron Dix, an astronomer, had identified as marker stones used by some ancient people as calendar regulators, corresponding to sunrise and sunset directions on particular days of the year, namely the solstices and equinoxes. The signs were at once identified as Bronze Age solar symbols, and associated Ogam of the Iberian type showed that the inscriptions were the work of Bronze-Age Celts of Iberian origin. *Photographs by Peter J. Garfall from casts prepared by Fell*

Symbols of sun worship–4. The New England sun symbols were thickly overgrown by lichen when discovered (top left), a fact that disproves claims that we were forging the inscriptions. Inscriptions of a like nature were later found elsewhere in New England, as exemplified by one from Raymond, New Hampshire (bottom left). In contrast to local attitudes, Portuguese archeologists were quick to recognize the correspondence of the American and Iberian material when it was drawn to their attention. Like the Iberian inscriptions, these American examples are to be dated to the late Bronze Age on account of the associated Ogam and Punic inscriptions. *Fell and Peter J. Garfall*

Symbols of sun worship–5. In Europe after the coming of Christianity, the old pagan sun symbols were adapted to serve an acceptable function within the approved canons of the church, for the monks were unable to detach the people from their mystic worship of the rotula. Left, the so-called Celtic cross, exemplified by the ancient Cross of Iona. Right, an old Basque tombstone in the French Pyrenees, in which the cross is formed from 5 sun wheels. Christian missionaries did not reach the New England Celts, so the pagan inscriptions in Ogam and Punic letters have remained intact in their original form. *Iona Cross from a replica collected by Elisabeth M. Foster, Edinburgh; photographs by Joseph D. Germano*

not known to Neolithic men, it is surprising to find that European archeologists have classified these inscriptions as a form of Stone Age art, known in Spain and Portugal as *Arte Esquematica,* a name given by the great French archeologist Henri Breuil. So far as the Ogam inscriptions are concerned, these and the associated Libyan and Phoenician texts must of course be removed from this incongruous classification and transferred to either the latter part of the Iberian Bronze Age or the earliest part of the Iron Age. The form of the associated Phoenician letters suggests to me a date around 800 B.C.

There is another type of Ogam found in Iberia, as exemplified by the rebus pictures of Cogul, in Lerida, Spain. A *rebus* is any style of writing in which the letters are so arranged as to suggest a picture of the topic to which the writing relates. We are familiar with it in advertising, for example, when a baker will place a sign above his shop in which the letters BREAD are made to form the shape of a loaf of bread. This style of writing was much more popular in former times than it is nowadays. There is a fascinating rebus at Cogul in which the Ogam letters are arranged along stem-lines that are alternately horizontal and vertical, thereby producing a stylized Picasso-esque picture of two stags, their legs and antlers supplied by the Ogam strokes, their bodies and necks by the stem lines. To this is added a drawing of a youth with bow and arrow. The solution is easy, as seen in the illustration on page 75. This style of Ogam is listed as number 24 in the Ogam Tract, but Macalister groups it with the others that he links with Finn's Ladder—that is, Ogam in which the stem-line can rotate into various positions. In the Ogam Tract oblique angles are also acceptable for the stem-line. Petroglyphs of the Cogul type are common in Sweden, and these might repay closer study, for they too may be rebus forms; but that is a topic beyond the scope of this chapter.

Yet a third type of Ogam can be recognized in Spain, corresponding to what the Ogam Tract calls *Cos-Ogam* and *Sron-Ogam,* classified by Macalister as *cryptocheironomy,* a long word that means secret communication by hand signs. The author of the Ogam Tract tells us that the strokes above, across, and below the stem-line represent the fingers, though he does not explain all the details. In *Cos-Ogam* a squatting man can use his shin bone as the stem-line (vertical, of course) and employ the fingers of each hand to form the one to five strokes on either side required to make the letters. Presumably the strokes that cross the stem-line are to be formed by simultaneously using corresponding fingers of both hands at once. The only value of such a proceeding would seem to be that two literate persons (for example, Druids) could exchange information in the presence of other illiterate persons (for example, clients

Ogam rebus as rock painting at Cogul (Lerida), Spain. This Picassoesque sketch of two stags and a hunter reads also as an example of Ogam with dissected stem-line, no. 24 of the Ogam Tract, yielding from left to right: L M-B D-M-V (hunter) C-S L-B. This may be construed as the Celtic roots "With the youth (is) a stag. The hunter bends his bow." Pictures such as these may be the relics of the schoolwork of young Druids, learning their letters. *Garfall and Germano*

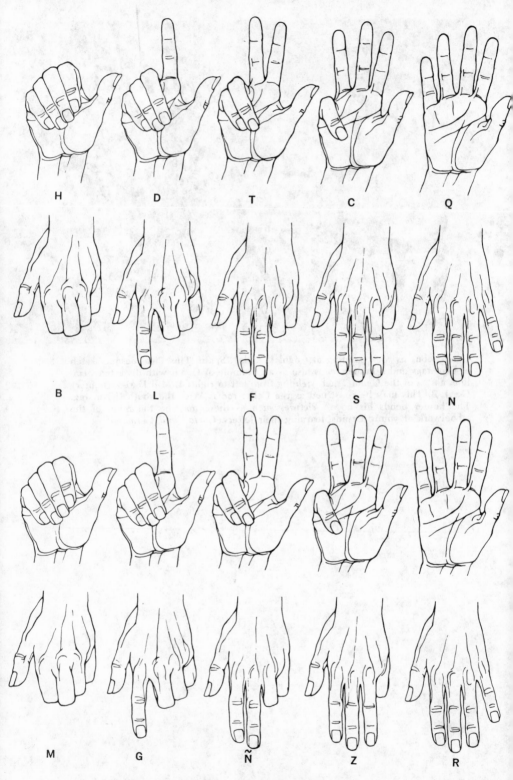

Ogam finger alphabet

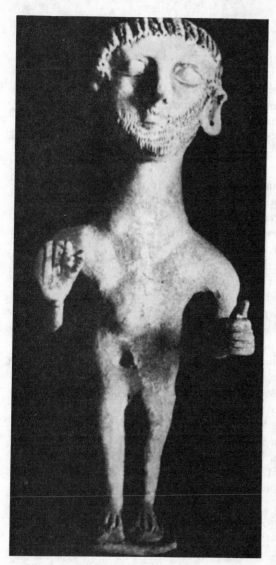

Inferred Ogam finger language as seen in funerary monuments from the ancient necropolis at Molina (Ibiza), Spain. Left, nude warrior whose hands signify his death in combat (Q-B). Right, woman with all digits of both hands extended, signifying mourning for death (Q-N). *Museo Arqueologica Nacional, Madrid*

at an oracle), and the illiterate consultants would not understand the communications. This is on a par with the rather clever techniques of mountebank mind readers whose performances used to startle our grandparents, only in that case the secret communication was by means of the initial letters of the patter invented by the intermediary who introduced the client to the blindfolded visionary. The other variety of hand Ogam mentioned by the Ogam Tract under the name *Sron-Ogam* is similar to *Cos-Ogam*, but the bridge of the nose is used as the stem-line.

In the illustrations you can see how the system apparently worked. I asked the artist who drew them, Lydia Wunsch, to make the letters in the way the Ogam Tract describes, and assigned the right hand to the upper staves (that is, the series from H to Q), and the left hand to the lower stave (letters B to N), while both hands at once yield letters M to R. The reason for assigning the hands in this way (instead of vice-versa) is that in the cemeteries of ancient Celtic sites in Spain there are found statues of deceased persons who are holding their hands in a peculiar way, with certain fingers extended, others retracted. You will see examples from Molina in Ibiza on page 77. Of course, the most likely explanation of these strange hand positions is that the figures are expressing a word in finger language. There are also well-defined differences between the manners in which people are depicted. The young male figures are commonly nude, and if nude they hold the five fingers of the right hand aloft while only the thumb is raised on the left hand (remember that when you face a person his left is your right). We know from classical writers that Celtic men went into battle nude. Hence these must represent warriors who died in battle. But the word that means "in battle" in old Goidelic is *qath*, pronounced as "kah." If we read the finger letters in the way I have suggested, then it turns out that the warriors are telling us that they died "in battle."

Now we can test out the hypothesis by seeing what happens if we read the fingers of other monuments in the same way. We then discover that the women (who are fully clothed and hold all five fingers of both hands in the extended position) are apparently saying Q-N. Since vowels are omitted, Q-N is how an Iberian Celt would spell the word *qaoin*, corresponding to the modern Gaelic and Anglo-Irish word "keen," meaning to utter lamentation for the newly dead, as at an Irish wake. It seems then that these ladies are saying to us something like "Weep for me," or as the French might express it, "Ayez pitié!"

In Celtic mythology, as Professor Proinsias MacCana of University College, Dublin, tells us in his book so titled, the wheel was the form in which thunderbolts are represented, and there is a fine embossed relief of the Thunder-God Taranis holding thunderbolts on a Celtic bowl in the

Taranis, the thunder god. Note the peculiar elevation of the thumbs. *National-museet, Copenhagen*

National Historical Museum in Copenhagen. Look at the hands of Taranis in the illustration. In each case the thumbs are elevated, a highly unlikely circumstance if one were to grasp two wheels of the size he is manipulating. Once again we suspect a concealed Ogam message. The ancient Goidelic word for thunderbolt is not known to us, but in modern Gaelic, *beithir* can have this meaning. I suspect that Taranis is saying B-H or "Bith," and that this may represent the sound of the word for thunderbolt in ancient times. In Chapter 12 you will note that one of the Iberian visitors to Oklahoma engraved two wheel-shaped objects on the Cimarron cliffs, together with the Punic-Iberian letters B-R-K, *baruk*, meaning thunderbolt in the Punic tongue. In that case it may perhaps commemorate the name of the visitor's ship. This, of course, is only a guess, but we do know that ancient ships were given names of that kind.*

The upshot of the examination I had made of Jim Whittall's extensive Iberian collections was to convince both him and me that we now had firm evidence that Celtic speakers who wrote in Ogam script, and hence were presumably Goidels, had once lived in Spain and Portugal. This finding, as will be apparent from the next chapter, has great significance for American archeology. As this book was written Jim made yet another visit to the Iberian sites, this time to pay special attention to the particular districts where the Ogam inscriptions tell us to expect other material evidence of the one-time presence of Q-Celts.

* Saint Paul traveled to Malta on the *Castor and Pollux* with 230 fellow passengers.

7

Mystery Hill

BY the beginning of May 1975, several signs began to warn us that there was a faint but real possibility that we might be on the verge of solving the most baffling problem of American archeology, namely the identity of the builders of the mysterious "root cellars" of the northeastern states and the date of their occupation. These signs were:

(1) The so-called "root-cellars" appeared to be the work of megalithic people; that is, they resembled corresponding structures in Europe dating from the Bronze Age and known to have been in use by the Celts in classical times.

(2) We now knew that Celtic inscriptions occur in Spain and Portugal, associated with Iberian Punic inscriptions, and in the vicinity of megalithic structures.

(3) Iberian Punic inscriptions were identified by me at sites near Boston to which I was taken by James Whittall. These inscriptions (see page 89) appeared to be the work of casual voyagers visiting America during the era of about 500–300 B.C.

Although my researches up to this time had been related to inscriptions of Europe and the Far East, Jim Whittall perceived that the parallels between the archeological settings in New England and in western Europe were now much clearer than had previously been realized. He now began to show me the files of photographs taken by Malcolm B. Pearson over the previous 35 years, illustrating the principal features of the so-called "root cellars" and other apparently megalithic structures. In company with Professor Norman Totten, Chairman of the Department of History at Bentley College, we studied these and pored over every detail we could make out, searching for traces of Ogam or other lettering that might disclose if any Celtic occupation had occurred. None could be detected. Re-

luctantly I had to tell Jim that unless there were inscriptions I could throw no light on the problem.

Nonetheless, despite these discouraging results Jim Whittall and I visited the best-known of the sites on June 14. This is Mystery Hill, New Hampshire, a complex of stone-slab chambers and associated henge stones oriented so that the sun sets behind particular standing stones on the days of the equinox and the summer and winter solstices (see chapter 7). The site covers approximately 60 acres, mostly occupied by second-growth woodland through which run peculiarly constructed dry-stone walls with tall, pointed, triangular stones occurring at regular intervals in the walls. It includes an area of about one acre covered by a maze of massive stone chambers with various other striking but puzzling features, such as the so-called Table of Sacrifice (page 84).*

Some of the slab chambers reminded me of the *dunans* ("little fortresses") of the ancient Goidelic Celts that I had studied in Scotland many years before. I was struck by the occurrence all over the site of flat flagstones of triangular outline, and these reminded me of the triangular slabs I had seen set above the lintels of dunans in northern Scotland. Although the things that I was shown that day by Robert Stone, the present owner and devoted protector of the site, made a profound impression on me, the one feature for which I was particularly alerted was, of course, whether or not any inscriptions had been found at Mystery Hill. It now turned out that such had indeed been found, and fortunately preserved in the museum on the site, but it had not been realized that the strangely marked stones carried anything that could be read as writing. Writing it certainly was that I saw before me, not the Celtic script I had hoped for, but severely weathered Iberian Punic script. Before I refer further to these, I should here interpolate some short outline of the history of the site as an archeological object.

When the first colonial settlers came to New England they found numerous stone buildings of one storey, circular or rectangular in form, up to 30 feet in length (usually half that).and up to 10 feet wide and 8 feet high or more. Some were completely sunken beneath the ground and were only discovered years later when a roof caved in or a plow or pick-axe penetrated the chamber. Others were partly buried or had mounds of earth covering them and trees growing from the top of such a size as to indicate an age of at least 250 years. Still others were wholly above ground or excavated into the side of a hill. All were made of large stones and included roof slabs weighing several tons. Many had elaborate "smoke holes" and other recesses built into the walls.

The colonists, asking no questions apparently, accepted these structures as the work of vanished Indian tribesmen and put them to use as

---

*The site at Mystery Hill is also known as "America's Stonehenge."

The so-called Table of Sacrifice at Mystery Hill, New Hampshire, is a large rectangular rock slab bordered by runnels that drain into a former receptacle placed at the front right corner. Although its function is still uncertain, James Whittall on his 1975 expedition to Portugal learned that some thirty similar grooved tables have now been discovered on ancient sites in that country, some of them known to be associated with burial grounds. *Norman Totten*

storage cellars for their root crops. Some were used as secret hide-outs by escaped slaves and others were made to serve as illicit whiskey distilleries. Most were referred to guardedly if at all as "root cellars," and in the course of time large numbers of them were dismantled and their stones used for making dry-stone walls. This latter fact is abundantly attested by the number of temple dedications we have since found in stone walls together with much other evidence as to the origin of the large stones in the walls.

The large complex of slab buildings now called Mystery Hill became the property of a settler named Pattee, who arrived in North Salem, New Hampshire, in 1823. In the following twenty-five years about 40 percent of the stone structures were destroyed or damaged severely by building contractors who visited the area to obtain stone for dams and bridges.

Until 1893 no one seems to have stopped to think whether these New England structures might have a remote origin. Almost everyone by this time supposed that their own forebears had built the "root cellars," and this became the accepted belief of archeologists, who began to speak of them as colonial in date. This is despite the fact that Professor Hugh

Morrison, Chairman of the Department of Architecture at Dartmouth College and a leading authority on colonial architecture, declined to accept this interpretation. The *Milford Journal* of April 26, 1893, carried an article by Daniel Fiske in which he drew attention to peculiar unexplained features of what is now known as the Upton Chamber, Massachusetts.

In 1928 the parents of Malcolm Pearson purchased the Upton property, not knowing that it contained the mysterious chamber. This, when noticed, engaged the interest of Malcolm, then a young man; and on learning of Olaf Strandwold's interest in Norse relics, Malcolm Pearson drew the former's attention to the structure in 1935. Meantime an article by a clergyman of Methuen appeared in the *Boston Globe* in 1936, making reference to unexplained "stoneworks" at North Salem. This proved to be the Pattee property, now called Mystery Hill. Shortly after, William Goodwin was directed to Pearson by Strandwold, and Malcolm took him to North Salem. Goodwin purchased the property and erected a protective fence about it. Soon after he began to restore and study the ruins.

Goodwin became convinced that the Mystery Hill chambers must be the work of Irish Culdee monks, and devoted the rest of his life to endeavours to prove this hypothesis. The discouragement he received from archeologists whom he consulted never led him to give up his views, but he was unable to convince any reputable authority that the structures were ancient. In 1950, after Goodwin's death, Malcolm Pearson inherited the property at Mystery Hill. He was not able to leave his professional work in order to live on the site, which accordingly became subject to vandalism. To avoid further destruction he was glad to lease it to Robert Stone, the present site director, in 1950, and in 1965 Bob Stone purchased the property, which he had already opened to the public and protected from further vandalism. Since that time archeological work has proceeded, though much hampered by lack of funds, for no professional archeologists could be found to support the theory of the antiquity of the site.

From 1960–1971 Geochron Laboratories, Cambridge, Massachusetts, made a series of radio-carbon determinations on samples of charcoal obtained by James Whittall at specified levels in Mystery Hill. Copies of the letters exchanged by Robert E. Stone and Harold W. Krueger on these determinations (see Bibliography) have been deposited in the Widener Library archives at Harvard University. These carbon analyses point to periods of occupation of the Mystery Hill site extending back to the second millennium B.C. Dr. Krueger, in a report dated September 18, 1917, stresses that one of the buildings that professional archeologists have claimed to be the work of Pattee in the nineteenth century is in fact penetrated by the roots of a tree whose carbon age is determined to be

Small megalithic chamber at Mystery Hill, North Salem, New Hampshire. The entrance faces south, and the proportions of the chamber suggest its possible use in connection with observation of the midwinter solstice by means of the sun's noon shadow. *Peter J. Garfall*

Two methods of roof construction employed at Mystery Hill, New Hampshire. Above, corbelling, using small slabs progressively overlapped toward the center and topped by small capstones. Below, lintels spanning the entire chamber, used where large flat slabs are available, leveling adjusted by wedges at left of ceiling. *Peter J. Garfall, Joseph D. Germano*

Subterranean chamber at Upton, Massachusetts. It was Pearson's interest in this unexplained building that led him to Mystery Hill, and hence to Goodwin's eventual purchase and protection of that important site. *Malcolm D. Pearson*

Archeologist James P. Whittall II with the Mill River stele, near Boston. The inscription in ancient Iberian letters warns passersby not to loiter as the site is a burial ground. Recently a stele with a similar inscription was excavated from an ancient cemetery near Hudade do Pêgo, in Portugal.

1690 A.D. ± 90 years. In 1988 the ruins are still considered by many to lack archeological context, despite these radio-carbon datings.

Two societies have been established by interested people who believe the stone chambers of New England are ancient structures. One, the American Institute for Archaeological Research, is particularly linked with Mystery Hill and was founded by Robert Stone. The other, the Early Sites Research Society, is the outcome of reviving an earlier society with a similar name established in Vermont and New Hampshire by Dr. Vilhjalmur Stefansson, Dr. Hugh Morrison, and other professional archeologists; this group is interested in all so-called "root cellars" and related structures. The Bibliography lists some documents relative to the Society's origins. Associated with Robert Stone in his work of exploring and protecting the Mystery Hill site are his son Dennis as general manager and various local residents. A small museum and refreshment center has been established on the site for the convenience of visitors, and thus the work of protecting the site has proceeded, fortified by the enthusiasm of the group and the belief that they are custodians to a part of America's remote past.

In this belief they are certainly correct. The inscribed stones I was permitted to study after my first visit to the site disclosed that one of the chambers on the site was dedicated to the Phoenician god *Baal*. The triangular tablet carrying this information in Iberian Punic script was found some years ago by James Whittall. The probability is that other chambers on Mystery Hill were dedicated to other divinities, and that the whole complex was a religious center and astronomical observatory. I alerted Bob Stone as to the probable importance of triangular stones as likely inscribed objects; he forthwith began a search for them.

On July 9, 1975, I obtained Bob Stone's permission to bring Professor George Carter to inspect the site, together with a party including Rene, George's wife Alberta, Os Stone, and some of Bob's assistants. George, like me, was deeply impressed by what he saw, and although he did not feel competent to judge such objects as the peculiar sacrificial table, he did sense the same antiquity as I had when confronted with the inscribed dedication in Iberian Punic to the sun god Baal.

And it was while we were examining the chamber where Jim Whittall had discovered the Baal tablet that the most important find up to that time took place. A shout from Bob Stone told us he had found another tablet in the adjacent dry-stone wall. As he brushed away the adhering dirt there came into clear view a line of Ogam script that read B-B-L. I could only conclude that this is in the same vowelless style as the Punic script and the same as the Portuguese and Spanish Ogam, and the reading was therefore to be taken as *Bi Bel,* that is, "Dedicated to Bel." *Bel* is the

One of Whittall's most important finds was this triangular dedication tablet, found in the ruins of a small rectangular stone chamber at Mystery Hill, New Hampshire, now recognized as a winter solstice noon transit temple-observatory. The inscription in Iberian characters reads, from right to left, "To Baal of the Canaanites (Phoenicians), this in dedication." Subsequently an Ogam dedication was also found by Robert Stone, showing that Bel (the sun god of the Celts) was identified with Baal of the Semitic peoples. *Peter J. Garfall*

Celtic sun god, long suspected (but until now never proven) to be the same god as the Phoenician Baal. One swallow does not a summer make, so we were still cautious, for Ogam-like markings can be produced occasionally by fortuitous means, though this inscription was very clearly and neatly cut.

As events quickly showed, we had the solution in our hands. Within ten days we were seeing dozens of Ogam inscriptions on another less-damaged but more remote site in central Vermont. It became clear that ancient Celts had built the New England megalithic chambers and that Phoenician mariners were welcome visitors, permitted to worship at the Celtic sanctuaries and allowed to make dedications in their own language.

The antiquity of Mystery Hill inscriptions could now be confidently set at about 800–600 B.C. (to judge by the writing style of the associated Phoenician inscriptions) and it was clear that Goidelic Celts were the occupants at that date, and in all probability the builders too. We all knew there would be a tough fight ahead to obtain a means of publication of our finds; and that indeed proved to be the case.

The full significance of the Mystery Hill complex did not at first appear clear, and for a while I thought there had been an initial Celtic occupation followed by a Punic phase. These problems were cleared up once we began work in the Vermont area. There were also additional inscriptions found soon afterwards at Mystery Hill, one of them showing that Celts still occupied the site as late as the century following the introduction of the reformed calendar of Julius Caesar in 45 B.C. Of this more is said later in this book. Before continuing the account of our Celtic inquiries I must turn to consider parallel studies that led us to realize that Celts were by no means the only visitors or colonists who came to the Atlantic shores of America. As has already been made clear, Phoenicians were certainly visitors to the Celtic sites, and in all likelihood were conducting affairs of their own over here. To this matter some attention must now be given.

8

Ships of Tarshish

BY the eighth century B.C. a group
of Syrian colonists had settled the lower reaches of the valley of the
Guadalquivir River in Andalusia, southwestern Spain, where they were
engaged in trading for metals mined by the natives, who seem to have
been mainly Basques. Eventually invading bands of Celts in ever-increasing numbers came down from the north, and by 500 B.C. they had overrun the whole region. Thereafter we hear no more of Phoenicians in this
part of Andalusia. Now, however, we have found their inscriptions in
America.

The city built by people in Spain was called Tarshish, and it is referred to by that name in the Old Testament. The Greeks called the city
Tartessos, and from this name comes the word *Tartessian,* used by epigraphers to describe the special script and dialect employed by the men of
Tarshish. The alphabet has been deciphered in part by Spanish epigraphers, and most of the residual letters have now been assigned their
phonetic values as a result of the discovery of Tartessian inscriptions in
Central and North America. The language can now be read with relative ease, for it proves to be no more than a dialectal variant of Phoenician. In fact, one wonders why the Tartessians bothered to devise their
own script, seeing they could equally well have employed the script of
Phoenicia itself.

From the Bible we learn that the ships of Tarshish were the largest
seagoing vessels known to the Semitic world, and the name was eventually applied to any large ocean-going vessel. On the coasts of Palestine,
where the ancient psalmists of Israel could watch the vessels of their
Phoenician cousins plying their trade with Lebanon and Egypt, the ships
of Tarshish became proverbial as an expression of sea power. On this coast
the east wind was feared by the sailors in Bronze Age times because it

could blow ships out into the Mediterranean, and most of the coastal vessels were unable to withstand the turbulence of the open seas. Thus, in
their naiveté as landlubbers, the Hebrews imagined that the same east
wind meant disaster for the ships of the Phoenicians too. (In fact, of
course, it would not.) So we find the poet of Psalm 48 expounding the
power of Jehovah as such that "Thou breakest the ships of Tarshish with
an east wind." Another reference to the ships of Tarshish occurs in the
book of Jonah, which describes how the prophet "went down to Joppa,
where he found a ship going to Tarshish; so he paid the fare thereof, and
went down into it to go with them unto Tarshish." Here, too, the ship is
no sooner dispatched from land than it immediately gets into grave difficulties with a tempest. The ships of Tarshish come under threatening
notice also in the book of the prophet Isaiah, and by and large it is rather
clear that the Tartessian ships were a source of envy or irritation to the
Jews.

Tarshish was ruled by kings, as we learn from Psalm 72, kings of comparable power to those who ruled over Sheba, since both are mentioned
in the same breath, and grouped with the princes of the isles, by which
is probably meant the Phoenician kings of Cyprus and Sardinia.

The merchants of Tarshish were famed for their wealth which, according to Phoenician sources, they obtained by trading with the docile mining communities of Andalusia, people who (so the Phoenicians say) set
little value upon the silver they extracted from the rocks of Spain. When
Ezekial sings the impending fate of Tyre, he mentions the passing glory
of the Tyrian fairs, to which merchants of Tarshish "brought a multitude
of all kind of riches, with silver, iron, tin, and lead they traded in thy
fairs."

Spanish archeologists have investigated the remains of the Tartessian
culture, and have found that it exerted a dominant role over southern
Spain, preventing the development there of the Celtic native culture
known as the Hallstatt and La Tête Iron Age. This situation even applied after 500 b.c., when the influx of Celts was so great as to change the
local spoken language to Celtic.

With so intimate a contact with the Celts from whom the metals were
obtained, it is not unlikely that the merchants of Tarshish may have been
associated with the trans-Atlantic migration of the Celts who came to
America. Indeed James Whittall, with whom I have discussed the decipherment of Tartessian inscriptions here in America, thinks that the
American Celts were deliberately brought here by Phoenicians, who
wanted mining communities to exploit American natural resources, and
with whom they could then trade. If this hypothesis is correct, then
Tartessian vessels would surely have played a major role in the Celtic
migration to New England.

The Bourne Stone, recording the annexation o
Massachusetts to Hanno, a Punic suffete (king o
governor) who may or may not have been the sam
as an historical Carthaginian suffete of that nam
Bourne Historical Society. Left, Malcolm D. Pea
son, whose photographic skills led to the deciphe
ment of the Bourne Stone, and whose early inte
est in the Upton Chamber and Mystery Hill i
New Hampshire led to the acquisition and prote
tion of the site by William Goodwin. He als
discovered the Running Deer inscription and w
a founding member with Vilhjalmur Stefansson o
the Early Sites Research Foundation. *Top photo b
Malcolm D. Pearson*

Pieces of metallic copper (above) found on the bed and shoreline of Lake Superior, and used in manufacture of tools and weapons (below) that closely resemble corresponding tools and weapons of the Old World in the late Bronze Age. Carbon dating of ancient metal workings on the Copper Peninsula, Michigan, sets the date at about 2000 B.C. Presence of silver nodules in the copper tools shows that they were made by cold-working, not from molten metal. All specimens in the Fell collection.

This interpretation of a sailor's life on a long voyage is the work of an Etruscan engraver. We know from the Greek writer Hesiod (about eighth century B.C.) that mariners only sailed in the summer months, and that they originally followed the coastline, putting ashore each night to cook a meal and sleep, setting out again the following morning. This engraving depicts such a shore landing. By the first century A.D. Greek captains were crossing the Indian Ocean from Aden to Ceylon, and evidence from cave inscriptions implies that Libyans were already crossing the Pacific in the third century B.C. For lack of records we cannot cite European authority for supposing that Phoenician and Iberian mariners were crossing the Atlantic at either of the dates just mentioned, but it is obvious that the Mediterranean cultural objects and writing systems could not have reached America by any other route than an Atlantic crossing. Hence we must infer that the surviving European records are defective, and that ocean passage was undertaken by late Bronze Age mariners, apparently unknown to their contemporary, Hesiod. The nudity of the sailors is consistent with summer voyaging in the tropics and subtropics, as also with much other evidence from Mediterranean sources. Caesar and other writers also refer to the nudity of Celts during campaigns. Thus this engraving is probably a good interpretation of ancient mariners' life at sea.

(*Data courtesy Erik Reinert, ex* **Gente,** *Argentina*) Whereas colonists from Iberia have left us inscriptions cut into the masonry of temples and on tablets buried in funeral mounds, casual visits by explorers are usually recorded as cliff inscriptions or on massive rocks near the coast. This one is exceptional for, although its Iberian-Punic text tells us that the men who engraved it were visiting mariners, it was found a thousand miles inland in caves in Paraguay. The explanation that Erik Reinert gives is that the Paraguay River is navigable to this point by sea-going ships. The inscription, in standard Iberian script (Diringer, 1968) reads in translation: "Inscription cut by mariners from Cadiz (Gedeth) exploring." The decipherment is explained in volume 2 of the *Occasional Publications* of the Epigraphic Society. Similar inscriptions made by permanent colonists will be found in chapters 2 and 11.

As this book is being written, very few Tartessian inscriptions have been discovered in New England, but those we have provide interesting information and show that other writings in Tartessian probably await discovery here. A few inscriptions have also been found in the region of West Virginia and Ohio, where their association with large burial tumuli resembling those of the Iberian Bronze Age point to important American colonies of these Phoenician navigators and merchant princes.

The first Tartessian inscription discovered in America is engraved on a rock on the seashore of Mount Hope Bay, Bristol, Rhode Island. In 1780 it was described and recorded by Ezra Stiles, who later became president of Yale College. Later the location of the rock was forgotten till 1874, when William J. Miller rediscovered it and made a drawing of the characters as he perceived them. Other versions, differing considerably, were made by Wilfred H. Munro (1880) and Edgar M. Bacon (1904). None of

Incised figure of high-sterned Tartessian hull, engraved on rock at Mount Hope, Rhode Island, originally discovered by Ezra Stiles in 1780. The steering oar is seen near the stern. Masts and sails are not indicated. The inscription, now severely vandalized, was photographed about 1940 by Malcolm D. Pearson, and is shown below the hull. It is believed to read in translation, "Mariners of Tarshish this rock proclaims." *Fell, Rommel, and Germano; Malcolm D. Pearson*

these versions is accurate or even remotely legible, the main reason for this being that other graffiti had been added over the years, and since the artists could not distinguish one script from another, their diagrams are meaningless.

It is a curious fact, but one well known to epigraphers, that modern graffiti added to an ancient inscription are almost always cut much less deeply than the ancient part of the inscription. At first sight this seems anomalous, for would not the ancient inscription be more weatherworn? The reason for the apparent contradiction is not hard to find. An ancient engraving, to have survived at all through 2,000 years on a rock that is exposed to weather, must necessarily have been cut deeply. On the other hand, the vandals who add their names and dates in modern times are simply casual visitors who do not arrive equipped with mallet and chisel for the express purpose of leaving an enduring monument to their passage. Instead, they happen to see what a previous person has done, become imbued with a sudden desire to leave their mark also, and can find nothing more serviceable than a pocket knife. With this unsuitable implement they contrive to mutilate the original while doing little more for themselves than to leave a readable advertisement of their names as the culprits who damaged a national treasure. Skilled epigraphic photographers also know that water, when applied to an ancient inscription and allowed to evaporate, has the power of exaggerating some chemical changes that occur in rock that has carried an inscription for many centuries. The art consists in photographing the inscription at just the right degree of evaporation.

Using this and allied techniques, Malcolm D. Pearson secured an excellent photograph of the inscription, in which, with his usual skill, he has been able to accentuate the deeper shadows cast by the ancient engraving, whereas the more shallow-ground letters of the modern vandals are readily distinguishable. However, Pearson's fine photograph was severely retouched by Olaf Strandwold, and the version he published in 1948 is undecipherable (though Strandwold thought he had Norse runes reading "There is a house over on the clearing").

It was not until 1975 that Pearson's original unretouched photograph came to my notice through the courtesy of James Whittall. Some months later at Union, New Hampshire, another inscription was discovered with excellently preserved Tartessian letters, and it then became clear that the Mount Hope inscription is also written in this style, though somewhat damaged by time, vandals, and erosion. Under the outline carving of a hull appears a single line of Tartessian Punic, reading from right to left, to yield

VOYAGERS FROM TARSHISH THIS STONE PROCLAIMS.

The script cannot of itself be accurately dated, but a likely estimate would perhaps be about 700 or 600 B.C. The voyagers were probably not explorers but rather merchants trading with the New England Celts who, by that date, would already be well-established fur trappers, and very likely also mining precious metals on those sites where ancient workings have been discovered.

The periodic arrival of Phoenician ships on the New England coast is attested by the Ogam inscription on Monhegan Island, off the coast of Maine (page 58). It is obvious that the flat-topped rocky islet would not have been set aside for the loading and unloading of Phoenician ships were they not regular visitors to America, with a predictable timetable of ports of arrival and departure at expected dates. It is also clear from the fact that the Monhegan inscription is given in the old Goidelic tongue of the New England Celts, that it was primarily intended as a notification for native American Celts who had goods for sale or exchange, to inform them where to bring their merchandise in order to be sure of meeting with customers from Phoenicia.

These inscriptions, therefore, suggest that organized international maritime commerce was well established in the late Bronze Age, that North American ports were listed on the sailing timetables of the overseas vessels of the principal Phoenician shipping companies, and that the same information was circulated to customers in America. As Monhegan Island lies some ten miles offshore it seems likely that the whole island was a trading station used by the Phoenician captains, with some organized ferry system for the transfer of goods to and from the mainland.

Over the four centuries that have gone by since European ships began to ply the New England coast in the sixteenth century there have been countless wrecks on the treacherous rocks and shoals, especially during stormy or foggy weather when visibility is limited. The hulls of these ill-fated vessels still lie on the bottom.

What, then, became of the many ships of Tarshish that once frequented these same coasts from 2,000 to 3,000 years ago? Certainly some, probably many, must also lie on the bottom, for sea travel was more dangerous in ancient times, and the storm waves could surely wreak more havoc upon the timbered hulls of Phoenician galleys than on the steel plates of modern ships. In particular there must have been many mishaps around Monhegan Island itself, and between Monhegan and the mainland, when occasional capsizes of lighters transferring cargo must inevitably have occurred. Archeologists who point to the absence of Phoenician glass and Iberian pottery from American sites should perhaps try looking in the places I have indicated on the basis of the inscriptions reported in this book. The shallow seabed around Booth Bay Harbor is where I would recommend scuba divers to start the search. Here the fleets of swan-necked galleys must often have ridden out a storm and dropped many an item overboard, either by accident or intention.

In the sixth century B.C. shipping was much more highly organized than we have hitherto believed. This is illustrated by letters that have been discovered written on metal sheets (*laminae*). The style is terse, sometimes legalistic as if drawn up by lawyers—and indeed this is very probable, for the signatures of the writers or consenting parties to an agreement appear in quite different handwriting from the body of the text. Because of their simplicity and directness, and because the matters referred to are transactions that we can readily understand, the decipherment of texts is made much easier than in the case of religious scriptures, where the subject matter was probably already obscure enough to contemporary readers, let alone those separated as we are by 2,500 years from the time of their composition.

Thus it was that in 1973 I was able to decipher the following letter, written on sheets of gold leaf, by Hiram Lord of Tyre. The language is Etruscan, as he is writing to a king of Lavinia (spelled *Luvenia* in the letter), near Rome. The letter was excavated at Pergi, Italy, in 1964. The text shows that the Etruscan language is a member of the Anatolian group of tongues, related thus to Hittite and Urartian. Dr. Reuel Lochore, a specialist in these tongues, has pointed out (1975) that many features of Etruscan life imply the probability that their tongue would have an Anatolian character, but that this letter is the first demonstration of the truth of that inference.

The script is that used in the Greek states of Italy and Sicily and in Etruria itself, a minor variant of the Phoenician alphabet in which vowels are introduced where the clarity of the text requires it. The date of the script is estimated by Italian archeologists as about 550 B.C., an estimate that is confirmed by the content of the document, for Hiram reigned from 553–533 B.C. The full details of the decipherment and the analysis of the vocabulary and syntax will be found in my original paper (1973), since reprinted in the publications of the Epigraphic Society. This particular letter deals with a shipment made from Tyre to Italy, and shows that extremely valuable cargoes were entrusted to the Tyrian vessels, in this case almost certainly one of the ocean-going or so-called Tarshish class.

FOR THE GODDESS,

WITH THE PRAYERS OF HIRAM

GREETINGS*

FOR IN AS MUCH AS his ambassador is bringing with all dispatch from Tyre a statue of *June-of-the-Stars* to the Palace of Thesarias Velianas, situate in Luvenia:

THIS IS A GIFT from a land far away for you to present to the priestesses. It is made of solid gold.

Have them measure its weight. The aforesaid man, Ambassador Qurvar, is to bring back to me a written declaration of the weight of the image, duly certified by them.

---

* In his commentary on this decipherment Lochore (1975) points out that it was a convention at this period for monarchs to communicate under the pretext of addressing one another's gods.

Lead lamina of Alcoa, cast of side 1 (above), and transcription of both sides (below) of Nara's agreement with the Greek merchant Makarios to take him from Cadiz to Tangier, thence to Oran, where he is to transship to another vessel on his voyage to Tyre, in Lebanon. About 500 B.C. See page 105 for translation. *Peter J. Garfall*

If in response to my inquiry a just measure is reported upon his return, then I, Hiram, will reward the man from my treasury.

But if the weight be too low, then by that amount it has been diminished I shall myself fine the man for his wickedness in desecrating the sanctuary of Celestial Juno over there. For such profanity to the goddess he shall relinquish his profit to me for the reimbursement of their treasury.

It would appear from this letter that the ambassador Qurvar must have been the owner of the vessel, since reference is made to his profit, which would have to be derived from the charge levied upon Hiram for carrying and delivering the cargo. The fine, as the letter makes clear, in the event of noncompliance with the terms of the contract, would be levied in addition to forfeiture of his normal profit.

A similar ambassadorship may well have been accorded any voyager of good reputation and adequate financial resources who happened to announce that he was about to visit a faraway land. This would explain why the Chinese Han Court records, for example, refer to Roman embassies in the second century A.D., though the Roman records themselves make no reference to such ambassadors. The validity of the Han Court records is unimpeachable, for the recorded dates and the name of the Roman emperor as given in the Chinese archives precisely match the western records, as I have pointed out elsewhere (1974).

Here now is a different type of shipping contract between a Greek merchant named Makarios and a skipper of Cadiz named Nara, both of whom have signed the contract on the back. It was found near Serreta de Alcoy, Spain, and consists of a lead lamina written on both sides. It is a curious fact that even at the early date its script implies (about the sixth century B.C.) the conditions less favorable to the hirer are set out in smaller print, on the back of the contract! The alphabet employed here is Greek, but the language of the contract is Phoenician. The words are abbreviated, and Greek influence is evident in the frequent insertion of vowels, because a native Phoenician would write only consonants. There was a Greek colony at Rodi in Catalonia to the east of Andalusia and it is possible that both the merchant Makarios and his lawyer may have been Catalan Greeks. The skipper's address is given as Cadiz, Andalusia, and for that reason the contract is drawn up in the Phoenician language, that of the home port of the vessel itself. Previous attempts at translating the document have failed for the very simple reason that the attempts were made by persons unacquainted with Semitic tongues, mistaking the phonetic values of several signs, and supposing that the back of the tablet is the beginning text. It is small wonder that the only outcome of those efforts was the conclusion that the lamina is written in an unknown tongue not belonging to any European family of languages. Despite this, one decipherer contrived to extract a few phrases that he translated as

"O Horror, O Horror!" a result that led him to conclude that the tablet deals with the soul's adventures in hell after death!

In point of fact the document is an exceedingly businesslike agreement set out in terse, abbreviated, but nonetheless readily comprehensible Phoenician, using words that are still to be found in all literary Arabic dictionaries to this day. With the original spelling of the place names shown in parentheses, it reads as follows:

A CERTAIN GREEK, his destination Tyre (*Tyr*), being desirous of traveling overseas by ship to Tyre, NARA hereby contracts to sail initially to the Cape at Tangier (*Tingis*) on the opposite shore* and then to proceed on the voyage with all dispatch to Oran (*Uran*).

AND IN DUE CONSIDERATION of the fare† this is the token, the entire balance outstanding in either hard cash or in merchandise of equal value to be on hand when the time comes to set out from Cadiz (*Gedir*), either on that (same) morning or on the previous evening, such (equivalent merchandise in lieu of balance of fare) to be kept separate: the merchandise is to be taken on board in an orderly manner, placed deep in the hold, under covers, protected by canvas against damage (from weather), and permanently marked as may be necessary "*Lot 160, Tyre, Lebanon.*"§

Whatever rich profit may subsequently accrue by good fortune** is from the outset renounced by the Greek: and whatever may remain (unsold) on board is also renounced by him, in accordance with this clause of the contract.

Upon arrival at the destination the token coin is thereupon to be made over to Nara as his profit, to retain absolutely or dispose of in Morocco (*Magarok*) as he may see fit, as compensation for his labors in assisting the Greek towards his destination, and in accordance with his desires

(Signed)   Verily NARA
Makari(ou) his signet††

It is apparent that Makarios would have to engage a series of skippers before he would reach Tyre if each skipper limited his range to a few hundred miles, as Nara did. This vessel, then, would not be a ship of the Tarshish class, but some smaller vessel of a value such that a single owner could afford to operate it, Nara doubtless being both owner and skipper.

---

* On the opposite shore of the Straits of Gibraltar as seen from Cadiz.

† The fare as far as Tangier.

§ Written *Tyr Leb.* In the Phoenician manner, the numeral is written 20 + 20 + 20 + 100.

** From the sale of the merchandise delivered on board as payment for the balance of the fare.

†† Makariou is the genitive (possessive) case of Makarios.

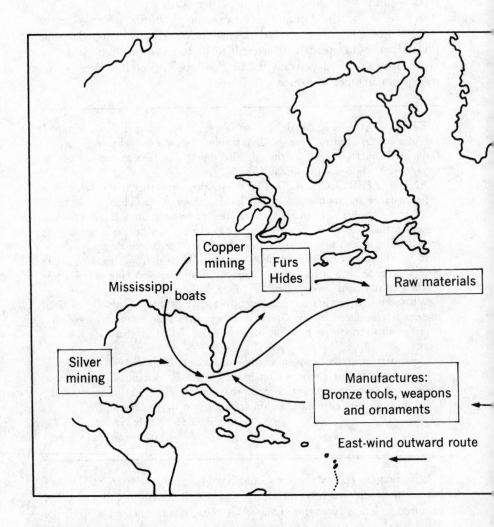

Inferred transatlantic trade patterns after 500 B.C. and until 179 B.C. The conquest of Egypt by Darius I in 525 B.C. and the successive rise of the Greek and
Roman empires effectively closed the eastern Mediterranean to Carthaginian
shipping. Carthage retaliated by closing the Straits of Gibraltar to all European
mariners. Under the guise of supposed Spanish and North African trade,
Carthaginian merchants exploited the North Atlantic resources, bringing to
Cadiz the copper of the Celtiberian settlements of North America, and the tin
of Cornwall, to provide the raw materials of a bronze industry, whose products
were re-exported to Britain, Gaul, North America, and West Africa. The Celts of
New England obtained a share of the American imports by supplying furs and

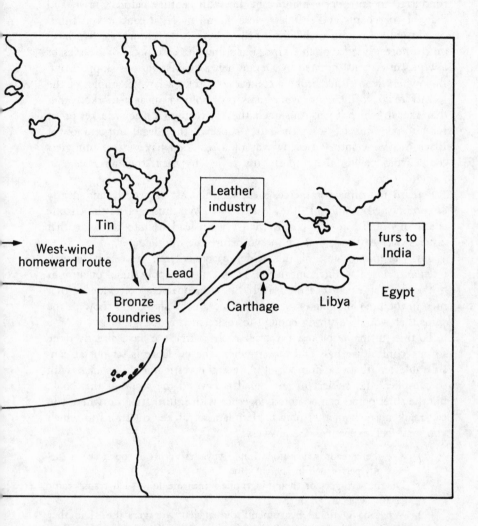

hides, both of which the Carthaginians re-exported to the eastern Mediterranean as supposed products of Gaul, the furs even reaching India. By the time the Romans conquered Spain and Carthage they had adequate alternate sources of these materials, and they took no interest in overseas shipping, having no merchant navy. The North American trade dwindled, the last phases presumably being operated by the maritime Celts of Brittany until their conquest by Caesar in 55 B.C. For 400 years after the Battle of Actium in 31 B.C. the Romans had no navy, since they had no rivals, and the memory of America apparently was lost. By 200 A.D. geographers believed that a voyage westward from Spain would lead to India and China, and this was the inheritance of Columbus.

These documents show that international maritime commerce was conducted in an orderly manner in the sixth century before Christ, and that the merchants and skippers were bound by legal contracts to fulfill certain obligations to each other. From the fourth century B.C. we have much more evidence of this kind, including the case notes of a series of lawsuits in Athens initiated by Demosthenes against various skippers and shipowners who either broke a contract or broke a law. Examples of the former relate to incidents where a skipper sold grain at a market other than that to which it was consigned, thereby reaping a black-market profit for himself; and a case of the latter concerns the illegal importation of Black Sea wine into Attica by way of a secluded bay where smugglers could avoid paying the import duty levied by the Athenian *Boule* on foreign liquor.

Foreign maritime commerce, then, was at least as orderly and nearly as complicated in ancient times as it is now. We must not let the chaotic conditions of life in the post-Roman era mislead us into thinking that orderly overseas trade was unknown before the middle ages.

But, you may protest, all this evidence comes from the relatively sheltered and closed Mediterranean Sea. How can you apply these conclusions to the vast context of oceanic travel? Show us one scrap of evidence that men in the pre-Christian era could cross oceans by ships, and show us the ships that would be strong enough to make such crossings.

To this justifiable protest my brief reply is that we have already done so in technical journals and books, where the evidence is set out at considerable length by a number of different investigators.* To deal with so complicated a subject in any detail is beyond the scope of this book, but the chief points can be noted, together with information on where you can read more about the subject. Here is a set of key questions to which you may well expect concise answers:

(1) Are there records of authenticated voyages across an open ocean successfully performed in ancient times?
(2) Do the voyagers or their biographers indicate how such transoceanic sailing was carried out?
(3) What navigational instruments did ancient voyagers use? Did they understand latitude and longitude and realize that the earth is spherical?
(4) What kinds of ships were used on ancient transoceanic voyages?

And here now are my very brief answers to these inquiries: Yes, we have well-authenticated records of actual voyages across the open ocean.

* See, for example: Barry Fell, *Life, Space and Time* (Harper & Row, 1974), and *Introduction to Marine Biology* (Harper & Row, 1975); George F. Carter, "Egyptian Gold Seekers and Exploration in the Pacific"; and Sentiel Rommel, "A Torquetum of 232 B.C.", both in *Occasional Publications of the Epigraphic Society*, vol. 2, 1975.

One of the first for which documentation exists is that of an expedition by an emperor of the Han dynasty of China in 140 B.C. The Emperor Wu, accompanied by many of his court officials, led the expedition from the Chinese capital of those times, Ch'ang An, in northern China. The ships first sailed 3,000 miles south, to pass through the Straits of Malacca, and then rounding the Malayan peninsula, they set their prows northwest to cross the 1,200 miles of open ocean and land at "Huang-Chih," identified by modern Chinese scholars as Conjeveram, near Madras. Here the emperor traded his cargo of gold and silk for precious gems, pearls, and rock crystal, returning home by the same route. The historian Pan Ku (2–92 A.D.) does not explain how the voyage was carried out, but it is believed that the seasonal monsoon winds were used. They would favor passages in both directions, provided the correct time of year was chosen for each start. Subsequent civil strife in China disrupted the trade route thus established and China withdrew from the outside world for nearly three hundred years.

Up to 30 A.D. the Greek shippers who operated the eastern trade routes for Mediterranean markets required three years for a round voyage to India and back, following the tortuous coastline of Asia, as Alexander the Great had done when he returned to Babylon from his Indian expedition. About 30 A.D. an Alexandrian skipper named Hippalos discovered how to use the monsoon winds to cross the Indian Ocean in the space of only three months. He returned from India in less than a year, thereby revolutionizing the trade routes. Within a year upwards of 100 ships were setting out for India each season, to return to Egypt laden with silks, spices, and gems in return for Roman gold. The vastness of this luxury trade led Pliny the Elder to deplore the flight of gold from Rome, and the countless Roman coins found in India show that his concern was well founded. Soon Ceylon and eastern India were added to the trade areas, as again the coinage shows. By 166 a merchant ambassador named Alexander had crossed the Bay of Bengal, to retrace the route of the Wu emperor, arriving at the court of Huan Ti, bearing gifts from Marcus Aurelius. These, and other similar voyages, did not follow the tedious and protracted route of the continental coasts, but struck boldly across the open waters. There can be no doubt that the merchant ships used the seasonally reversing monsoon winds to aid their progress, for no ship (other than naval vessels) could afford to carry a crew of rowers and yet still remain solvent.

As to the navigators' knowledge of the shape of the earth, and of latitude and longitude, this was well based from the time of Eratosthenes onwards. In 239 B.C. Eratosthenes had calculated the circumference of the world as being about 28,000 miles, an error of excess of only 13 percent. This means that the degree of latitude was mistakenly thought to be

some 69 nautical miles instead of 60 miles, its true value. This error was
not so great as to forbid successful ocean crossings with a predicted landing point. Longitude was calculated by dead reckoning, a method that
continued until long after the time of Columbus. For lack of a magnetic
compass, bearings could not be taken in cloudy weather, but the stars and
the sun and moon provided data at all other times. The astronomical
observations were set into an early type of astrolabe which, combined
with the cross staff for measuring the elevation of the midday sun or
other celestial objects at the time of their meridional passage, yielded a
direct reading of latitude. By 150 B.C. a mechanical computer had been
added to the navigational equipment, which could now perform the
operations of an astrolabe merely by cranking bronze gears and matching
dials. The remains of one of these instruments now rest in the National
Museum in Athens, recovered from an ancient wreck by divers. The manner of operation of these highly technical instruments is now known to us
and may be found by consulting the journals that deal with the history
of science.

The discoveries of the Greek and Roman inventors did not just suddenly arise *de novo*. We know that many instruments had been developed by earlier navigators, and that each generation improved on the
work of those that had gone before. Maps of the constellations show
that early voyagers were well aware of the fixed reference point in the
heavens, the pole of rotation of the stars, even though in those days no
bright star marked the position of the pole. It is a mistake to think that
the so-called age of navigation (of Vasco da Gama and Bartolomeo Diaz
and Christopher Columbus) was something entirely new, ushered in by
the circumstance that around 1400 A.D. a bright star of the constellation
Ursa Minor moved over the position of the pole as the Earth's axis slid in
accordance with precession. As we now realize, ancient navigators knew
always where the true pole is located even when there was no polestar,
and after the third century B.C. we have maps showing the position of the
celestial south pole also, proving that navigators were then crossing the
equator in the southern parts of the Pacific Ocean.

As to the relative sizes and strengths of ancient ships in comparison
with those used by Columbus, medieval Europe of 1492 was in a state of
nautical skill that the ancients would have regarded as benighted. Columbus's whole expedition could mount only 88 men, carried on three vessels
of which two were only 50 feet in length, about the size of a small Boston
fishing boat. Contrast that with the Pharaohs of the Ramesside dynasty,
1200 B.C., who could mount expeditions of 10,000 miners across the Indian
Ocean to the gold-bearing lands of South Africa and Sumatra. Julius
Caesar's triremes carried 200 men, yet he found his ships outmatched in
size, height, and seaworthiness by those of the maritime Celts.

The discovery of the so-called Pedra Lavrada inscription in Phoenician script engraved on stone occurred in Parahyba Province, Brazil, in 1886. A translation by Da Silva Ramos was published in French in 1939, and the following is an English rendering:

"This stone monument has been cut by Canaanites of Sidon who, in order to establish trading stations in distant lands, mountainous and arid, under the protection of the gods and goddesses, set out on a voyage in the nineteenth year of the reign of Hiram [i.e., 536 B.C.] our powerful king. They departed from Ashongaber in the Red Sea, after having embarked colonists in ten ships; and they sailed in company along the coast of Africa for two years. Subsequently they became separated from the flagship, and carried far away from their companions. Ten men and three women arrived here on this unknown coast. Of whom I, the unhappy Metu-Astarte, servant of the powerful goddess Astarte, have taken possession. May the gods and goddesses come to my aid."

This document, of which the original stone inscription is now apparently lost, has been declared a forgery by Professor Frank Cross of Harvard University. On the other hand, Professor Cyrus Gordon maintains its genuineness, and has issued a more recent translation. Since hundreds of obviously genuine inscriptions found in the United States have similarly been declared to be forgeries or marks made by plows or roots of trees, by persons who have not studied ancient inscriptions, there is no obvious reason at this time for doubting the authenticity of the Parahyba text.

9

Celtic Sea Power

THE rise and fall of Celtic sea power has been so strangely neglected by most historians and archeologists as to prompt much skepticism when first I began to report Celtic inscriptions in America. "I can't say I ever heard that the Celts were seafarers," was a typical comment. Those who recall that Julius Caesar described the ancient Britons as mostly naked savages, wearing only iron torques about their necks, sometimes with the skin of a beast cast over the shoulders, think of the Britons as having nothing better than one-man coracles for crossing water.

Nothing could be further from the truth. In fact, most of Book III of Caesar's *De Bello Gallico* is devoted to the greatest naval battle he was ever called upon to mount. And his adversaries? None other than the Celts of Brittany, whose fleet was swelled by the arrival of a flotilla they had summoned from their allies in Britain! The combined Gallic and British naval armament comprised an immensely powerful force, numbering, so Caesar tells us, no less than 220 ships, all larger than and superior in construction to those of the opposing Roman navy under Admiral Brutus.

These Celtic ships, Caesar says, were so soundly constructed that they could outride tempestuous or contrary winds upon the very ocean itself without sustaining injury.* It is clear that these fine vessels, which towered over the Roman galleys, had the capability of crossing the Atlantic Ocean *vasto atque aperto mari,* "upon the vast open sea," as Caesar indicates.

But who were the Celts to which Caesar refers, and how did they come to be in possession of such naval might? To answer that question, let me retrace the steps of my own inquiry into the background of the Roman observer's commentary on the events of 55 B.C.

* *De Bello Gallico,* books III, XIII, 1.

After receiving word of my identification of Ogam inscriptions at various localities in Portugal and Spain, Jim Whittall began to make plans to return to the Iberian peninsula to follow the new leads in the Douro river valley and other sites that seemed likely to add to our understanding of the origin of the New England Celts. Just before his departure he drew my attention to some standing stones in Brittany that seemed to him to have inscribed markings much resembling one of the classes of Ogam script given in the *Book of Ballymote* and a newly discovered Ogam inscription in Newfoundland reported by Dr. Robert McGhee, professor of archeology at Memorial University.

Jim's suspicions were well founded, and to my surprise I now had before me a series of Goidelic inscriptions from Vendée, apparently the first to be recognized in France. The translations disclosed funeral epitaphs of Celts of the Q-group, for the formula "son of" is rendered on the stones as M-C or M-Q, the vowels omitted as in the Iberian and New England examples (differing from the Newfoundland inscription in this respect, and suggesting that the voyagers who cut the Newfoundland record did so several centuries later).

The Vendée stones were originally discovered in 1904, dispersed over an area of about one square kilometer, on a farm called La Vaux, near Saint-Aubin-de-Baubigné between Poitiers and Nantes. They range in size from two to nine feet high and, in addition to the Ogam lettering, carry images of men and horses as well as the rounded markings called cupules (which are also found in New England). According to my decipherments the gravestones gave the names and fathers' names of some individuals of whom at least one had died through violence (*Sabal was slain*), and at least one appeared to be a mariner (M-C F-M-L, which I read as *Son of the Pirate*).

I wondered who these hitherto unsung Celtic buccaneers might be, and began to see if they could be traced. As a first possible trail I consulted with numismatists as to what ancient Celtic coinage might have been discovered in the Vendée, because ancient coins often indicate by their design the principal activities of the people who used such coins. As, however, Gallic coins before the age of the Caesars nearly always are imitations of the gold *staters* of Philip III of Macedon, all I was able to learn from the ancient coins was that the Vendée region had been occupied by the Veneti tribe and their allies. In the area of the La Vaux farm it appeared that these allies were called the Namnetes, after whom the city of Nantes takes its name. It seemed at first as if this inquiry had been of little help.

Guide books to the Vendée region of Brittany were my next quarry, and from these I learned that such French archeologists as Ernest Desjardains have come to the conclusion that the probable shape of the

The discovery of the West Indies, perhaps around 800 B.C., is here recorded in Ogam script, and old Celtic language, by Mab (or Mabo), a Celtiberian sea captain who left this inscription cut on a rock at Barouallie, Saint Vincent Island, in the southern Antilles. From above downwards it reads S-L M-B Ia-R-G-H N-S Io-H-M-L-K, or, with vowels inserted, Seal Mabo Iargh-Innis iomalach ("Mabo discovered this remote western isle"). Slightly restored, from a photograph originally obtained by Thomas Huckerby in 1913. *Malcolm D. Pearson*

coastline of Brittany in classical times was such as to suggest that Caesar's naval battle with the Celts may have taken place in the marshy estuary of the River Loire rather than at Quiberon Bay, fifty miles further north, where tradition has it. If the inferences of Desjardains are correct, then the naval battle could have occurred within the tribal territory of the Namnetes, allies of the Veneti and presumed occupants of the land where the La Vaux inscriptions had been discovered. This hint was enough to send me to Book III of Caesar's commentaries, and hence to the eyewitness account Caesar has given us of Celtic shipping in his own time.

Now although I belong to a generation that read Caesar in high school it so happened that in my sophomore year Book III of *De Bello Gallico* was not prescribed. Unfortunately so in my opinion, for as now became apparent we had missed out on one of the most informative accounts of ancient seamanship to be found anywhere in the classical literature.

So I now learned to my surprise that, unlike the Gauls of the interior, several of the tribes that inhabited the coastal lands of northern France were skilled sailors whose chieftains were united in a maritime alliance under the leadership of the Veneti of Brittany. Caesar lists these maritime Celts, and they include the Veneti themselves of Armorica, together with their neighbors the Curiosolites of the Channel coast, the Venelli of the Channel Islands and the Cherbourg region, the Namnetes of Nantes, and further south the Pictones and Santones of the Bay of Biscay coastlands, as well as the Lexovii of Normandy. Caesar further mentions that when the battle was looming up, the Veneti also summoned allies from among the tribes of Britannia. These, then, were the Celts whose combined resources placed a fleet of 220 ships off the estuary of the Loire, ready to do battle against the might of Rome early in the summer of 55 B.C.

And what ships they were! Even Caesar, hard-boiled man of action as he was, waxes almost lyrical as he describes the splendid fleet of swan ships, high-prowed and graceful, that now rounded the headland to close in upon the Roman galleys in the roadstead below the island where Caesar was to watch the sea fight.

Whereas the Roman triremes and biremes lay low in the water, deep-keeled and helpless in shallow waters, the Celtic ships towered high above them, on flat keels that made them maneuverable in the estuary. Although a keel prevents a ship from drifting before the wind (making leeway), it is not in fact a necessary feature; no one denies the ocean-going capability of the Viking ships, yet their exhumed remains show them to have been flat bottomed. Hence there is no need to doubt Caesar's assertions.

The Celtic vessels had tall masts whose yards and cordage carried sails sewn from beaten hides, their leather far more serviceable in the rough

Atlantic storms than the Egyptian linen of the Roman *vela*. These were
ships propelled solely by wind and by the skilled seamanship of skippers
who knew how to harness the air currents to their will, even sailing into
the wind, to Caesar's bewilderment. Because no Celt would demean himself by rowing an oar, the thwarts on which a Roman skipper would expect
to seat his galley slaves were replaced in the ships of the Gauls by far
stronger and better chosen beams. These were ships bound firmly against
the buckling action of ocean rollers by iron chains,* where the Roman
galleys had only ropes to tie the timbers together. The Celtic anchors
were made entirely of iron, a detail which (since Caesar mentions it)
makes us suspect that Caesar's own ships may still have been using the
wooden-fluked stone anchors that they had copied from their former
Carthaginian enemies.

Because of their superior size and height, mariners on the Celtic ships
could cast their arrows and spears downward to the decks of the hapless
Roman galleys beneath. The armament of iron chains protected the larger
ships from being rammed by the Roman skippers. It was midday when
the two fleets engaged, and the disadvantage of the Romans was at once
evident. They were outnumbered and outweighed, despite the fact that a
Roman trireme would carry 200 men.

In this dangerous situation the forethought of Brutus had seen to it
that an appropriate secret weapon had been taken aboard the Roman
ships. Knowing themselves to be poor sailors, no match for the Carthaginians during the Punic wars, the Romans had long ago invented the
grappling iron to lay hold on the enemy so he could be boarded and de-
feated as in a land engagement. Now again Roman military genius came
to the aid of naval mediocrity. A sharp, hook-shaped device called a *falx*

* Hypozomata, as the Greeks called them.

Libyan ships employed oarsmen as well as sails, and could therefore journey in
any direction, irrespective of the wind. The upper picture, from an ancient Libyan
mosaic, shows the mariners nude, indicating that voyages were only performed in
the summer season, as was also the custom among the ancient Greeks.

No detailed picture of an ancient Celtic ocean-going ship has yet been discovered, but from the account of them given by Julius Caesar we can recognize
most of the characteristic features of Celtic ships in the bas relief of a Tartessian
ship found in Lebanon. Save for the steering oar near the high stern (to the
right of the illustration), there were no oars, and the ship relied upon wind
power, utilized by skillful adjustment of the yards carrying the heavy leather sails.
Caesar notes that the Celtic ships were able to travel on the open ocean, and
were strong enough to withstand tempest and high waves. He records that the
Roman galleys of his own fleet were much inferior to the vessels of the great
Celtic navy that gathered to attack the Romans in 55 B.C. *Peter J. Garfall, Gerald
Heslinga*

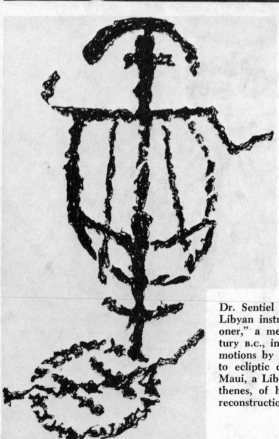

Dr. Sentiel Rommel, with mechanism of ancient Libyan instrument called the Tanawa, or "Reckoner," a mechanical calculator of the third century B.C., intended to aid the study of planetary motions by converting position angles from polar to ecliptic coordinates. Below, cave drawing by Maui, a Libyan student of the astronomer Eratosthenes, of his Tanawa, used by Rommel in his reconstruction of the instrument. *Peter J. Garfall*

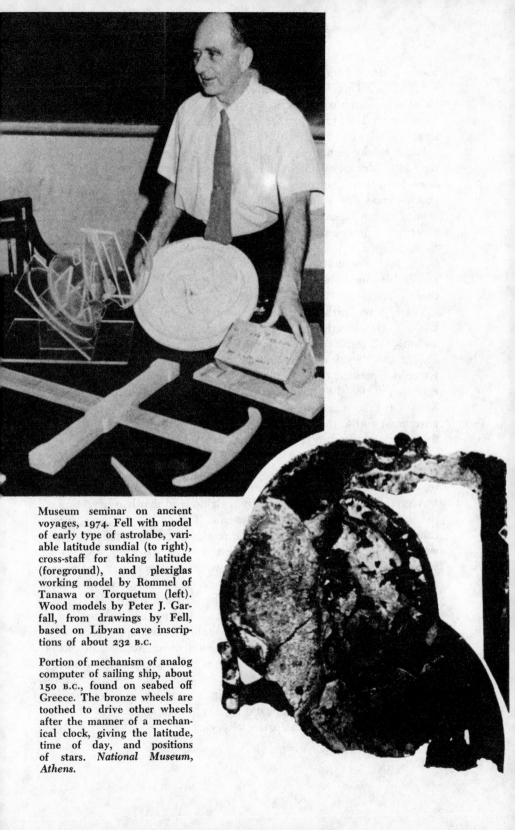

Museum seminar on ancient
voyages, 1974. Fell with model
of early type of astrolabe, vari-
able latitude sundial (to right),
cross-staff for taking latitude
(foreground), and plexiglas
working model by Rommel of
Tanawa or Torquetum (left).
Wood models by Peter J. Garfall, from drawings by Fell,
based on Libyan cave inscriptions of about 232 B.C.

Portion of mechanism of analog
computer of sailing ship, about
150 B.C., found on seabed off
Greece. The bronze wheels are
toothed to drive other wheels
after the manner of a mechanical clock, giving the latitude,
time of day, and positions
of stars. *National Museum,
Athens.*

had been devised and taken on board in advance in large numbers. It was attached to a long line. The *falces* were hurled into the rigging of the Celtic vessels, after which the Roman oarsmen drove ahead while the steersman turned his pintle to veer away. The tautened *falces* sheared the stays and wrought havoc with the Celtic cordage.

Faced by the certainty of being outmaneuvered by this new strategy, the Celtic admiral (whose name is not given) ordered his ships to withdraw from the engagement. At this juncture nature came to the aid of the Romans. The wind suddenly dropped, leaving the Celtic fleet becalmed without means of propulsion. Admiral Brutus seized his chance, ordered the grappling irons thrown, and the battle now reverted to the Romans' specialty, hand-to-hand combat on stationary decks. The entire Celtic fleet was destroyed or captured while the Romans still had 80 serviceable ships, with which Caesar later, in September of 55 B.C., carried the war across the Channel to Britannia.

There is no further mention of British or Gaulish naval vessels in Caesar's commentaries, nor does Tacitus in the century that followed give any space or consideration to native naval might. It seems that the battle against the Veneti was the end of Celtic sea power in classical times. Except for periodic truculence by British chiefs against Roman economic exploitation, for the most part the Celtic aristocracy willingly adopted Roman manners and luxury under the sweet persuasion of competent governors; and so the Celtic lands settled down to four centuries of relative prosperity and peace. By the time the Saxon pirates appeared off their eastern coasts, the Britons had forgotten their seamanship as well as most of their martial arts, and ruin soon followed, ushering in four more centuries of ignorance and misery.

Across the Irish Sea, however, lay a Celtic land that had never known the Romans as conquerors. It is true, as Tacitus relates, that Agricola contemplated adding *Hibernia* (as he rendered the name Ibheriu) to the empire, thinking thereby to extinguish the last sparks of nationalism among the Britons of Britannia, who would no longer gaze with envy upon the Irish visitors occasionally to be seen in British ports aboard the ships of merchants engaged in the Irish commerce. Agricola also welcomed to his governor's mansion at least one Irish king, thrust out by rebellious subjects, and the Roman's hospitality was candidly based on his intention to establish a puppet administration under Imperial protection. But the uproar in Caledonia that soon after ensued, followed in turn by a recall to Rome, prevented his accomplishing this end. Soon afterwards Agricola fell victim to the envy of Domitian, succumbing to a mysterious illness which, the Roman public did not fail to note, coincided with a new health plan instituted by the palace physicians.

The independence of Ireland was thus maintained until the rescript of Honorius withdrew the legions from Britain to defend the Eternal City itself, by now facing the hordes of barbarians that broke upon Europe in the fifth century A.D. No sooner was the *Pax Romana* at an end than fleets of Irish raiders (*scotti*) began to ravage the western shores of Caledonia, later to settle there and still later to fuse with the Pictish Celtic tribesmen, establishing the kingdom of the Picts and Scots. Other Irish *scotti* crossed the Irish Sea to Wales, the Feni of central Ireland giving rise to the Gwynedd in North Wales, and the Desi of southern Ireland to the Dyfed of South Wales. Still later these Irish colonists were to be expelled by the P-Celtic Cymru, leaving behind their Ogam monuments in the Gaelic tongue.

Obviously none of these sea crossings could have been performed in coracles, so Ireland evidently had either retained, or subsequently acquired, a fleet and sailors to man her ships. Similarly the fleeing Britanni of Cornwall, as the Saxon invasions grew more serious, took ship to Armorica, there to join the Celts of seagirt Brittany. By the seventh century Irish and Breton sailors could look to the western ocean once more, as their ancestors had done a thousand years before, as a possible means of access to lands more peaceful than ravaged Europe.

The illustrations in the manuscripts, however, show that the Irish vessels of the dark ages and medieval period were little more than enlarged coracles, made of a framework of wood, over which hides were stretched, in the manner of a kayak large enough to carry six or eight men. A relic of paganism is apparent in the bull's skull on the prow, countered by a Christian cross in the stern. Such fragile vessels may have made channel crossings in calm weather, but it seems unlikely that so stormy a sea as the North Atlantic would offer safe passage to any so foolhardy as to seek it. The Irish monks preserve a tradition that one of their number, Saint Brendan, crossed the Ocean to discover sundry marvels.

Whether there be truth or not in the Irish tradition of Brendan's voyage to the westlands, we appear to be on the verge of finding American relics of some such later phase of Celtic seamanship, to judge by Professor Robert McGhee's newest find, mentioned earlier in this chapter. Add to this the illuminating contributions of Dr. T. G. E. Powell (see Bibliography) of the Department of Prehistoric Archaeology at the University of Liverpool, and we begin to sense a developing image of yet earlier Irish or Goidelic exploits upon the great waters. Let us now attempt, however hesitantly, to turn the clock backwards a thousand years before the Saxon invasions.

The city of Tarshish, whose sailors occupied a commanding role upon the ocean in the far-off days when the Hebrew prophets foretold the doom of Tyre, was itself destined to fall victim to Carthaginian envy. The Guadalquivir valley was overrun by Iberian Celts, doubtless with the connivance of Carthage, and the Tartessian merchants now paid imposts to Punic Cadiz. No longer could the Tartessian allies, the Greeks of Catalonia, make the passage through the Straits of Gibraltar, save with the permission of Carthaginian sea lords, sparingly granted. It is believed that this change occurred about 530 b.c.

Thus the middle part of the sixth century b.c. would seem to be the latest possible date for American settlements here attributed to Tartessian inspiration or leadership. If tradition is correct in reporting the actual *destruction* of Tarshish in 530 b.c., then the Mount Hope inscription in Rhode Island can be of no later date.

The Iberian Punic dedication tablet found in the temple of Bel at Mystery Hill refers to the god (or perhaps to the dedicators of the tablet) as "of Canaan." The name *Kana'ni* (Canaanite) was used to refer to them- selves by both Carthaginians and the Lebanese Phoenicians of Tyre and Sidon. Does the Mystery Hill inscription mean, then, that it was a dedica- tion made later than 530 b.c., by Iberian visitors under the cultural dom- ination of Carthage? I suspect so. By the same reasoning, we are obliged to date it no later than about 146 b.c., when Carthage in her turn fell under the onslaught of Rome. Thereafter no ships could be expected to reach the Americas under Punic sponsorship.

What now of the Manana islet inscription, near Monhegan Island, which I have translated as an Ogam Celtic notice reading *Cargo plat- form for ships from Phoenicia?* The Ogam alphabet used is one that differentiates the letters G and K, unlike most of the New England Ogam, where voiced and unvoiced velar consonants are not distinguished. The fact that the distinction *is* made might well suggest to us that the Mon- hegan inscription is a late one. The word supposed to mean Phoenicia is spelled F-N-K, presumably to be read as *Finiki,* matching the Arabic *Finiqi.* That seems plausible enough, seeing that the extensive Greek influence in southern Spain would have familiarized the Celts with the Greek name *Phoinikoi,* "Men of the Purple," by which they designated the Canaanite dispensers of purple cloth.

But there does remain an alternative possible reading. The form F-N-K might well refer to the Feni people of Ireland, a self-governing kingdom whose citizens were well acquainted with ships at the time when the Romans withdrew from Britain, as Dr. Powell has shown (page 301). This matter cannot be satisfactorily resolved at the present exploratory stage of our American researches, but it does give us pause to examine likely events in the progress of Celtic apprenticeship upon the sea in the centuries before the first written records occur.

So long ago as 1943 Jacquetta and Christopher Hawkes were stressing the apparent continuity of Celtic physical traits in the prehistoric sites of Britain from the time of the Urnfield People (about 1200–900 B.C.) onwards, giving as their opinion that recognizably Celtic speech was already being used in Britain at that period. The same authors noted that the so-called bluestones of the Stonehenge monument seemed to date from about Urnfield times, and that they had been traced to a source in Pembrokeshire by geologists. This would require a journey by sea of some 400 miles, surely the task of ships rather than coracles.

By the late seventh century B.C. we find in the so-called *Massiliote Periplus,* of uncertain authorship, indications that the Celtic-speaking Iberians had knowledge of distant lands called *Ierne* and *Albion* (Ireland and Britain). It seems rather unlikely that a people so adventurous as the Celts would sit idly by while Tartessian ships visited Andalusia to trade with them, without some at least of the young Celtic fishermen taking service on the famed ships of Tarshish. Indeed, I think it inevitable that the Tartessian art would have been acquired by some of the coast-dwelling Celts—and these, as the Iberian Ogam inscriptions now disclose, were Q-Celts or Goidels.

Is it not likely, then, that the various maritime Celts whose settlements in Gaul were later to come to the attention of Julius Caesar came originally from a part of Iberia where Tartessian tutelage gave native Q-Celts the art of oceanic navigation? The Goidelic character of the inscribed stones of La Vaux is consistent with such a view. It is generally thought that the earliest Celtic invaders of Britain were Q-Celts, so there could well have been a long tradition of involvement with coastal navigation among those Celts who were later to acquire the skills of the Veneti and their allies.

I have set down this chapter in the sequence in which the relevant facts have come to my attention. I began with the destruction of Celtic sea power under Caesar, for that is the clearest documentation we have of the subject; then my discussion ranged forward and backward in time from the point of reference supplied by Caesar, namely the summer of 55 B.C. The treatment is necessarily speculative, but perhaps it may open our eyes to the kind of evidence we should now be alerted to seek in the soil of the Americas, or upon the continental shelves of both New England and Europe, where storm-wrecked Celtic ships may perhaps lie encrusted with the growth of sea-floor denizens.

A decade after this chapter was first published, the truth of Caesar's words was demonstrated by Dr. Margaret Rule and her colleagues of the Guernsey Archaeological Trust when, in 1985–6, they brought to light a wreck of a Celtic trading ship that sank around 125 A.D. Its timbers are of solid oak two feet thick.

10

The Celts in America

BOTH on-site investigations and historical research had now shown that Celts from the Iberian peninsula were *responsible for the Ogam inscriptions* we find on ancient stone buildings in New England. In all probability the same Celts *were the actual builders* of the structures on which their inscriptions occur. It is also clear that the Celts, by virtue either of their own skills or those of their Phoenician neighbors in Spain, *were capable of sailing to America* to colonize any lands that appealed to them. The evidence now in our hands furthermore shows that Celts in considerable numbers *did in fact settle here,* particularly in New England. For America's Celtic inscriptions could not have been an independent American invention! Celts must have come here to write them.

This, therefore, is the place to say something about Celts as people, how they looked in ancient times, and how they lived. Then it will be a logical step to review their activities in America as evidenced by the remains of their handiwork.

First, as to their appearance. Various ancient writers, notably Julius Caesar, Strabo the geographer, and Diodorus have left accounts of the Gauls and ancient Britons. They described them as a fair-haired race, blue-eyed, very high spirited, boastful, quarrelsome, courageous in war, with a love of ornamentation. Warriors and men of the lower ranks went naked (at least in the warmer seasons of the year, when war was considered appropriate); the women were accustomed to wear garments; both sexes delighted in massive metal arm, neck, and waist bands. They lived in rude hovels in clearings in the depths of the forest; their huts were made of interlocked boughs over which animal hides were stretched. In winter the men wore a cloak made of animal hide, though their chieftains used rich cloth obtained from Phoenician or other traders.

Now these descriptions do not specifically relate to the Celts of Spain and Portugal, but rather to the Celts of France, Britain, northern Italy, and the lands to the north of Greece. In Iberia the invading Celts, who may have entered the peninsula from France about 1000 b.c., soon became much intermingled with an earlier Iberian people. These original Iberians seem to have been the ancestors of the modern Basques, a theory first advocated by the explorer naturalist Wilhelm von Humboldt. According to Humboldt the Basque Iberians had occupied Europe long before, in the Stone Age, and had later been displaced by successive waves of invaders, the various tribes of the Celts and Teutons. Humboldt supposed that the dark-haired people of Ireland, parts of Scotland and southern France, and much of Spain and Portugal were descendants of the old Iberian Basque stock, their language now changed through contact with later invaders.

Humboldt's theory fell into disfavor, mainly because it was supposed that the ancient Iberian language is enshrined in the Iberian inscriptions of Spain and Portugal, which no one seemed able to decipher (an example of these supposedly undecipherable Iberian inscriptions is the contract of Nara and Makarios given in Chapter 8). Of course that argument is false and in reality most of the supposed Iberian inscriptions actually comprise Punic language, written in a local Iberian script. Some, however, are Basque, such as the funeral tablet of Queen Bengerd, and others are Celtic. So in reality we are back to where Humboldt started. I personally favor his theory, and believe that the dark-haired strain of Irish and Scots Gaels, as well as the other dark-haired Celts, are the product of ancient intermarriage of Celts with Iberian Basque stock, the language of the Basques having all but suffered extinction in the process of integration.

It therefore seems likely to me that the bands of Iberian Celts who crossed the Atlantic must have included many brunettes of original Basque Iberian extraction, though speaking the Goidelic branch of Celtic. They were probably about as mixed as we modern inhabitants of America are, blondes and brunettes intermingled.

But what about the skeletons? Don't they tell us anything about their owners, whether they were tall or short, and what clothes if any they may have worn? A good question, except that there *are* no skeletons to study as yet. Gravestones we have aplenty, their owners' names engraved in Ogam, but there are no bodies, alas. Why? Because all the gravestones we have so far found have been dragged away from their original positions by the colonial farmers of the eighteenth century, and built into the dry-stone walls that now crisscross the farmlands and second-growth woodlands of New England.

When we first recognized the gravestones this past spring, we began to try to reconstruct the actions of those colonists in the hope of identifying where the bodies had originally been buried. So far no traces have turned up. There is a great deal working against us, unfortunately. Nearly all the rocks of New England are ancient granites and gneisses and schists with a high acid content. This means that the soil also is acid, and bones scarcely survive a hundred years in such soil. In contrast, the Celtic lands of France and England are largely limestone or chalk; the soil is alkaline, and bones last much longer. However, we hope to locate original burial sites by stone artifacts buried with the bodies. Metal, unfortunately, unless it be gold, deteriorates and vanishes in acid soil, but nametags or ornaments carved from stone could survive, and perhaps lie somewhere beneath the soil awaiting discovery.

Numerous bronze adzes and other tools have turned up over the years,

Comparable copper and bronze artifacts of New England (left) and of the Iberian Peninsula (right). *Drawn by James P. Whittall* **(1976)**

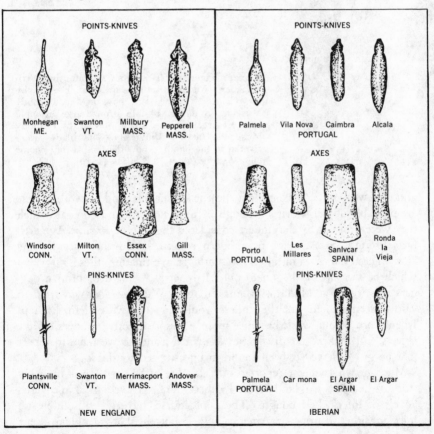

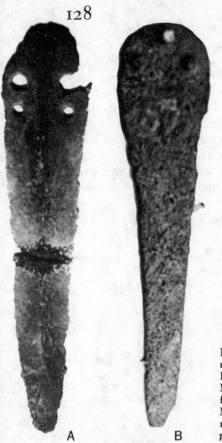

A   B

Bronze daggers of Celtic type: A, found in Merri-
mackport, Massachusetts, shortly after 1900 by
Dr. C. A. Kershaw, and now in the Peabody
Museum, Andover; B, late Bronze Age example
from El Argar culture, Spain, now in the Peabody
Museum, Harvard University. The blades were
riveted to the handles, now decayed. *From photos
published by James P. Whittall (1970)*

and also weapons, for example a spearhead, daggers, and a sword. These
are probably of Celtic origin, though up until now the museums to which
they were brought by the finders considered them to be Bronze Age artifacts brought to America by modern collectors and then accidentally
"lost" here. James Whittall is presently reinvestigating these finds, on
which he has already begun to publish reports. A hoard of bronze daggers was found at Madison, Maine, in 1924; William Goodwin tried in
vain to secure them, but the finders would not part with them. Perhaps
when word of our work becomes more widespread, other finders of like
objects will make their discoveries known. Meantime we have to report
that no graves have yet been found in undisturbed condition.

Much of what Caesar reported of Celtic life as he saw it was probably
true of the New England Celts. I expect they too lived in skin-covered
hovels of interlocked boughs. These, of course, have left absolutely no
trace in either Europe or America. No doubt the New England Celts

were hunters, too, though a quern for crushing grain found near the temple of the Mother Goddess at South Woodstock may be of Celtic provenance. Clothing would doubtless match that of the European Celts, skins serving as the raw materials for the majority, the wealthier people obtaining cloth from Phoenician traders by bartering skins or metal ores.

All this, of course, is sheer speculation. But what about the permanent structures that the Celts left behind, besides the bare tombstones that lack bodies?

The permanent structures we find are of the class called megalithic; that is, made of large undressed boulders to which have been added more carefully trimmed stone roof-slabs and lintels, often weighing several tons each. This is very interesting, for although exactly the same types of construction occur in the Celtic lands of Europe, many of these massive objects have been considered to be the work not of Celts but of some race antecedent to the Celts.

It is a peculiarity of European archeology texts that the books that deal with the Celts say very little about megalithic structures and in fact say virtually nothing at all about any buildings made by Celts. It is as if the European Celts were quite clever, civilized beings who somehow forgot to erect any buildings. On the other hand, the European archeology texts that deal with the megalithic buildings of Europe say little if anything about the people who built them.

Now, is it not extraordinary that in America, and in particular New England, we can recognize all the main types of megalithic structures that our European colleagues report from Europe, yet our structures are associated in most cases with pagan Ogam inscriptions that betray their Celtic origin? Are we to suppose that New England, too, had its mysterious megalithic builders who were then followed by Celts, and that the Celts afterwards added their inscriptions to the megalithic buildings they found here? I do not find that hypothesis at all convincing. In my own view the megalithic buildings of New England are the work of Celts. That their European counterparts do not carry Ogam inscriptions must surely be due to the known fact that the early fathers of the Christian Church forbade their followers to go near the pagan monuments or, if they needed the stone for holy purposes, advised them to convert the heathen building to a church or monastic cell, first taking care to erase the offensive written matter.

There is clear evidence that some of the megalithic monuments of Europe are indeed very ancient, antedating the Celts, though the Celts chose to use them, as indeed the Romans did sometimes. But that does not mean that all such megalithic monuments antedate the Celts, or that

Malcolm Pearson

James Whittall

the Celt was so helpless as to be unable to build a building should he require one. Now we can take a look at the chief classes of megalithic monument, and the names appropriate to each.

Best known on account of their bizarre appearance are the *dolmens,* a Breton word meaning *stone table.* Other names are used in Ireland, but these are not sufficiently well known to detain us. A dolmen is a memorial to a chief or to some event of importance, and takes the form of a huge central boulder, sometimes ten tons or more in weight, supported on three, or four, or five vertical stones like pegs. Good examples are to be seen at Bartlett, New Hampshire, and North Salem, New York. Other examples occur in Maine and at Westport, Massachusetts, the latter of relatively small proportions.

These American examples exactly match those known from Europe and the Middle East. The oldest proven examples are from 4500 B.C., much antedating the Celts in Europe, and showing that the design reached Ireland at that date. No archeologist or geologist in Europe has ever suggested that dolmens are the work of glaciers. Indeed there was no ice age in countries like Syria anyway, yet dolmens are widespread there. Occasional perched blocks of stone called erratics are found on ledges, hills, or mountains, dropped there by the retreating ice sheet that had swept the boulder before it, but it has never been found, nor is it considered feasible, that a glacier could erect several boulders of exactly the right height and then neatly deposit on top of them a giant capstone. Yet some archeologists here, when faced with the evidence of megalithic dolmens, have claimed that they are the work of ice. American glaciologists have made no such statements, deeming such structures to be the work of agencies other than glacial ice, an opinion coinciding with that of their European and Syrian colleagues.

In France a curious intergradation can be observed between the rudest and most ancient dolmens, through later varieties where the support stones are neatly squared off into four vertical faces, then through yet another variety where the vertical pegs have been cut into cylindrical squat columns, terminating, in one extreme medieval example, with the giant capstone, in all its primitive formlessness, resting neatly upon four architectural columns of the Tuscan order! The American examples are

Two of America's largest dolmens, both of the type called cromlech, in which the capstone is not flat, like a table, but hemispherical and massive. Above, the largest of all, at North Salem, New York. The 90-ton capstone is supported on five erect pegstones. Below, at Lynn, Massachusetts, with a 50-ton capstone, supported on 3 pegstones. These megaliths resemble those of Europe that date back to about 2000 B.C.

ABOVE: Dolmens at Westport, Massachusetts, and Carrezeda, Portugal *(photo James P. Whittall II)*.

OPPOSITE PAGE: Above: Large dolmen of cromlech type at Bartlett, New Hampshire *(photo Charles J. Hepburn)*. Below: Dolmen of cromlech type at Trelleborg, Sweden *(photo Joseph D. Germano)*.

all of the early type, which is in any case by far the commonest variety everywhere else. In Ireland the dolmens are rather small, resembling a Massachusetts example at Burnt Mountain, and our Irish colleagues believe that these were originally tombs, completely covered by earth that has since been eroded away.

The construction of a dolmen, especially those that are found at the tops of hills, must have involved immense labor. The vertical peg stones would first be erected, then a great mound of earth piled over them to permit the captone to be levered and dragged to the top. After the capstone was set in place, the earth would be removed, allowing the huge boulder to sink on to its supports.

Analogous methods of construction would be used for a second type of megalithic monument found widely distributed in New England with a few examples in neighboring states. This is the *slab-roofed chamber*, a rectangular or square building, the sides made from natural boulders or large slabs of stone, roofed over by either one large square slab of about a half-ton or a ton in weight or, in the case of the larger examples, roofed by a series of lintel stones weighing up to three tons each. These are so numerous as to forbid listing particular examples, but reference may be made to the illustrations in this book. Structures of similar type occur in Europe, ranging in age from the youngest so-called *souterrains* of Scotland, some dating from the period of the Roman occupation, to much older examples from the Bronze Age, some or most having been used as tombs for tribal interments. The late examples from Scotland and Ireland were used for occupation by families, apparently during periods of stress, such as the Norse invasions perhaps.

The American examples have been considered to be the work of "colonial farmers," and termed "root cellars." The absurdity of this interpretation is sufficiently demonstrated by the facts in the accompanying table.

In Table 3, the data Sections 1 and 2 are the result of the researches of Byron Dix, an ardent amateur astronomer who has been investigating these alignments since 1973. His observations* were made entirely independently of my own work on the inscriptions, noted in Section 3 of the table. The miscellaneous inscribed material of Section 4 has been observed by John Williams and others. It is obvious that most slab-roofed chambers are temples.

A visit to a well-preserved megalithic slab-roofed chamber, such as the Pantheon near South Woodstock, is an experience never to be forgotten.

---

* See articles by Byron Dix in volume 3 of the *Occasional Publications of the Epigraphic Society.*

TABLE 3

Characteristic Features of the New England Slab-roofed Chambers

---

(1) Like their European counterparts, the New England slab chambers nearly always face toward the east, with a prescribed pattern of deviation from true east that can be related to the solar cycle.

(2) The long axis of the New England slab chamber almost invariably lies along one of the following astronomical axes:

    (a) Pointing due east; that is, declination zero, the sunrise point on the days of the vernal and autumnal equinoxes.

    (b) Pointing to declination $+23\frac{1}{2}°$ on the eastern horizon; that is, the sunrise point on the day of the summer solstice.

    (c) Pointing to declination $-23\frac{1}{2}°$ on the eastern horizon; that is, to the sunrise point on the day of the winter solstice.

    (d) Some other well-defined astronomical axis such as due south; that is, the direction of maximum elevation of any celestial body being used to calculate latitude by means of an astrolabe.

(3) The outer surface of the door lintel and/or the lower surface of the door lintel and/or the inner face of the door lintel carries (in well-preserved examples) an Ogam dedication to one of the Celtic gods, usually to Bel. The dedication may include the name of the god written in Phoenician letters as well as in Ogam. The dedication may occur on the vertical porch slabs.

(4) The inner walls or ceiling lintels commonly carry other inscribed material, including phallic carvings.

The impressive ceiling slabs and the length of the chamber combine with its antiquity to impart a feeling of awe. This particular temple carries lintel dedications to Bel (the Sun god), and portions of dedications to other gods can be discerned. Hence our proposed name Pantheon. It is oriented to face the midwinter sunrise point, $-23\frac{1}{2}°$ declination. The original mound of earth under which it was buried is still intact, with large trees growing over it, yet so high is the door lintel that a tall person can enter without stooping, a most unusual feature in any slab chamber.

These temples usually have a square smoke-hole above the altar at the inner end; it may be cut into a circular slab of rock about two feet in diameter, or else merely comprise a chimney made of several stones. A rectangular window-like vent, with a covering louver, may also occur in the ceiling near the smoke-hole. These fittings seem to indicate that an altar fire was kept burning at the inner end of the temple.

There is no observed connection between the divinity to whom a temple is dedicated and the astronomical orientation of a temple. Thus of two temples at Woodstock one is oriented due south, the other to the winter solstice sunrise. A small chapel dedicated to Bel on Dix's Calendar Site 1, near South Royalton, Vermont, is oriented to declination zero, facing the vernal and autumnal equinoctial sunrise point; another, nearby, faces due south.

Above, chamber, South Woodstock, a rectangular stone temple oriented so that its long axis is aligned with compass bearing 123° which, for latitude 43.5° N, corresponds to the horizon azimuth of the rising sun on December 22, the winter solstice. Thus, on the day of midwinter, the sun can be seen from the altar as rising midway between the two piers forming the front wall. Date, some time after 433 B.C. Below, inner altar region of oracle chamber at Mystery Hill, New Hampshire. A slotted rectangular opening in the ceiling appears to be constructed to admit a ray of light onto the altar, but the details remain to be investigated. *Peter J. Garfall, Joseph D. Germano*

Massive lintel stones cap the ruins of a temple at Danbury, Connecticut, shown by John Williams to be oriented to the midwinter sunrise. Engraved inscriptions in the vicinity relate this structure, and others nearby, to the sun god Bel. The inscriptions include Ogam and Punic Iberian, and also the Mediterranean equinox symbol of the circle divided by a diameter, symbolizing equal day and night. The Danbury complex is provisionally dated to ca. 800–600 B.C., coeval with the Vermont and New Hampshire megalithic monuments. *Malcolm D. Pearson*

Outdoor altars to the Celtic gods are found in central Vermont, notably along the old Celtic highroad that runs through South Woodstock. Altars dedicated to the sun god Bel are identified by the three subscript staves of the Ogam alphabet, spelling the letters B-L (above). The middle photograph shows part of the natural rock altar of Bel, carrying a square incised libation bowl, covered by moss as when first found by Fell in 1975. The lower photo shows a cast of the same bowl prepared after removal of the moss. Ruins of a large temple occur beside the altar, several of the masonry blocks also carrying the Ogam inscription B-L, one in addition also carrying the name of a king who apparently dedicated the temple. *Peter J. Garfall, Fell and Peter J. Garfall, Fell and Germano*

The outdoor altar of Apollo or Mabo-Mabona, god of youths, whose name means Hero-of-Heroes or Youth-of-Youths, located at South Woodstock, Vermont. The inscription, reading in part from the left, gives the consonants of the name of the god, M-B-M-B-N. The lower photograph is a view from above of the carved rectangular seminal libation bowl, with runnel, apparently used during rites of initiation of youths of the tribe. It is cut into the horizontal surface of the altar, to the upper left of the inscription on the vertical face. The line drawing to the left shows an exactly comparable libation bowl, with side runnel, recorded from Portugal by Professor Adriano Vasco Rodriguez in 1961. *Top photo by Joseph D. Germano, John Williams, bottom photo by Peter J. Garfall, Fell*

Ancillary wall or ceiling decorations generally relate to the divinity to whom the temple is dedicated. Thus the small chapel of Bel at Calendar Site 1 carries a quadripartite square, a symbol of the sun, appropriate to the sun god. The temple of the Mother Goddess Byanu beside the pond at South Woodstock, Vermont, carries on its ceiling a lightly punched and stained representation of Tanith, the Mother Goddess of the Phoenicians. Phallic symbols have no obvious relationship to the dedication, for a large ceiling phallus appears in the same temple of Byanu at South Woodstock, Vermont, and small phalli are also found in the Pantheon at the same locality.

Why should the structures identified as temples have their long axes directed towards the particular sunrise points on the horizon, as indicated in the table? A full answer is given in Chapter 13, but a short answer would be as follows. A typical Celtic temple is rectangular with a narrow entrance doorway in the middle of the eastern wall and the smoke-hole (and hence the altar) at the opposite or western end, these two features lying along the long axis. There are no window openings, the only light admitted coming from the doorway. Suppose you are standing in the chamber at the South Woodstock site in Vermont. The long axis points to declination $-23\frac{1}{2}°$ on the eastern horizon. This means that on the three or four days of the winter when the sun reaches its southernmost limit (nowadays from about December 21 to 23), a person standing at the altar and looking through the entrance opening will see the sunrise. On all other days of the year the sunrise will not be visible to him. Evidently, then, the orientation of the temple must be to provide a dramatic event on the selected day or days of the year appropriate for that temple, in this case the four days of the midwinter festival. It is logical to assume, therefore, that each temple was associated with one or other of the festivals of the Celtic year, much in the same way as Christian churches are usually dedicated to some particular saint whose feast day is one particular day of the year, and whose congregation therefore makes a special celebration at the church on that day.

The sun's motion is relatively slow at the time of solstice, so the midwinter

Ogam inscriptions in Oklahoma discovered by Gloria Farley throw light on the otherwise surprising occurrence of Celtic divinities in the archeology of that state. The voyagers apparently ascended the Mississippi, Arkansas, and Cimarron rivers, and left inscriptions and burial mounds. Above left, wooden mask resembling the antlered god Cernunos, from Spiro Mound, Oklahoma, Museum of the American Indian. Above right, bas relief of Cernunos from Celtic bowl, National Museum, Copenhagen. Below, cliff engraving of Romano-Celtic phase, showing young horned God. Letters M M presumably stand for Mabo-Mabona, whose name may be a more ancient equivalent of Cernunos of Gaul. *Cast by Gloria Farley, photo by Peter J. Garfall*

and midsummer festivals were necessarily spread over several days. In contrast, near equinoctial times the sun moves faster, and so the celebration of the spring and autumn festival was a more precise matter, each equinoctial festival occurring at sunrise on one particular day only. Thus, since the festival at the equinoxes was shorter, and hence less important, it is not surprising to find that a temple such as the one dedicated to Bel on Dix's Calendar Site 1 (near South Royalton, Vermont), where the axis of orientation lies due east and west, corresponding to the equinoctial sunrise and sunset directions, the temple itself is more modest, indeed no more than a small chapel. Here, we may guess, the tribal gathering was not at the equinoctial chapel, but on the nearby calendar site itself, where the Druids would be engaged in the astronomical observations.

These calendar matters, linked with Celtic religion and hence reflected in the physical orientation of their religious buildings, are undoubtedly to be traced back to an ancient cult of sun worship, and certain symbols widely distributed across the Old World at sites where the sun was worshipped in ancient times occur also on the walls or lintels of some of the Celtic temples in New England. They are also found at some other sites linked with various tribes of North American Indians, and there can be no doubt that the Indian shamans acquired these symbols from contact with ancient colonists in America such as the Celts.

The sun, as the giver of warmth that promotes the growth of all vegetation, both the forest foliage and the edible crops, and whose annual return after the winter months ushers in spring and the birth of the young of many wild animals, came to be regarded as the *Giver-of-Life*, a phrase that appears in the ancient Semitic Creation Hymn preserved by the Pima people of Arizona and Mexico (see Chapter 11). Thus any discussion of the role of the Celtic temple is bound to relate to the annual solar cycle whose astronomical axes determine the orientation of the temples and the dates of the year when any given temple celebrates its own special festival.

It is clear that the astronomical orientation of the various temples of the New England Celts is one of the most decisive facts showing that these structures cannot possibly have been built as root cellars by early colonial settlers in modern times. The farmers who cleared the land of forest in the eighteenth century were country people from England and Wales, Scotland and Ireland. Their names are on record in the town archives of New England, often also on memorial stones since erected in the public places, and still more conspicuously exhibited in the charming country graveyards, in the heart of the temple country of South Wood stock, for example. Here in the pioneers' burial ground we read the names of the fathers and mothers who first came to South Woodstock, their

The Eye of Bel–1. Until 1975 the subterranean stone chamber at the McIntosh farm near South Royalton, Vermont, was thought to be a colonial root-cellar. In the summer of that year Rene Fell (above, with cast) and Marjorie Chandler removed the soil over the entrance to disclose a deeply engraved stone lintel carrying a dedication in Ogam Celtic letters and a Phoenician monogram, showing that the building was dedicated to the sun god Bel. In the lower photograph of a cast of the lintel the Ogam letters read, from left to right, D-G B-L, to be read as Degos Bel, Temple of Bel. The pupil and lower eyelid are formed from the Phoenician letters B-L (Baal). An inscription within the chamber reads "Pay heed to Bel, his eye is the sun." *Bottom photo by Peter J. Garfall, top photo by Joseph D. Germano*

The Eye of Bel–2. In 1975 Byron Dix, while carrying out astronomical research on the function of the standing stones at Calendar Site 2, near South Woodstock, Vermont, discovered this engraved inscription on a large prostrate stone carrying worn Ogam letters. Here shown as a cast, with the incised markings painted in white, the inscription is seen to be Ogam, reading upwards B M-H-G, believed to represent the old Celtic words Bi amharg, or Observation stone. Subsequently similar inscriptions were recognized at Mystery Hill, New Hampshire, and when photographs were taken to Portugal by James Whittall, corresponding inscriptions were identified by Portuguese archeologists. It is believed that the distortion of the Ogam letter G to resemble an eye indicates either the eye of the god Bel (i.e., the sun) or perhaps was intended to convey the purpose of the observation stone to the illiterate. *Byron Dix, Peter J. Garfall*

The Eye of Bel–3. After the identification of the sign of the eye of the sun god at sites in Vermont, more severely eroded examples at Mystery Hill, North Salem, New Hampshire, were recognized. On this cast of part of the surface of a standing stone, upper right, the inscription appears to be identical with that of the Vermont Calendar site 2, near South Woodstock, reading therefore "Observation stone." Osborn Stone believes the monolith is related to lunar observations. *Peter J. Garfall and Fell*

The Eye of Bel–4. Following identification of the first example at Mystery Hill, Fell next found a more severely eroded eye inscription on an erratic boulder in the same line of sight as the summer solstice sunset stone of the Mystery Hill calendar complex. Shown here as a painted cast, no readable Ogam letters are discernible. *All casts in the Eye of Bel series were prepared and deciphered by Fell, photographed in color by Garfall, and rendered in black-and-white by Joseph Germano.*

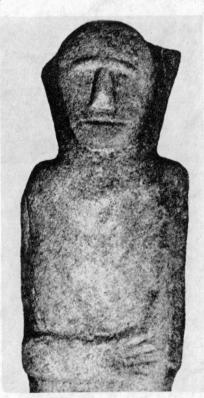

The Celtic Herm–1. A herm is a rectangular block or column of stone having a human head or skull carved at the upper end, and set into the ground as a grave marker or as an image to a god. In 1904 some carved monoliths were found at La Vaux in Brittany carrying representations of herms (top, from Joseph Dechelette), accompanied by Goidelic Ogam lettering giving the names of dead warriors and sailors. The crosses may indicate a Christian date. The figures at bottom are from the pagan Celtic sites near Wurttemberg, Germany, in the Landesmuseum, Stuttgart. The right figure is part of a double-faced image. The left is a fragment carrying Ogam letters M—Q-M ("noble youth"). The Ogam of the Breton example at the upper left reads T-UI-UI F-S-D-H, and apparently means "The two men named Tawi laid to rest."

The Celtic Herm—2. A badly eroded massive herm was found in 1975 by John Williams in central Vermont, near remains of stone temples dedicated to Bel and to Byanu in the high country near Reading. It carries no readable inscription and the head lacks detail. It still stands nearly erect, and libation bowls are cut in nearby rocks. This may be an archaic image of Bel, antedating the more sophisticated sculpture of the South Royalton sites. *John Williams and Joseph D. Germano*

Celtic art is characterized by the manner in which natural figures, such as birds and animals, pass insensibly into geometric elements in the design. The motif at the upper left is from a Cocle dish, Panama, in the Peabody Museum, Harvard University. The other three are from the *ceramica negra iberica* of Spain, in the Museo Numantino, Soria, Spain. As Celtic inscriptions and other artifacts occur in Florida and west to Oklahoma, it may be inferred that perhaps Panamanian potters came under the influence of these southern Celtic outposts.

Celtic motifs from the old world and the new. Above left, Cocle bowl, Panama, in the Peabody Museum, Harvard University, drawn by Gerald Heslinga. Other figures are from *ceramica negra iberica* in the Museo Numantina, Soria, Spain, after Jose Camon Aznar, Las Artes y los pueblos de la Espana Primitiva, Espasa-Calpe, Madrid.

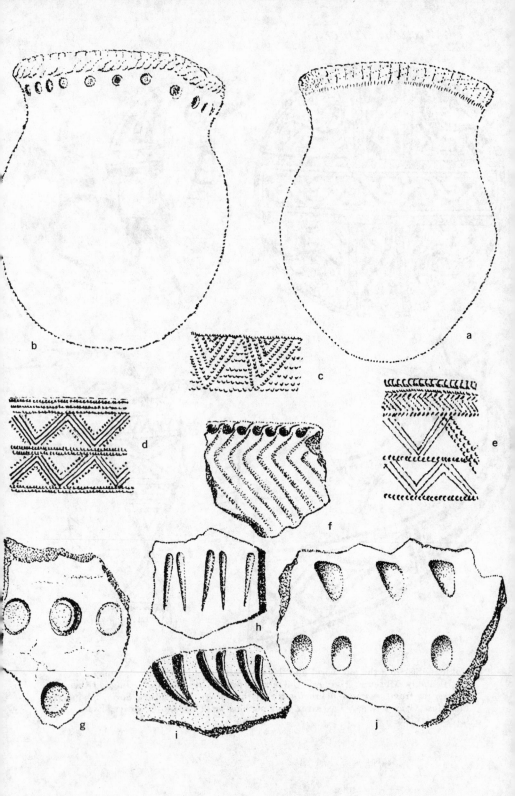

b

a

c

d

e

f

g

h

i

j

children and other relatives. The simple inscriptions show that these were certainly no band of astrologers or philosophers imbued with druidic learning. To assert that these megalithic buildings are merely "root cellars" built by the colonists is unjustified. Even supposing that by some unexplained means the colonial farmers were able to inscribe Ogam and Phoenician dedications on their "cellars," this would by no means explain the systematic orientation of the cellars with respect to the ancient rites of the Celtic solar year.

Monoliths, also called standing stones, are among the most characteristic features of any Celtic landscape, in New England no less than in Europe, though as yet we have not found American examples so impressive as some of the giant monoliths of Brittany. Some appear to have been monuments to dead heroes. Others perhaps marked a battle, a crowning ceremony, or some other event long remembered but now forgotten. We have collected some photographs of monoliths in Vermont, some now overturned, though capable of being erected again should such be the wish of their custodians, the present landowners. Standing stones often occur in threes, especially in straight lines of three. The magic properties of the number three are remembered to this day by the Gaels, and in Scotland when I was a student I was taught the following ancient prayer:

> Comnadh tri mo dhuil,
> Comnadh tri mo run,
> Comnadh tri mo shuil,
>   Agus mo ghlun gun chlaon,
>   Mo ghlun gun chlaon!

> May three aid my hope,
> May three aid my love-making,
> May three aid my eye,
>   And my knee from stumbling,
>   My knee from stumbling.

Celtic burial urns from Iberian and North American sites. Bell-shaped, unglazed urns were introduced into the Iberian Peninsula near the close of the European Bronze Age, and it is considered by Portuguese and Spanish archeologists that Celts of the Urnfield culture of France brought these ceramics into Spain around 800 b.c. They usually have an incised geometric pattern, especially around the rim. Their purpose, when buried in funeral mounds, was to hold ashes of the dead. Vase a, above, is from Marles, Barcelona, and the similarly shaped vase b is from Owasco, New York. The incised patterns c and d are from Las Cogotas, Portugal, and that of figure e is from New York. The other rim sherds are from Amoskeag, New Hampshire (coll. James P. Whittall); the impressed circular and oval decorations (seen also in the New York vase, b) are paralleled by a similar decoration in ware from archeological sites in Majorca (*fide* Salvatore Trento, personal communication); the New Hampshire examples are from an area believed to have been in Celtic occupation.

The sacred bull of the Iberian Celts is here replaced by a bison, an animal that formerly roamed the northeastern region of the United States. This sculpture, in the style of the Celtic sculpture of Iberian sites, was found in the Lawrence area of the Merrimack River valley, Massachusetts. Other evidence of a Celtic sculptor's work in Massachusetts is the finding of part of a carved human leg near Haverhill. *Malcolm B. Pearson*

How you get inside depends on the temple. Above right, Fell emerging from a small hole leading down into the completely subterranean temple of the Eye of Bel at the McIntosh site in the White River area. Below, Robert E. Stone, director of Mystery Hill, shelters from 95-degree summer heat in the equinoctial porch of the temple of Bel on the hills above South Royalton, Vermont. *Photos by Peter J. Garfall*

Rings of stones, sometimes double rings, with or without a central stone, also characterize Celtic lands, Vermont and Connecticut included, Burnt Mountain in Massachusetts, and other New England localities. In Ireland they range in diameter from ten feet upwards, and those of America are of similar dimensions. Their functions are not really known, and probably varied. Some seem to have been religious or astronomical, having an east–west axis marked by extra stones; others may have been no more than protective fences around a grave tumulus. Some seem to have been the outer limits of a hut or wigwam. Two sketches from my notebooks illustrate these small circles of puzzling purpose. The circle represents the protective power of a deity, and in the prayers of the Hebridean fishermen when the sun rises Alexander Carmichael recorded the following lines that may well come down from pagan times, for the circle was the symbol of the sun god Bel:

> Dia dha mo chaim,
> Dia dha mo chuairt,
> Dia dha mo chainn,
> Dia dha mo smuain!

> God be my enfolding,
> God be my circle,
> God be in my words,
> God be in my thoughts.

Perhaps the last couplet was added in Christian times.

When the Celt of old had lived his span of days, his friends and relatives held a wake for the departed, the *feill* of the Irish or *gwyll* of the Welsh, and after much loud *caoin* (keening or lamentation) his body was laid to rest in earth. Many ancient heroes of New England sleep among the Green Mountains in the soil they once trod. Their simple tombstones give just their name and the name of their father, occasionally also the word "alas" is found, as on the grave markers of the Celtiberians of the Susquehanna valley. The names we read are older forms of names that many a Celt yet carries: Da or Dai, Lu or Lew, Hu or Hugh, Yoghan (Ewan or Evan), Gab (Gavin) and many another yet to be recorded. So here in the quiet beauty of the mountain valleys lie the remotest ancestors of how many modern American families, themselves the descendants of those who stayed behind in Europe but whose progeny eventually followed the ancient urge to cross the wide ocean to the western lands. Truly the mountain pastures of Vermont are hallowed soil. The Gaels have preserved the ancient prayer of one who is about to be laid to rest, a lesson in humility that still can have meaning for us:

Caimich mi a nochd
Eadar uir agus earc,
Eadar run do reachd,
Agus dearc mo dhoille

Bury me by night,
Amid the pastures and the herds,
Amid the mystery of thy laws.
    My unseeing eyes.

This poem of resignation is addressed to a deity called, with typical Celtic periphrasis, Thou Being-of-laws-and-of-the-stars, some creator god of the old philosophy that the Church adapted to Christianity. Has any modern faith more to offer by way of comfort? The ancient Celt looked into his future after death and accepted the end of existence as a mere personal detail. Perhaps therein lay the strength that carried him across an ocean to settle a strange and hostile shore.

Collapsed megalithic structure near Castledearg, County Tyrone, Ireland, dating from about 2000 B.C. The Ogam inscription may have been cut 1,000 years later; it is written in the early style, without vowels (Ogam consaine). Photographs and peels made by Warren Dexter, James Whittall, and David Barron (ESOP vol. 16, 1988) yield a text relating to omens in the flight of birds.

LW

11

The Celtiberians

THE men of Tarshish established colonies in eastern North America, the settlers probably drawn from the native Iberians (that is, Celts and Basques) of the Guadalquivir valley in Andalusia. That they could not have included many Phoenicians is apparent from the lack of sophisticated material cultural objects at the sites so far investigated. Rather, these colonists must have been accustomed to the rude manner of life of the Iberians before the arrival of Phoenician traders in Spain but, like many colonial peoples, they had acquired the language of their colonizers, in this case the Phoenicians, and some at least of their chieftains were literate in the Tartessian manner of writing the Phoenician (or Punic) tongue. These inferences are drawn from the documents found in their chieftains' burial mounds.

The first authenticated find of an engraved Phoenician tablet in an American archeological context was that of a Tartessian inscription found in 1838. This tablet was excavated from a burial chamber found at the base of Mammoth Mound, in Moundsville, West Virginia. Although the Tartessian alphabet had not then been deciphered, the similarity of the inscription to Iberian writing was recognized, and in the contemporary reports of the dig, the mound and its contents were attributed to European visitors. Man-made burial mounds, or tumuli, are characteristic of many royal graves of the European Bronze Age.

The notion that Europeans had visited and even settled in North America in ancient times continued as an acceptable hypothesis in the archeological periodicals for the ensuing forty years. Then, sometime around 1870, the opinion became widespread that there had been no such callers before Columbus. The Moundsville tablet was forgotten, or dismissed as a later intrusion that had accidentally fallen into the mound, or been surreptitiously introduced by some irresponsible person; others thought it was a Cherokee artifact of quite modern date, unconnected

This engraved tablet, inscribed in Iberian script and employing the Punic language, shares some of its vocabulary and all its basic style characters with the historic tablet of Tasach, excavated in 1838 from the foot of the Mammoth Mound at Moundsville, Grave Creek, West Virginia. Thus it is clearly related to the Iberian culture of Moundsville. It was found in a stream bed in central West Virginia, and erroneously supposed to be of Viking origin. Its vocabulary is found in standard Semitic dictionaries, and yields the following translation, the script matching that given in Diringer's tables:

(1) The memorial of Teth
(2) This tile
(3) (His) brother caused-to-be-made

Compare the inscription and the translation with the data given for the tablet of Tasach in chapter 2. *Ceramic cast courtesy Dr. Clyde Keeler, photo by Joseph D. Germano*

The Pontotoc stele, found in Oklahoma, is apparently the work of an early Iberian colonist in America, as the script is that known otherwise only from the Cachaoda-Rapa region in northern Portugal. It depicts the life-giving rays of the sun descending upon the earth beneath. To the left the Iberian Punic letters spell "Start of dawn," to the right "Dusk," with the crescent-ship of the moon. Two of the panels contain Ogam Punic, partly illegible, but sufficiently clear to disclose the phrases "When Baal-Ra rises in the east, the beasts are content, and (when he hides his face) they are displeased." These identify the inscription as an extract from the *Hymn to the Aton* by Pharaoh Akhnaton, here translated into Iberian Punic. Further study of this remarkable stele is still in progress. Although Akhnaton's hymn dates from the thirteenth century B.C., this American version can scarcely be older than about 800 B.C. The engraver was interrupted, covered over his work with soil, and never returned to complete the blank panels. *Gloria Farley, Weldon W. Stout*

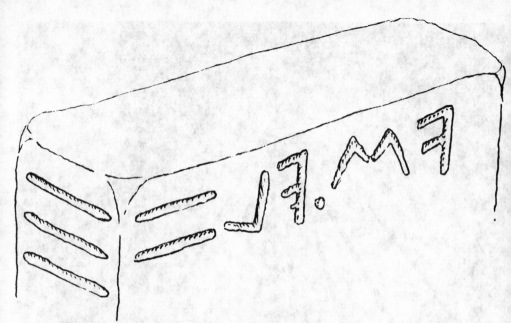

"Haga rests here" is the purport of the bilingual inscription on an ancient grave-stone found at Bache, Oklahoma. The South Iberian script reads from right to left H-L-L H-G. The Ogam script to the left, in the style of Cachao da Rapa in northern Portugal, reads from below upwards H-G. The name Haga is probably cognate with modern Arabic Aga, meaning "chief." This stone, which yields a phonetic value for the Ogam sign for G, could be substituted for the Iberian inscription (c) cited in the Appendix (*Cracking the Code*), thereby making the decipherment of the American Ogam inscriptions totally independent of European materials. Such independent decipherment, however, yields a result that matches that derived for strictly European inscriptions. *Gloria Farley*

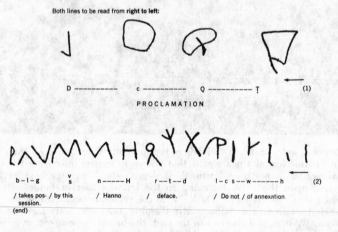

Both lines to be read from **right to left**:

D ——— c ——— Q ——— T   (1)

PROCLAMATION

b – l – g   v̆ / s   n —— H   r — t — d   l – c s — w —— h   (2)

/ takes pos- / by this   / Hanno   / deface.   / Do not / of annexation.
session.
(end)

Decipherment of Iberian inscription on the Bourne Stone, found at Komassakum-kanit, Cape Cod Bay. From *Occasional Publications* of the Epigraphic Society, v. 2, no. 44 (1975).

Approximate vocalization
1. Takidh
2. hawasa. Il datar. Hannu sha galaba.

Translation
1.   A PROCLAMATION
2. of annexation. Do not deface. By this Hanno takes possession.

Roman	Iberian	
	Massachusetts (Bourne)	Southern Spain
b		
g		
d		
ḍ		
h		
w		
ḥ		
ṭ (th)		
q		
l		
n		
ṣ (sy)		
c (i)		
r		
š (sh)		
t		

Alphabets of the Bourne stone and southern Spain, compared.

Sound	Style of Syria and Lebanon (Phoenicia) 800–600 B.C.	Style of Punic settlers of Iowa 800–600 B.C.	Style of Punic settlers of Spain 800–600 B.C.
b	⟍ᐸ	૧,૬	⟍ᐸ,૬
g	⟍	>	>
d	◁	△	△
h	⊒	∏	∏
w	Y	↑,	↑,Y
z	I	∨,н	∨
ḥ	目	‖‖‖	‖‖‖,目
ṭ	⊕	ℬ	☼
k	⊁,Ɏ,Y	⊓⊥ʎ	⊁,K
l	∠	⋋⋌	∧
m	ᗰ	⋎	Ⱳ,ᕹ
š	WW	∀	∀
ꞌ, i	O	O,:	O,:
s	⧧	Ꙅ	Ꙅ
t	✝	Ψ	Ψ

The Phoenician (Punic) colonists of Iowa used an alphabet that shows clearly that their homeland was in the Iberian peninsula. The Iowa inscription was found at Davenport in 1874, and is written in the Iberian alphabet whose sound values were determined in Spain 60 years later. Failure to identify the Iowan alphabet led archeologists until now to suppose that the Davenport finds were fraudulent.

with the so-called Moundbuilders, a word coined for a supposed phase of Woodland Indian culture on the east coast. Interest in the Moundsville tablet was revived in 1948, when Olaf Strandwold declared it to be Norse and, by what means no Norse scholar can fathom, contrived to read it as: "I knelt on the island, Øn's Yule site on meadow island. Now the island is a sanctuary where holy things are hoarded." To obtain this peculiar translation he was obliged to duplicate letters, turn some upside down, ignore some parts of letters, and assign more than one sound to the same signs. The effect of this unfortunate Norsemania was mainly to discredit epigraphy in America, and the view hardened that Columbus was in fact the first European visitor to these shores.

By 1968, when the English epigrapher Diringer brought out tables of the comparative phonetics of the Iberian alphabets, it was already possible to read numerous Semitic words and phrases in the various Spanish inscriptions in the Iberian scripts. Spanish scholars, however, had meantime become interested mainly in the classical era, particularly the Greek settlements of Catalonia, where vowel signs had been introduced into the writing system by changing the sounds of certain Phoenician letters. Thus the Andalusian texts, which retain the ancient Semitic manner of writing only with consonants (and semivowels such as y and w), were seen as untranslatable writings in an unknown language. It is almost as if the Spanish epigraphers had set their minds against reading Semitic texts, for they do not seem to have noticed the Phoenician character of the Iberian and Tartessian inscriptions. This is the more surprising since no less an authority than H. N. Savory in England gave a masterly review of the Phoenician characteristics of the Tartessian culture and its viability in the face of Celtic inroads, in his book *Spain and Portugal,* published the same year (1968) as Diringer's Iberian tables. So it is not altogether strange that several more years elapsed before the Iberian character of our American inscriptions could be detected and proved.

Such has been the checkered history of the Tartessian inscriptions of West Virginia and Ohio. Interest in them was renewed in 1974, when Professor George Carter in Texas noticed the similarity of many of the letters in his copies of these tablets to letters I had then recently reported from Libyan inscriptions. He forwarded copies of the American tablets to me for study. I could see that they carried a script of the Iberian group, related to the Libyan but with many differences from it. I could also see that the reading direction must be from right to left and that Phoenician words occur in the inscriptions, though often abbreviated or spelled differently from the more usual dictionary forms. The style was terse, rather like creole or pidgin-English, suggesting that the writers may have been using a language other than their native tongue. Although I was not at

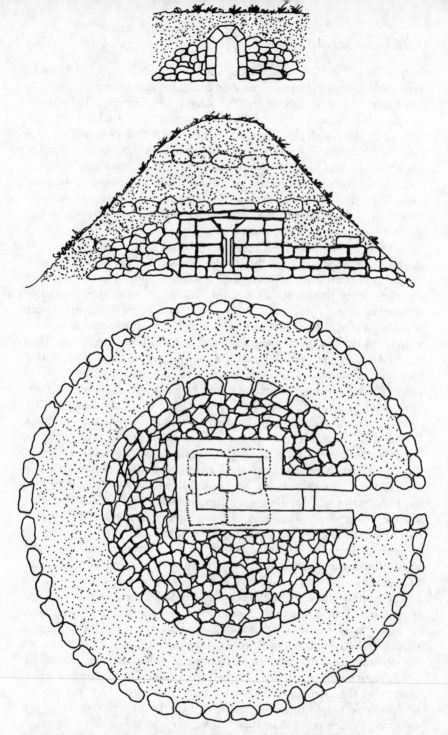

During the Bronze Age Iberian chiefs and kings were buried in mounds of varying size, similar to this example from Portugal, the body being placed in a stone-lined chamber about 60 feet deep beneath the summit of the mound or *tumulus*. The corresponding mounds of eastern and middle United States had timber chambers rather than stone, but they contain similar archeological remains to those found in Iberia, including mortuary inscriptions in Iberian script and language, like that cited in chapter 2 from Moundsville, West Virginia.

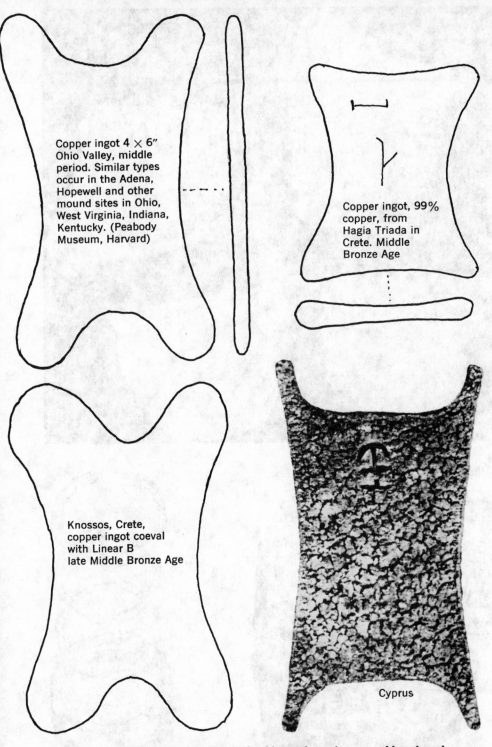

Copper ingot 4 × 6″ Ohio Valley, middle period. Similar types occur in the Adena, Hopewell and other mound sites in Ohio, West Virginia, Indiana, Kentucky. (Peabody Museum, Harvard)

Copper ingot, 99% copper, from Hagia Triada in Crete. Middle Bronze Age

Knossos, Crete, copper ingot coeval with Linear B late Middle Bronze Age

Cyprus

American mound sites have yielded considerable numbers of copper tablets shaped like the hide of an animal; the function of these was unknown, and they were namd "reels." However, in 1896 in Cyprus, and subsequently in many Mediterranean excavations, corresponding Bronze Age copper objects, recognized now as ingots used as international Bronze Age currency, have been found. The American examples indicate an international trading system extending to the Atlantic states.

Pottery appears abruptly in northeastern American sites, suggesting that it was introduced by visitors or settlers from Iberia during the Bronze Age. Above left, rim sherds from a collection made at Amoskeag, New Hampshire, by James P. Whittall II, from a deep horizon prior to dam construction. The geometric pattern of incised parallel lines in chevron form resembles Iberian ware of the Bronze Age. Below left, a sherd collected at Raymond, New Hampshire, by William Goodwin's group. Below right, five copper armbands, resembling those of the European Bronze Age, found in the burial mound of Tasah when Mammoth Mound was excavated in 1838; this find was associated with a Celtiberian inscribed tablet, deciphered on page 158. *Top photo by Joseph D. Germano, left photo by Peter J. Garfall*

Portrait figurines and also figures of animals appear as handles or rim decoration in Iberian pottery during the latter half of the first millennium B.C., and Portuguese scholars attribute their presence to the influence of the Greek settlers, as also to Punic influence. Similar terracotta figurines form the handles or decoration of North American pottery from the Mound Burials, as seen in these examples. The European features and the Iberian form of the headdress are noteworthy. From S. D. Peet, *The Mound Builders*, 1892. *Left, Gerald Heslinga, Buffalo Museum. Right, Peabody Museum, Harvard University*

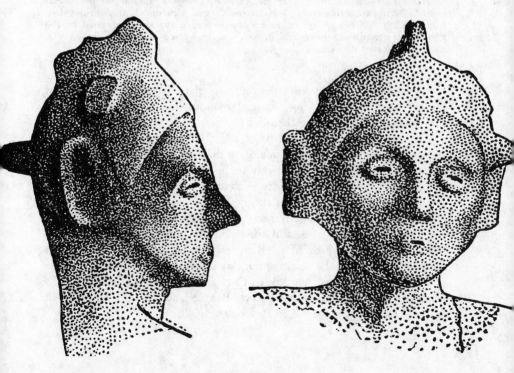

The Phoenician at home and abroad retained his characteristic high-crowned hat, the *hennin*, worn on formal occasions. It is here illustrated by two terracotta figurines. Left, an American example, excavated from a Mound Builder burial mound. Right, a figurine from Hagia Irene, Cyprus Museum. Both figurines date from the 8th to 6th century B.C. For a comparison of the alphabets used by the Phoenician colonists in Iowa and in southern Spain, see page 162. From S. D. Peet, *The Mound Builders*, 1892.

first informed by Carter as to the source of the tablets, I could tell from the text that they came from funeral mounds, for words answering to these meanings occurred in the brief phrases.

The translations should still be regarded as tentative until we have a fuller documentation of the Andalusian dialects, but I think the versions offered in this book are not likely to be grossly in error. The lack of vowels, with resultant uncertainty as to the precise words intended, is the main cause of difficulty to the epigrapher.

The Celtiberians, as already noted, were a mixed assemblage of tribes speaking several languages, and one of the constituent nations must have been the Basques. Nowadays Basque-speaking people are found in Europe only around the shores of the Bay of Biscay and the adjacent parts of the Pyrenees Mountains between France and Spain. Modern Basque is rendered in two main forms, French Basque and Spanish Basque, but each comprises a number of local dialects.

In 1975 I was introduced by American colleagues to Marjorie Chandler of New Hampshire, curator of inscriptions for the New England Antiquities Research Society. In her custody are some 450 inscribed stones collected in the 1940s by the late Dr. William Strong from the lower part of the Susquehanna valley in Pennsylvania. Many of these are inscriptions from the graves of early settlers, and the variety of scripts and tongues on the stones tells us that these were Celtiberians of Basque, Celtic, and Punic origins. A few examples of the Basque stones given here will illustrate the modest nature of the settlement, about which we know very little else at the moment. Much more research needs to be done in the Pennsylvania area. Even as I write this chapter a young archeologist visitor from Harrisburg tells me that the specimens from the Strong collection in that city's museum are kept out of sight and the inscriptions are referred to as marks made by plowshares!

Another, and in some respects richer, source of evidence regarding the Celtiberians is known. The Pima peoples of the Southwest are a loosely knit confederation of tribes governed by *makai,* a word translated as magician or wizard, and evidently related to the old Semitic word *magi,* with the same sense. During 1901–1902 Frank Russell, an ethnologist of the U.S. Bureau of Ethnology, lived with the Pima and transliterated into roman letters the ancient Creation Chant which at that time was still remembered by the makai. It was published in 1908 by the Bureau, together with a crude attempt at a translation. In truth, while every praise must be accorded Russell for thus preserving the Chant, his translation is very inadequate for, as he himself reports, the archaic words in the Chant often baffled him. Here is a sample of his attempted translation:

> Earth-Magician earth make. Come see what you intend.
> Round make come, see what you intend.
> Earth-Magician mountain make come, see what you tell,
> Smooth make come, see what you tell. . . .*

Small wonder that uninformed people tend to think of Amerindian languages as childish and even incoherent! Sheer literary murder has been done here, all unwittingly.

The plain truth is that the devoted ethnologists who collected the ancient literature of the Amerindians lacked the linguistic skills to realize what they were doing. Russell, and apparently every other investigator, failed to recognize the Creation Chant as an ancient Semitic hymn.

Although the language is Punic and most of the words in it are no longer used by the Pima, the subject matter of each section of the chant

* *Twenty-Sixth Annual Report of the Bureau of Ethnology,* Washington, D.C., 1908.

The 500 inscribed stones collected in the Susquehanna valley by the late Dr. William Strong comprise Celtiberian, Phoenician, and Basque grave markers from a Bronze Age settlement, about 800–600 B.C., though mistakenly dismissed as "marks made by plows" by some professional archeologists. Above, Marjorie Chandler and Fell with the Strong collection. Below, grave marker; casts of both sides of stone recording the death of a Punic speaker named Q-S; the Y-shaped mark is the letter Wa, signifying mourning. *Peter J. Garfall*

was correctly identified by Kamal Tkak, the magician who dictated it to Russell. Section 1, dealing with the creation of the earth, for example, and Section 4, relating the creation of the sun, are so titled in Russell's translation. It is evident that in the course of time the Pima language diverged so much from the original Punic that the latter could no longer be understood by modern speakers, in the same way that a modern English speaker can scarcely comprehend a word of the Anglo-Saxon Gospels unless he has training in the archaic forms of the old English language. Here now, for comparison with Russell's attempt at translation, I give the translation as I believe it should be rendered, using a *Semitic* dictionary:

In the beginning the World-Magician created the earth.
As time went by he set plants upon his handiwork.
By magic, water for irrigation came into being, and so vegetation arose upon his handiwork.
Then the World-Magician created rains by magic, to water his handiwork, so the crops would ripen.

The whole remarkable Creation story continues for page after page in the bureau's annual report, rendered there as nonsensical English. If read as Semitic, however, the text unfolds a conception of the Creation as poetic and logical as any to be found in ancient scripture. Thus, failure to apply comparative linguistics to the Amerindian tongues has led in this instance to major errors in our understanding of the whole spectrum of American history, and the role of Mediterranean peoples in it, as well as doing grave injustice to the cultural tradition of the Amerindian peoples. In the case we are considering the errors disclosed lead me to propose the following corrections:

(1) The Pima tribe speaks a Semitic tongue evidently derived from that of the Iberian Punic colonists who settled America 2,500 years ago.
(2) The Pima have preserved with remarkable fidelity the ancient religious scriptures of these early Iberian Punic colonists.
(3) These scriptures have a poetic and literary quality wholly obscured by the grotesque mistranslation to which they have been subjected.
(4) The false notion that Amerindian tongues evolved as unique American phenomena has led to a classification of them that does not express their true affinities.

Should anyone claim that the Pima example is an atypical case, the claim may be subjected to examination by reference to other Amerindian tongues. In the next chapter of this book it is shown that the language of the so-called Zuni tribe (more correctly the Shiwi or "Nomads") is a tongue directly derived from the Libyan speech of North Africa, in which the Coptic, Middle Egyptian, and Nubian vocabulary is overwhelming.

TABLE 4

Extracts from the Sacred Creation Chant of the Pima Indians
(*Semitic roots in the Arabic text are given in their
dictionary form, in Roman script.*)

a. Pima
b. Arabic
c. English translation

1. a. Tcu-Wutu-Makai   tcu   wutu   nata   mi.
   b. Taqna-Watan-Makana   taqna   watan   nataj   mia.
   c. The-Solid-Earth-Magician   the solid   earth   created   in the beginning.

2. a. Aku   ka   niyiata   hasit   co   ony-i.
   b. Aḳd   kan   niyat   hasida   ka   ana i.
   c. He set   on his handiwork   herbs   as   time passed.

3. a. Sikala   mu   nata   miakuka.
   b. Siqaya   mu   nataj   makraqa.
   c. Irrigating   water   he created   by magic.

4. a. Nyuita   hasit   co-onyi. (*da capo* from 1)
   b. Niyat   hasida   kana-i.
   c. On his handiwork   plants   came into being.

5. a. Tcu-Wutu-Makai   talaku   nata   miakuka   nyuita   hasi   yana.
   b. Taqna-Watan-Makana   dalaqa   nataj   makraqa   niyat   hasida   yana.
   c. The World-Magician   rains   created   by magic   on his handiwork   so crops   bore fruit.

6. a. Tapi-nyi   mu   nata   miakuka   nyuita   hasi   yana. (*da capo* from 5)
   b. Dabib-nyi   mu   nataj   makraqa   niyat   hasida   yana.
   c. Ever-flowing   waters   he created   by magic   on his handiwork   so crops   bore fruit.

7. a. Tcu-Wutu-Makai   tcu   wutu   nata   himlo,   himlo,   himlo,   hu mutco-o. (*bis*)
   b. Taqna-Watan-Makana   taqna   watan   nataj   ḥaml,   ḥaml,   ḥaml,   hu muḍiya.
   c. The World-Magician   the solid   earth   created,   and fruits   upon fruits   upon fruits   he created.

8. a. Tcu-Wutu-Makai   tava'-ku   nata (*bis*)   himlo, himlo, (etc.)
   b. Taqna-Watan-Makana   dauha-kau'   nataj   ḥaml, ḥaml.
   c. The World-Magician   fruit trees   created   fruits upon fruits.

9. a. Tcu-Wutu   tapa   Şihait   con yo-ka-ana,
   b. Taqam-Watan   tabba   Sahida   kaun ya-kauna,
   c. The Earth   now established,   the Universe   continued to form,

10. a. Tavangu   tapa   sitco   mama   tcu-u.
    b. Tabina   tabba   šatta   mamar   taka.
    c. Animals   were created   of diverse sorts   at times   preordained.

The Creation of the Sun

11. a. Vanyingi   tars   ai.   Wu   nata   kahi   Hiya-nyi   tamai,
    b. Bunyan   turs   auj.   Hu   nataj   qahir   Iḥya-nyi   ţamih,
    c. He raised   the sun   on high.   He   created   the mighty   Giver-of-Life   aloft,

12. a. Ya   ahai!   Punan   ait   ko-o! (*bis*)
    b. Ya   aya!   Bunyan   ata   kaya!
    c. What   a marvel!   Raised up   to bestow   warmth!

13. a. Si-iya   ldi   takio,   wopa   himu   kahowu.
    b. Swiya   ladi   taqs,   wabl   hamma   quhula.
    c. He regulated   the sharpness   of the weather,   giving rain   in heat   and drought.

14. a. Tait   cun   yuku,   sapava   Mununaa! (*da capo* from 13)
    b. Tiyat   kaun   yakana,   sabaka   Muniya.
    c. The design   of the world   continuing,   shaped   by Destiny.

The Creation Chant then goes on to deal with the Creation of the Moon (Pima *mar,* Semitic *amar*), the celestial vault or atmosphere (Pima *howa,* Semitic *hawa*), premonitory warnings of an impending Flood, the Flood itself, referred to as a submergence or subsidence (Pima *rso,* Semitic *rusub*), and the eventual salvation of chosen beings who survived the Flood. It is interesting that the Pima priests (*makai,* wizard, matching the Semitic *makana* and *magus,* magician or wise man) not only have preserved this ancient Semitic epic as a remembered sacred history, but also have retained the sacred words of the ancients, such as *Tars* (the sacred disk of the sun, matching *Turs,* with the same sense) which, it will be remembered, we found written in Phoenician and Ogam characters on the cliff face at Cachão da Rapa, a relic of the Iberian Bronze Age.

It is therefore not unlikely that the New England Celts may also have been in possession of the Flood story, indeed of the whole Creation story, in view of their shared Phoenician hieratic terminology in Iberia itself.

The existence of the ancient Semitic Creation Chant in America has not been noticed before. The excerpts given here are therefore the first published evidence of yet another aspect of the continuity of Amerindian culture with that of the Mediterranean. So far as the Pima language is concerned, it is of course obvious that its linguistics must be entirely reexamined so that the correct place may be assigned it among the Semitic creole languages.

Pending the further progress of my work I presently think of the Pima as descendants of some Celtiberian tribe that had been converted to the use of the Punic language by Phoenician colonists in Spain, and whose more adventurous members migrated to the Lands Beyond the Sunset under Phoenician leadership. They probably spoke a creolized form of Punic, "Pidgin Punic" you might say, of which the present-day Pima speech is the modern descendant. In the same way, in Europe, the creolized forms of Latin used by the Celtic tribesmen of France during the Roman occupation eventually gave rise to the Old French language, just as similar transformations occurred in parts of Spain, Portugal, and Italy.

It is quite in the cards that somewhere in the United States there are still spoken derivatives of the ancient Basque tongue, too. A fascinating letter I received from a Shoshone Indian who had been traveling in the Basque country of Spain tells of his recognition of Shoshone words over there, including his own name, whose Shoshone meaning proved to match the meaning attached to a similar word by the modern Basques. Unfortunately I mislaid this interesting letter. If the Shoshone scholar who wrote to me should chance to see these words I hope he will forgive me and contact me again. The modern Basque settlers of Idaho may perhaps bring forth a linguist to investigate matters raised in this chapter.

12

The Libyans of Zuni

THE coming of the Libyans is still one of the most mysterious of the colonial episodes of American history. We have so far found relatively little in the way of coastal inscriptions to tell us the time of their arrival, or of their portals of entry into the land. Just a few tell-tale written fragments from scattered points, including one from as far north as Quebec, one from California, and others from cliff faces along the Arkansas and Cimarron Rivers in the southern Midwest; and nothing else. Nothing more until the year 1879, when the U.S. Bureau of Ethnology was established and began their investigations of the Zuni country of New Mexico.

Unusual features of the Shiwi and Hopi tribes had already come to the attention of Professor J. Walter Fewkes (like me, a marine biologist at the Museum of Comparative Zoology at Harvard) and of James Stevenson. Continued work by these and other parties led to the publications of important memoirs and the preparation of Zuni linguistic and lexicographic materials. Although the vocabulary soon made it plain that the Zuni language is related to no other Amerindian family of tongues, no attempt seems to have been made to determine if it had external affinities.

While examining Pueblo materials in the Peabody Museum of Archeology at Harvard University, my attention was attracted to a white leather sun-disk that, according to its label, had been obtained from New Mexico after a religious ceremony of the Shiwi (Zuni) in 1891. On it are painted the Libyan letters T-M, a formula adopted in Egypt as the phonetic rendering of *Atum,* the primeval sun god of North Africa. The Libyan language, as I have shown elsewhere, is basically Egyptian combined with Anatolian roots introduced by the Sea Peoples who invaded Libya, while the written form of the language is like that of the Phoenicians, alphabetic but using only consonants. The records of the Bureau of Ethnology for 1891 disclose that Dr. Matilda Stevenson attended all the solar-solstice ceremonies of the Zuni clans, winter and summer, in that year, and that she collected some cult objects. Her report (Stevenson, 1904) includes a number of photographs and paintings in which well-known solar-cult motifs of the Mediterranean type are visible on the altars, though she did not identify them as such.

For these reasons I examined the etymology of the Zuni language, using vocabularies that Bernard Leman located for me in the Widener and other libraries. The results of this inquiry convinced me that the Zuni tongue is largely derived from North African dialects, the linkage being very marked with Coptic, Middle Egyptian, and Nubian of the Nile Valley. While there is evidence of much loan vocabulary, too, from adjacent tribes (from the Algonquian dialects to the north and the Mexican tongues to the south), the main vocabulary in my opinion is North African.

My conclusion, then, is that the Zuni language should be reclassified as an American branch of the North African group, which otherwise comprises the belt of so-called Afro-Asian tongues of mixed Semitic-Hamitic origin, stretching from the Moroccan Berber area near Gibraltar across the southern coastlands of the Mediterranean to Somalia in the east, and including in former times the ancient Libyan, Ancient Egyptian, Coptic, and Ethiopian (Amharic) languages. In view of the discovery of ancient Libyan inscriptions in the places I have indicated, and the evident concentration of such few inscriptions as we have in the southern parts of the United States, I think it probable that the ancestors of the Shiwi people of Zuni are the same visitors from Libya who cut the ancient inscriptions.

During the 1930s excavations in New Mexico by a Harvard team and associated investigators, including Harold Gladwin, brought to light a previously unknown style of pottery now called the Mimbres ware, from the type locality of the find. The vessels are decorated in black, white, and red and carry paintings of people and animals, together with other motifs that have been regarded as merely decorative. However, in my opinion these motifs are actually derived from original inscriptions in the Libyan alphabet and descriptive of the scenes depicted in the paintings. Gladwin's dating of the finds by dendrochronology (tree-ring dating) indicates a date of about 1200 A.D. The question of the supposed inscriptions requires further study.

The illustrations accompanying this chapter suggest that among some members of the Zuni priesthood there persisted into recent historical times a vestige of the Libyan writing system, such that certain religious objects would be inscribed with "magic" symbols that are, in reality, the written Libyan words for those objects, as exemplified by the sun-disk inscription already mentioned.

The principal evidence, however, of Libyan settlement in North America rests in the essentially North African word content of the spoken language of the Zuni people today. The matching pairs of words from New Mexico on the one hand and from North Africa on the other are so numerous, and the phonetic relationships so evident, that it is possible to set out the rules of phonetic mutation that govern the derivation of the Zuni language from its Libyan parent language. These phonetic rules are of the same kind as another series I demonstrated in 1973, linking the Libyan language with that of Polynesia. The Polynesian people, like the Libyans themselves, are descended from the Anatolian Sea Peoples who invaded the Mediterranean around 1400 B.C. and, after attacking Egypt and suffering a series of defeats as the Egyptians record, eventually settled Libya. Later the Libyan seamen were employed by the Pharaohs in the Egyptian fleet, and still later the Libyan chiefs seized control of Egypt to establish the Libyan dynasties. Thereafter Libyan influence spread far and wide, especially in the Indo-Pacific region, where the Egyptians mined gold, as in Sumatra. During the Ptolemaic period (after Alexander the Great conquered Egypt) Libyan seamen in the service of the Greek Pharaohs explored widely, some of them settling parts of the Pacific.

The foregoing inferences, based largely on linguistic studies, have forced us to discard the theory that traced the Polynesian settlements to supposed immigrants of uncertain origin in East Asia, for the early Polynesian inscriptions are essentially Libyan both as to the alphabet and the language. Linguists such as Professor Linus Brunner in Europe and Dr. Reuel Lochore in New Zealand have found this new interpretation to be consistent with their own researches into the sources of the languages of Malaysia and Polynesia.* It also explains the occurrence of Greek words in the Polynesian tongues. As Professor Brunner has pointed out, the Greek colonies in Libya used a dialect of Greek in which certain consonants replace those of Attic Greek, and it is in the Libyan form that the Greek words of Polynesia occur. The Anatolian elements in Polynesian have been the special study of Lochore, and these too are now seen to be consistent with a Libyan origin of the Polynesians, for we know from the ancient Egyptian records that Libya was settled by the Anatolian Sea Peoples.

If, therefore, my inference with respect to the Libyan affinity of the Polynesian tongues is valid, as appears increasingly likely (most recent support coming from linguists in Israel), I think that the equivalent evidence now coming from my studies of the Zuni language is likely to win support when the analyses are examined by linguists. (The Zuni

---

* See e.g. Brunner and Schafer, *Malayo-Polynesian Vocabulary* (1976).

etymological dictionary has not yet appeared in print.) So it is in this context that I here propose a new view of the origin of the ancestors of the Shiwi people of Zuni. I think they are the descendants of Libyan voyagers who crossed the Atlantic some time before about 500 B.C.

AN ANALYSIS OF THE ZUNI LANGUAGE[*]

The Zuni tongue, with its apparently limited vocabulary (only some 1,200 words have been recorded) makes remarkably broad generalizations in the use of words. Thus *ate*, whose original Coptic sense is *fluid*, in Zuni serves also for *blood;* and the root employed to mean *bleed* matches another Coptic word having the basic sense *to be red*. A word of this kind is classed by linguists as what is called a stative (a part of speech implying a state of being). It is like a verb and adjective rolled into one. Another example of Zuni word economy is the use of a Coptic root with the original sense *to be humble*, now fulfilling in Zuni the role of a verb meaning *to crawl*. Again, a word that in Coptic has the sense *to prick*, in Zuni acquires the meaning *to copulate*, more or less as the ancient Anglo-Saxon used the verb *prician*, its modern use confined by convention to conversation between males. These features of Zuni speech suggest that it may have been derived from the limited and racy vocabulary in colloquial use on board Libyan navy vessels by conscripted fishermen or employed by Libyan seamen serving on the ships of Tarshish or Carthage.

The Mauri script proper to the Libyan tongue was probably brought to North America by the officers on board such ships. It seems doubtful if any literary work was brought to America, for the Bureau of Ethnology records do not disclose any ancient compositions among the Zuni that could be compared with the Creation Chant of the Pima nation. The subject, however, requires fuller study, for undoubted Libyan inscriptions in the Libyan script occur on cliffs and on land markers in states such as Oklahoma, as the explorations of Gloria Farley have demonstrated.

Loan Words. Modern Zuni speech contains numerous loan words derived from Spanish and English. A much older loan vocabulary is also evident from American sources. Examples are words like *zi* (hair) and *ahha* (take) from the Otomi language of Mexico; words like *pu'a* (break) and *tachchu* (father) from the Aztec language of Mexico; a few

---

[*] A fuller treatment is expected to appear in the *Occasional Publications of the Epigraphic Society.*

other words such as *pilha* (bow) and *ma'* (well) from the Huasteca language of Mexico; also *pizulliya* (circle) and *lashokti* (ear) from the Mayan language of Mexico. This Mexican element indicates former extensive contacts with the peoples of the south. Some northern contacts are also evidenced by words such as *moqqa* (shoe, sandal) of the Algonquian group.

Basic Vocabulary. This is essentially North African, comprising a large Libyo-Egyptian element similar to Coptic, to which have been added Ptolemaic roots brought to the Egyptian and Libyan lands by Greek settlers in the wake of the Spartan colonization of Libya in the eighth century B.C., and the conquest of Egypt by Alexander the Great and his successors, the Ptolemies, during the last four centuries B.C. There are also roots of Nilotic origin, probably introduced to the Egyptian and Libyan speech by Nubian slaves.

Phonetic Mutation. Over the course of time languages tend to change in accordance with rather definite rules. By comparing the original spelling of words in Coptic (which was written phonetically), and the present-day pronunciation of the corresponding words in Zuni speech, we can elicit the laws of phonetic mutation for the Zuni language. They turn out to be almost identical to those already demonstrated for the Polynesian languages, which are also derived from the Egypto-Libyan group, though with a strong Anatolian element (lacking from Zuni). These are the principal rules of phonetic mutation:

(1) Zuni consonants are the *devocalized equivalents* of the *voiced African stops.* In plain language, that means that the Zuni speaker never allows his larynx muscles to vibrate when he utters a consonant. As a result he does not pronounce Egyptian b as b, but makes it sound like p. Put your fingers on your larynx, and pronounce b and p; you will feel the vibration of the muscles each time you say b. So we call b a voiced stop, and p is its devocalized equivalent. Similarly, Zuni t replaces African d; Zuni s or sh replaces African z; and Zuni ch (like Spanish j) replaces African g.

(2) Voiced sonants of African words are retained in Zuni. This simply means that sounds like m and n in Egypto-Libyan do not suffer change in Zuni.

(3) Liquid sonants of African words (l and r) are represented in Zuni by l and lh.

(4) African semivowels (i, y and w, u) remain unchanged in Zuni.

Pure vowels were not written in ancient scripts, so we cannot say what changes, if any, may have occurred in these sounds.

Ancient Libya was a kingdom located around the shores of the Gulf of Sirte, to the west of Egypt. Its light-skinned inhabitants were drawn from the mixed population of Anatolian sea-peoples who invaded Libya around 1250 B.C., native Berbers, and Spartan Greeks who settled the eastern margin of the Gulf coast. The Greek influence persisted in the American Libyan settlements at least until circa 1100 A.D. when the tortoise at left was painted by a Mimbres Valley potter in New Mexico. The Libyan language, written alphabetically from left to right or from right to left, and also vertically, was used in New Mexico, as the painting of the American catfish, above, shows, for the three letters written on the fish spell the Libyo-Egyptian word N-A-R, meaning "catfish." The photograph has been printed in reverse, and in this state the letters read from left to right. The painting is dated by tree-ring evidence to circa 1100 A.D. *Top photo courtesy of Peabody Museum, Harvard University, left photo courtesy of Gerald Heslinga, Buffalo Museum*

Sound	Style of Tunisia and Numidia	Style of Libyan settlers of Iowa	Style of Libyan voyagers in Pacific (Ancient Maori)
b	⊙, ⊡	⊡	⊡
g	V, ∧	V	Γ Ⴀ
d	⊏	⊨	⊏
w	‖	‖	‖
z	⊓, —	⊓	—
ṭ	⊓, ⤚	⊙	⊓
k	⇑		↓, ↓ⵑ, ⇑
l	=, ‖		=, ‖
m	⊔	∪	∪
n	ǀ	ǀ	ǀ
r	O, ᗡ, □, ◁	o	O, □
š	M	M	
A, '	•, ◁	•	•,)
t	X, +	X	X, +

Libyan inscriptions employ the above alphabet, but the language is nearly the same as that of Ancient Egypt. The language was first deciphered from North African bilingual Latin-Libyan tombstones by Fell (1973). Thus the Iowan text, originally found in 1874 and later condemned as a forgery, is in fact genuine, for it could not possibly have been forged. Other Libyan inscriptions have been found in Quebec, New Hampshire, Pennsylvania, and Oklahoma. They also occur on Pacific Islands and in Chile. On linguistic grounds Fell derives the Polynesian language from ancient Libyan (with some Anatolian and Asian elements). In North America the language of the Zuni Indians is also derived from ancient Libyan, and occasional Libyan alphabetic signs occur in Zuni art. Ancient Libyan was also written in the Mimbres valley in New Mexico 700 years ago.

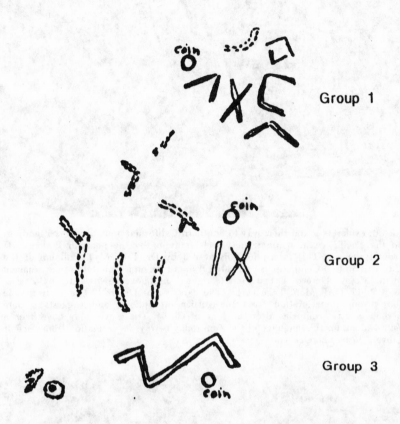

Group 1

Group 2

Group 3

Rock-cut inscription found by Bureau of Land Management archeologist C. R. Morrison in northwestern New Mexico, near the present Zuni Reservation. Dr. Don G. Rickey, Chief Historian for the Bureau, sent the photograph to Fell at Harvard for decipherment and, in his subsequent report (Rickey, 1978), he says: "Professor Fell replied that the inscription is written in the Libyan alphabet used prior to the Moslem conquest about 700 A.D., and it reads as follows:
  Group 1: "This (place) is for the sacrament of marriage"
  Group 2: "In seclusion implant semen in the maiden (or pure one)"
  Group 3: "As the token (of marriage)"
Dr. Rickey, on receiving this decipherment, goes on to say: "Since the identification of pre-700 A.D. Libyan is considered a unique and controversial phenomenon by nearly all southwestern archeologists, I met with Professor Boulas Ayad, Professor of Ancient Languages, University of Colorado, to submit the Morrison diagram to him for a second evaluation. Professor Ayad studied the diagram carefully, and gave it as his opinion that the inscription is indeed in the Libyan alphabet, and that it had to do with a marriage or fertility sacrament in a hidden place. His decipherment differs only slightly from Professor Fell's report. . . . He stated that such fertility-marriage practices were widespread in the ancient Middle East." (Rickey, 1978)

Libyan explorers found their way to Southern California, probably by sea landings on the Pacific coast, made from vessels sent out by the pharaoh Ptolemy III around 232 B.C. This inscription, discovered by Dr. Edward J. Pullman of the U.S. Exploration Company, is replicated from a rock on a mountain range adjacent to the Mojave Desert. It reads, left to right, from above downwards, S R-Z, R-Z. W-R Z-MT ("All Men, Take care, Take care. Great Desert"). The writing style shows some deterioration from the earlier inscriptions, and suggests a date perhaps several centuries after the time of Christ. The graver may have been a Zuni Indian, for the language of the Zuni today betrays its derivation from ancient Libyan. *Joseph D. Germano*

Chief Ras left this bilingual autograph to record his exploration of the Cimarron River in Oklahoma, probably around 500 B.C. Gloria Farley obtained this latex impression from a shelter under a rock overhang on the river cliffs. Above right, the Egyptian hieratic letters T-P (Chief). The eye symbol itself is the Egyptian hieratic word R-S ("Watchful"). The two Libyan letters, cut into the eye sign, also spell R-S. Bilingual Egypto-Libyan inscriptions in North America probably reflect the lasting influence of the Libyan pharaohs upon the Egyptian navy. In later centuries, when the Greek Ptolemies ruled Egypt, their Libyan queens continued to promote the interest of the navy, still manned largely by Libyan mariners. *Malcolm D. Pearson*

Chief Ras, who wrote his name in Egyptian and Libyan on the Cimarron cliffs, also left another bilingual autograph in Libyan and Iberian Punic. Here, in a plaster cast taken from a latex mold by Gloria Farley, we see to the left the Libyan letters R-S ("Wakeful" or "Watchful") and to the right the North Iberian letters spelling his name in Punic Pa-Ya-K ("Early awake"). Here, as elsewhere in North America, the multilingual inscriptions attest to the mixed racial and linguistic structure of early American colonies. This autograph may date from around 500 B.C. Gloria Farley's outstanding discoveries in Oklahoma have made Heavener one of the major centers of research in ancient American epigraphy. *Joseph D. Germano*

"The elephant that supports the Earth upon the waters and causes it to quake," so reads the Libyan inscription on this votive tablet found at Cuenca, Ecuador, and replicated by Dr. Clyde Keeler. The Libyan script, in the finest style, matching that of King Masinissa's monument at Thougga, Tunisia, dates to the latter half of the third century before Christ. The letters read, from left to right, and from above downwards: A-B-Y G-B S-R-D M-T M Z-D. Aby is the ancient Libyan (and Egyptian) word for the African elephant, depicted above the inscription. Californian tablets, on the other hand, employ the ancient Sanskrit word Gaja, used in India even today for the Asiatic elephant. Thus knowledge of elephants was brought to the New World by voyagers from both east and west. *Clyde Keeler and Malcolm D. Pearson*

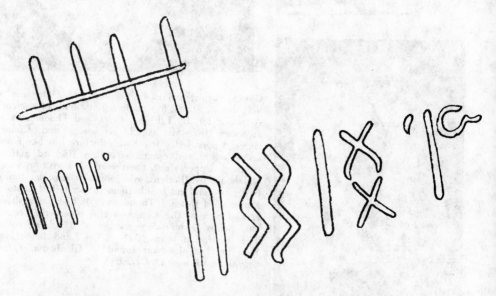

"A crew of Shishonq the King took shelter in this place of concealment." So read
the Libyan inscriptions found by Forrest Kirkland painted under a rock overhang
of the Rio Grande cliffs in Texas. The two Ogam lines to the left read D-G (took
shelter), and Z-D-H (hidden place). The Libyan letters read, left to right, S
Sh-Sh-N-Q-A N-B (Crew of Shishonq the King). Several kings of this name ruled
Libya and Egypt between 1000–800 B.C., an era when North African voyagers
began to explore the New World. Inscriptions such as this show that the Libyans
made use of both the Ogam and their own native Numidian alphabets in writing
the Libyan language.

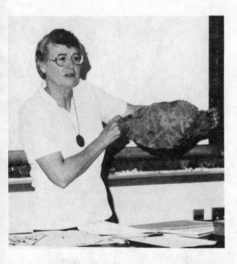

Gloria Farley, epigraphic explorer of Oklahoma and neighboring states, has made notable finds of ancient inscriptions left by Libyans, Celts, and Phoenicians who ascended the Mississippi, Arkansas, and Cimarron rivers. Upper left, Mrs. Farley lectures on her finds to archeologists and epigraphers at a Harvard gathering in 1975. Upper right, the record of a visit to western Oklahoma by Iberians, who engraved circular thunderbolt signs, and cut beside them (upper left of photo) the Punic word B-R-K ("Thunderbolt"). The photo shows a cast of part of the Cimarron cliff where the record is cut. Below, a boundary marker of a Libyan colonist. The inscription reads T N R-T ("Land belonging to Rata"). This also was found in Oklahoma. *Peter J. Garfall and Joseph D. Germano*

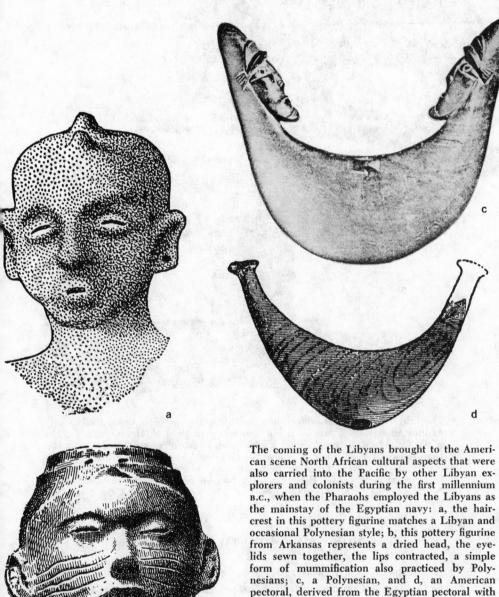

The coming of the Libyans brought to the American scene North African cultural aspects that were also carried into the Pacific by other Libyan explorers and colonists during the first millennium B.C., when the Pharaohs employed the Libyans as the mainstay of the Egyptian navy: a, the hair-crest in this pottery figurine matches a Libyan and occasional Polynesian style; b, this pottery figurine from Arkansas represents a dried head, the eyelids sewn together, the lips contracted, a simple form of mummification also practiced by Polynesians; c, a Polynesian, and d, an American pectoral, derived from the Egyptian pectoral with a head of Ra at either cusp, an ornament spread abroad by Libyans (a,b,d, from S. D. Peet, *The Mound Builders,* 1892).

The Libyan colonists introduced into North America not only distinctively North
African art styles and language, but also representations of African animals. The
African elephant, carved to form a pipe-bowl, is one of several similar examples
from Iowa; when originally found in the Davenport mounds and in the neighboring areas, they were taken to be mastodons, and later dismissed as modern
forgeries, since it was not then considered possible for foreign art to have entered
North America before Columbus. From S. D. Peet, *The Mound Builders*, 1892

HOW THE PHONETIC LAWS WORK

By means of lists of words in matching pairs the laws are elicited and
demonstrated. Complete lists cannot be given here for obvious reasons, but
single examples will serve to explain the way in which the changes occur.

1. *Labials* (consonants made with the lips).
    a. African b becomes Zuni p, as in African *toobe* (pay) and Zuni
       tapi (pay).
    b. African f becomes Zuni p or w, as in African *fuka* (pour) and
       Zuni *po'qa* (spill).
    c. African p equals Zuni p, as in African *Pukula* (steam) and Zuni
       pokhli (smoke).

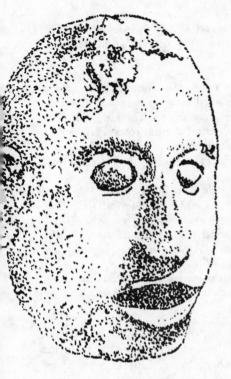

The builders of the original Hopewell Mounds appear initially to have been mainly Libyans. In classical times Libyans were still for the most part an olive-skinned European stock, of mixed Anatolian, Greek, and Berber derivation, speaking an adoptive language of the Egyptian group, though retaining also many words of Anatolian and Greek origin. The appearance of negroid types in the sculpture of the mounds, however, indicates that many crew members of the Libyan ships must have been Nubians, and that as time went by they intermarried with the Libyans. This head, from Seip Mound, Ohio, exemplifies the Nubian stock. The Nubians probably introduced the high style of sculptured African animals, soon adapted to form pipe bowls as the colonists adopted the Amerindian predilection for tobacco. So far as is known (in 1976) the Nubian hieroglyphic alphabet was not one of the imports, and indeed the Hopewellian culture seems quite early to have become illiterate. This might reflect a "slave revolt," in which the few literate aristocrats were eliminated.

2. *Dentals* (consonants made against the teeth).
   a. African d becomes Zuni t, as in African *dessew* (shrine) and Zuni *teshqi* (shrine).
   b. African t equals Zuni t, as in African *ta* (flat land) and Zuni *ta* (flat land).
3. *Palatals* (consonants made against the palate).
   a. African ch equals Zuni ch, as in African *chme* (sow seed) and Zuni *chima* (sow wheat).
   b. African ch can also become Zuni k or sh, as in African *chol* (honeycomb) and Zuni *ḵali* (honeycomb).
4. *Velars* (consonants made in the throat).
   a. African g becomes Zuni ch, as in African *gaba* (assemble) and Zuni *chapa* (assemble).
   b. African K becomes Zuni k or q, as in African *ḵoe* (place) and Zuni *ḵwe* (place).
5. *Liquid sonants* ("tongued humming").
   African l and r become Zuni l or lh, as in African *lol* (bed) and Zuni *lhelo* (take a nap); African *loḵ* (gentle) and Zuni *liḵa* (gentle); African *eri* (go) and Zuni *ela* (move); and African *hru* (pleasing) and Zuni *elu* (pleasing).
6. *Nasal sonants* ("nose humming").
   a. African m equals Zuni m, as in African *mou* (cat) and Zuni *musa* (cat).
   b. African n equals Zuni n, as in African *na* (of) and Zuni *na* (of).

7. *Sibilants* (hissing consonants).

   African s and sh equal Zuni s and sh, as in African *she* (go, move) and Zuni *shi* (go, move); and African *sike* (grind meal) and Zuni *sako* (ground meal).

8. *Hamza* (throat click).

   The click or momentary pause is a sign of a discarded consonant in English dialects. For example the word *butter* is pronounced *bu'er* in many country dialects, and *bottle* becomes *bo'l*. The same rule operates in Zuni with respect to its ancestral African roots. For example, African *ponk* (pour out) and Zuni *po'qi* (pour out); African *kya* (water vessel) and Zuni *k'a* (water); African *fukula* (to burrow) and Zuni *pok'a* (rabbit).

9. *Semivowels* (y and w which intergrade with i and u).

   a. African w equals Zuni w or u, as in African *waa* (self) and Zuni *waya* (self).

   b. African i and y equal Zuni i and y, as in African *Itn* (sun disk or *Aten*) and Zuni *yati* (sun); African *eine* (to be like) and Zuni *'ina* (to be like).

Grammar of the Zuni language: This has many features recalling the Coptic language, but a discussion is impossible without going into great detail.

In ancient Numidia (part of modern Tunisia) the Libyans wrote from left to right, but in areas adjacent to Phoenician settlements, as in the neighborhood of Carthage, and in southern Spain, Libyans who settled there adopted the Semitic habit of writing from right to left. In southern Spain the Libyan immigrants adopted some of the southern Iberian forms of letters, such as the triangular sign used for the stressed semivowel aleph (accented a), and the mirror-image-D-shaped sign used for r. Thus the Libyan word for catfish, *Nar,* would be written *raN* by Libyan writers in southern Spain. Now it is a remarkable fact that on Mimbres pottery from New Mexico a painting of an American catfish occurs (genus *Ictalurus,* having 8 barbels, as opposed to the Libyan species, which has 5 barbels), and painted on the fish are the Libyan letters reading *raN.* This can only mean that Libyan settlers brought to America both the writing system and the actual word for catfish used in North Africa, and somehow the people of the Mimbres valley were using this around 1200 A.D. when the pottery was made. The case of the Atum sun disk has already been mentioned, and is another example of such transference. Another would seem to be the symbols woven into the kilt worn by the Hopi snake priest who led the snake dance of 1891. This kilt is now preserved at Harvard, and shows alternating symbols which may be read as the Libyan letters W-ṭ repeated as a decorative motif. Is it merely an accident that W-ṭ is the spelling adopted by the Egyptians (and presumably by

Libyans) for the name of the sacred serpent known to the Greeks as the uraeus, and worn by the Pharaohs as a forehead ornament symbolic of divinity? It is facts such as these that force us to recognize that Libyan writing as well as Libyan language must once have been current in some southwestern regions of North America.

13

The Druids
of New England

IN Chapters 5 and 6 it was shown that the New England Celts employed an Ogam alphabet of at least 12 symbols, identical with those used in Portugal and Spain in the late Bronze Age, about 800 B.C. The New England signs also carry the same sound values as those of the Iberian peninsula; when Iberian sounds are assigned to them, they yield phrases appropriate to their contexts. Representative words are given on the following pages.

The chances that two such similar events can take place independently can be calculated by the mathematical theory of probability. It turns out that there is less than one chance in 430,000,000 that identical 12-letter alphabets could arise independently in two unrelated civilizations. For the 17-letter Ogam alphabet of Monhegan, Maine, and Ireland, the chances of independent origin in these two places are less than one in 300,000,000,000,000. This is just another way of saying that there is zero probability of such a double event. In other words, the people who wrote the Celtic Ogam inscriptions of Iberia and Ireland must be the same people who wrote the corresponding inscriptions of New England. Thus there is no probability that the New England inscriptions are the work of Amerindians, unless the Amerindians should themselves be derived in part from Iberian Celts. This possibility is discussed in Chapters 16 and 17.

In this chapter I shall show that the nature of the buildings and other standing-stone constructions found in New England is such as to compel us to assign these objects to the labors of Europeans familiar with the astronomical discoveries of Mediterranean philosophers. They are in fact observatories. And as these observatories are often inscribed with Celtic

TABLE 5

Representative Vocabulary from Druidic Inscriptions

A selection of readings from old Ogam inscriptions lacking vowels (found mainly in Vermont, with some additions from other areas). All readings are to be treated as tentative, since the subject is still in the exploratory stage and decipherments therefore cannot be final. On the basis of Punic letters found on the same or related steles, this Celtic vocabulary is believed to date from about 800–300 B.C. Thus it is much older than the oldest known British Ogam inscriptions.

AS WRITTEN	TO BE READ AS	MEANING
B	bi	to, preposition, loan word from Punic
B	bi, bigh	stone, stele, pillar
B-B	bab, pab	penis, phallus
B-G	bog	swell, let it swell, erect
B-H	bho	from
B-H-L	Baal	Baal, servant of Baal or Bel (proper name)
B-Ia-Ñ	Byanu, Beanu	Beanu (Goddess), Woman, She-of-the-yoni
B-L	Bel	Bel (Sun God)
B-L	balios	town, city
B-L-Ñ	blian	loins (possible alternative reading for M-D-Ñ in eroded inscription)
B-L-T-Ñ	bealltuinn	Beltane (May Day)
B-S	bas	slain
B-T-B-H	batabh	for the ships
C-D-H-H	cuidh	cargo
C-H	cah, gah	rays, heat
D	Dai	Dai (proper name)
D-B	dubh	black, dark; Dark-haired (proper name)
D-G	degos, tegos	temple, covered building
D-Ia-D	dayad	divine, of the gods
D-L-M	dalma	bold (also proper name)
D-M	Dam	stag (also proper name)
D-M-D	damadh	stags, of the stags
F-D	fad	distance
F-G	faic	eye, to see, as in M-H-M-H B-L, G-L-N F-G, "Benevolent is Bel, His eye is the sun."
F-M-L	fomor	sea-rover, pirate
F-N-C	Finici, Feniach	(1) Phoenicia (2) of the Feni (an Irish tribe)
G	Gi?	Guy (proper name)?
G-B	Gabh	Gavin (proper name)
G-B-D-H	gabadh	peril, danger
G-L-Ñ	grian	sun
G-M	gim	winter
H	Hu?	Hugh (proper name)?
H-M	Ham	Ham (proper name)
H-M-H-L-G	amharg	observation
XI	haon-deug	eleven
Ia-B-G-G	Iabagag	Habakuk (proper name, Punic loan word)
Ia-G-H-Ñ	Ioghan, Eoghan	Ewan
Ia-N-D	ianod	place, precincts, home
Ia-L-G-L-Ñ	Iargalon	(of the) Lands Beyond the Sunset, America
Ia-s-G	uisge	fluid, water, to inseminate
L	la	day

AS WRITTEN	TO BE READ AS	MEANING
L	Lu	Lew (proper name)
L-B-D	lebed	platform, wharf
L-D	lidh	grassy slope, green slope
L-G-H	Lughi	of Lug (proper name); could also be read as Righ, king, royal
L-H	Luhi	of Lu
L-Ia	Luia	vent, chimney, vagina
L-Ia-G	Liag	stone, pillar, monolith
M	Mo	elder, senior (see M-B M)
M-B	mab	son, son of
M-B M	mab Moi	son of the elder; i.e., son of a father of the same name as the son
M-B-M	Mabimos?	"Heroic" (proper name)
M-B-M-B-Ñ	Mabo-Mabona	"Hero-of-Heroes" (Celtic Apollo)
M-C, M-Q	mac, maq	son (of), Goidelic form not known from New England (see M-B)
M-C-M, M-Q-M	macamh	noble son (on Goidelic funeral stones of warriors)
M-G	muig?	fog, cloud (uncertain reading)
M-G-G	Magog?	proper name on stele (not yet found in New England, but occurs as place name)
M-H	mathair	seemingly abbreviation of word "mother"
M-H-M-H	math-math	good, benevolent
M-H-G	amharg?	abbreviation of word "observation"
M-H-M-B	Mathair-Mabo(na)	"Mother-of-Heroes" (title of goddess Byanu)
M-D-Ñ	meidhinn	loins, pelvis
M-Ia-B?	mabi?	of a son, for a son?; see S-Ia-M
M-Ia-L	meall	hill, mountain
M-S	mios	measure, measured
S-B-H	Seabh	Seabh (proper name, = Sorrel); (Vendée stele only)
S-B-L	siobal	fisherman (Vendée stele only)
S-G-M-B-H?	Sgiambhi?	(for) Fair-Haired (used as proper name)?
S-Ia-M	seam	prayer, petition; hence following
S-Ia-M-M-Ia-B	seam-mabi?	"our prayer for sons"? (cut on stele of Mother Goddess near yoni altar)
T-H	tuath	north

identifications, their builders must have been those Celtic philosophers who were called Druids.

In the second century after Christ an Illyrian geographer called Strabo wrote an account of the Celts in which he mentioned that their learned men were distinguished under three categories. These he called (1) Bards, who were responsible for composing, preserving, and performing music and poetry; (2) Vates, who were priests responsible for carrying out sacrifices to the gods; and (3) Druids, who studied natural science and philosophy.

Julius Caesar, after his invasion of Britain in 55 B.C., wrote an account of the Druids, in the course of which he said:

They have considerable knowledge of the stars, and of their motions, and of the dimensions of the Earth, and the Universe around. Also of science in general, and of the powers and spheres of influence of the immortal gods. These subjects they debate, and also teach to their young students. [*De Bello Gallico,* books VI, XIV.]

Modern studies of the megalithic monuments of Britain, such as the famous one at Stonehenge on Salisbury Plain, show that some of these structures served as astronomical observatories for regulating the calendar by the observation of the annual cyclic motions of the sun and other heavenly bodies, caused by the revolution of the Earth in its annual orbiting of the sun. Although there is uncertainty as to who actually built the megalithic buildings in Europe, it is certain that the Celts, the Druids in particular, made use of them.

Now, one of the most important findings of our work in Vermont has been the demonstration that certain megalithic monuments are related to

The Druids' Throne, on a hillside near South Royalton, Vermont. The Ogam letter D (formed from two vertical strokes) is carved into the apex of the stone block, overlooking the countryside for miles around. Similar but smaller stone thrones have been found in New England from Long Island Sound north to the Canadian border. *John Williams, Joseph D. Germano*

astronomical functions of a like nature to those of Britain and other parts of Europe, and that some of them carry Celtic inscriptions referring to their astronomical functions. In this study Byron Dix, an astronomer, and I have collaborated. But before he and I were able to define these functions for the Vermont monuments, Robert Stone of North Salem, New Hampshire, had already done the pioneering investigation at Mystery Hill. Here, even before any inscriptions had been found at all, Bob satisfied himself that an observatory existed on the site he studied.

Let me introduce the subject by quoting from my field diary of last summer:

June 21, 1975, *Grian-stad* of the Gaels, Midsummer Night, about 7:30 P.M. A reverent hush falls over Mystery Hill as the waiting assemblage of watchers follows the slow decline of the sun. We are participants in America's most ancient ceremonial, the scientific regulation of the calendar. No Ogam inscription has yet been found here, yet my thoughts inevitably turn to Caesar's account of the Druids. I am reminded also of another summer sunset I witnessed on Celtic soil, when the glowing disk sank behind the silhouetted Hebrides, and all the peak of Quineag behind me gleamed like fire.

It was Bob Stone who first discovered the solstice monoliths in 1965, and we are his guests on the tenth anniversary of the find: Midge Chandler, Norman Totten, Peter Garfall, Rene and myself, with other visitors and many of the local people of Derry and North Salem. There are parents, grandparents, children of all ages, all gathered here at the appointed hour, waiting and watching. New arrivals appear from the woods, others join us from time to time from the slopes below or emerge from silent ruins. Soon only the photographers continue to seek better vantage points, the rest of us content to stand and wait. As I look at the children among us, even a babe in arms, I cannot help thinking how close a parallel our group must present to so many ancient gatherings of the tribe on this same hill, to witness the same event we are now seeing. And I think too, of the Pima and the Zuni in the dry lands of Arizona and New Mexico; for it is the first day of their four day midsummer festival, and although sunset comes three hours later for them, already the *makai* of the sun god will have set his sights upon the magic mountain where they, too, will see the sun meet the horizon at the appointed notch at the appointed hour.

And then, so swiftly it seems over before we fully comprehend it, the solar disk comes down, touches the tip of the monolith now silhouetted in black, and disappears into the fiery afterglow. As we slowly make our way down through the woods in the darkening twilight I think we are all conscious of the unseen presence of those shadowy observers of long ago who had seen the identical event that we had witnessed, and whose bones, or what remains of them, must lie buried in the soil somewhere near at hand. I remark to Bob, "I believe the day will come when such crowds will gather here that you will have to issue tickets for reserved standing room only."

Interior view of the large winter solstice sunrise temple at South Woodstock, Vermont. According to measurements by Byron Dix (left) the dimensions of the two entrance piers show that they were used in observation of the lunar track, and in the prediction of eclipses. The lintels overhead span 10 feet and each weighs about three tons. *Peter J. Garfall*

Libation bowls occur widely in Iberian and New England Celtic areas. Some, as the South Woodstock example pictured, catch natural rainwater, and are most often found on the summits of hills, beside phallic or other monuments. Deer now use them as drinking places after rain. *Peter J. Garfall*

ABOVE: Sculpture cut in bedrock at Searsmount, Maine, now in the Sturbridge Village Museum, Massachusetts. It depicts a Druid wearing a chaplet of oak leaves and acorn, executed in the style of Celtic artists in Ireland.

BELOW: Portion of an ogam consaine inscription found in Oklahoma and comprising an invocation to the god Mabo-Oengus to engender fruits; details of the translation are given in ESOP vol. 16, 1987. Photos by Malcolm Pearson (upper) and Mark Farley (lower).

Discovery of the Beltane Stone at Mystery Hill, August 31, 1975. In 45 B.C. Julius Caesar instituted throughout the Roman Empire a new reformed calendar devised by the Greek astronomer Sosigenes. The date of the spring equinox was now set at March 25, and the new year was set to start on January 1. The Celts of New England, however, retained the old Celto-Greek New Year that began on the day of the spring equinox; in other respects they followed the revised Roman Calendar, presumably in order to facilitate business arrangements with overseas traders from Spain and Portugal. May 1, the great Mayday festival of the Celts, called Beltane, now fell on the thirty-ninth day of the year, a fact recorded in the Romano-Celtic inscription on the stone at Mystery Hill. Owing to changes in the earth's axis (called precession) the equinox day has since moved forward to March 21, so that Beltane now falls on day 43 of the Celtic calendar. Hence the Beltane Stone dates from about the time of Christ, when the Mayday festival occurred on day 39 of the New England year. In the picture are Daniel Leary (left) who found the stone, Osborn Stone, and Fell. The inscription, reading in Latin numerals XXXVIIII LA (Day 39) is shown below. The fallen monolith, now in the Mystery Hill museum, once formed a part of the calendar circle, it is inferred. *Peter J. Garfall; Fell and Germano*

Circles of standing stones varying from 10 feet in diameter upward are common in Ireland and are also known in North America. Giant rings of the Stonehenge type are peculiar to Britain. The function of the rings in many cases is unknown. The smaller ones may have served merely as boundary fences around graves or house sites. They are commonly called Druids' Circles, and it is possible that some may have served for religious rites. This would seem to have been the case with the Ungava circle, in Quebec, shown above and recorded by Professor Thomas E. Lee. A circle of large stones, 15 meters in diameter, occurs at Big Basin, Santa Cruz Mountains, California (see page 309), and was evidently used at the time of the winter solstice sunrise. One of the largest circles (lower picture) is located at Pleasanton Ridge, northern California, and measures 90 feet in diameter. Photo: Russell Swanson.

Standing stones that have a large central aperture cut into them are called Men-a-tol (Stone of the hole). Illustrated above is a well-known Men-a-tol located in Cornwall, England, at Land's End. Many folk superstitions persist as to the supposed magical power of such stones. For example, naked children were passed three times through the hole and then dragged along the grass in an easterly direction—this ritual being held to cure tuberculosis. The aperture probably represents the vulva of the Earth Mother. In some cases Men-a-tol appear to have served as entrances to burial chambers. Illustrated below is an American Men-a-tol located at Jefferson, New Hampshire. Photos by Donald L. Cyr (above) and Charles J. Hepburn (below).

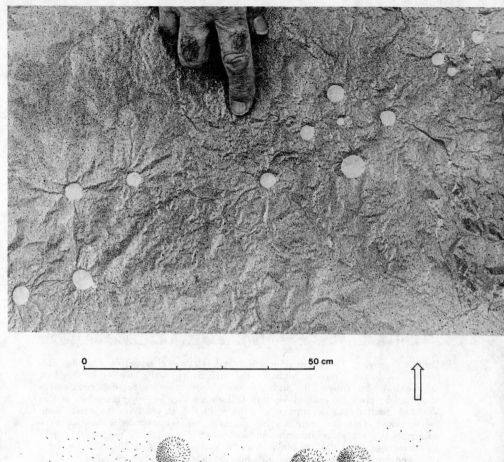

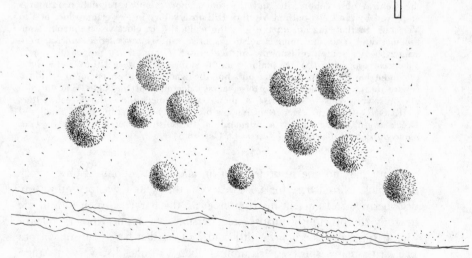

Druidic cupules—2. Cupules are occasionally arranged to form star maps. Above, constellations around the north pole, engraved on 20-foot monolith (now recumbent), South Woodstock, Vermont. On the left is part of Cassiopeia; in the center, the present polestar; upper right is Ursa Major. The drawing is by Dr. Fernando Lanhas, Museum of Ethnology, Porto, of cupules found at Montedor (Viana de Castelo), northern Portugal. This Portuguese version is apparently a map of the same region of the sky, but seen in mirror image (the mapping convention depends upon whether one transfers to the engraving the arrangement of stars as seen by looking up at them, or as seen by projecting them from the sky to the map). *Top, cast by Fell, photo by Peter J. Garfall; bottom, drawn by Dr. Fernando Lanhas, Porto*

Druidic cupules–3. Druidic mathematical and religious charts from chamber site, South Woodstock, Vermont, showing the meridian and the relative positions of the Central observation site and the four major calendar regulation azimuths employed by the Celts both at Mystery Hill observatory in New Hampshire and in Vermont. In the diagram on the left, the azimuths, in clockwise sequence from the meridian, are: midsummer solstice sunrise, midwinter solstice sunrise, midwinter solstice sunset, midsummer solstice sunset. The meridian points due north. These correspond to the five major standing stones at Mystery Hill. On the right, the same basic azimuths are set out, but the whole has been enclosed within a square outline, to simulate a tortoise, a sacred animal of the Celts. The tortoise may also be seen to comprise a monogram formed from the Greek letters CHELONE (tortoise). Hence it is possible that this diagram is originally of Greek origin, but serving as a mnemonic of the solstice directions. *Cast by Fell, photo by Peter J. Garfall and Joseph D. Germano*

Before 1965 no one suspected that an ancient astronomical observatory could have existed here for 3,000 years. In that year I was beginning my decipherments of ancient inscriptions from the Far East, soon to lead me to study the previously unsuspected Persian astronomical observatory of Mount Lavu in eastern Java: little did I know that barely 30 miles from Harvard a fellow spirit was stumbling upon a similar discovery in America. I asked Bob to recount for this book what he remembers of the circumstances, and this is how he tells it:

In 1964 I noticed many large standing stones in the woods around the site, and the following year I theorized that they might have had an astronomical function, though I had no idea as to how correct this was to prove. My first suspicion was that the area around the so-called Table of Sacrifice might be the primary viewing site, and that the standing stones might mark positions of sunrise and sunset for particular days of the year, significant perhaps for the unknown people who had built the site.

So I began to cut swaths through the woods to make it possible to see the standing stones from the central sacrificial area, also to bring into unobstructed view the horizon beyond the stones. Using a transit telescope and a compass I began to realize that some of the stones at least had a definite relationship to important astronomical axes.

On December 21, 1970, after four consecutive years of work, the sky remained clear and we now observed the sun slowly descending towards the monolith that we had recognized as marking the solstice. From the viewing area near the sacrificial table, some 500 yards away, we saw the sun above the monolith, behind which it then set. Later researches showed that some of the stonework in the viewing area had been removed by William Goodwin, and that the true viewing position had apparently been a stone platform 30 feet to the north of the Table of Sacrifice.

Robert Stone will surely be remembered by archeologists for this basic discovery, for it was the first clear indication that the ruins on Mystery Hill are indeed the work of a people who regulated their calendar in the same way as the builders of the megalithic sites of Europe. Bob enlisted the aid of his cousin, Osborn Stone, in identifying the other principal monoliths, and radially arranged avenues were cut through the woodlands to give clear views. This work is still continuing. The winter sunset

Winter solstice, chamber at South Woodstock, Vermont. *Joseph D. Germano*

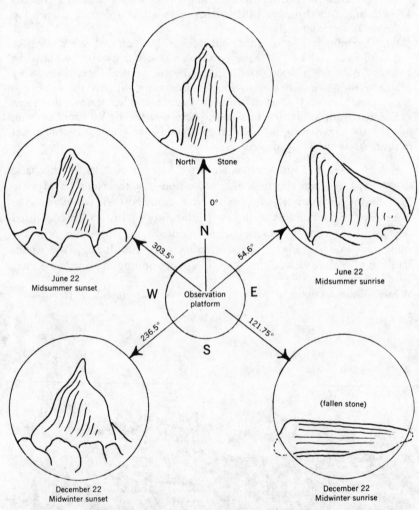

North   Stone

0°

N

303.5°   54.6°

W   Observation   E
platform

June 22   June 22
Midsummer sunset   Midsummer sunrise

236.5°   121.75°

S

(fallen stone)

December 22   December 22
Midwinter sunset   Midwinter sunrise

The Calendar Circle at Mystery Hill, New Hampshire, a Celtic astronomical observatory still in process of extrication from the forest overgrowth. The azimuth angles shown are those actually demonstrated by a transit telescope without special leveling, the mean deviation from the calculated values being even so only some minutes of arc. Compare this chart with the Druidic cupule charts on page 203. (Drawn by Fell, with practical aid from Osborn Stone; the stones shown in the circles are as they actually appear in the telescope field when sighted from the observation platform. November 1975.)

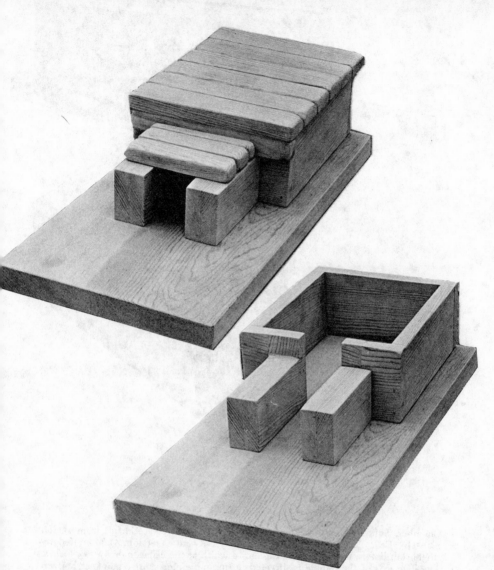

Equinoctial sunrise temple observatory, dedicated to Bel, located at South Royalton, Vermont, modeled by Peter J. Garfall from sketch plans by Fell and Castleton College students. The main temple area, or *cella*, lies behind the narrow east porch, which constitutes the observatory chamber. The cella was partly destroyed by colonial farmers who tore off the lintel slabs for other purposes and caused the walls partly to collapse. The east porch is still intact. Its lintels terminate about 12 inches from the end of the porch walls, suggesting that the first lintel is missing. This, however, is not so because (1) the exposed face of the existing first lintel carries the dedication inscription and (2) the shadow of the lower edge of the outer lintel coincides at sunrise with the inner end of the observatory porch on the two equinoctial days, March 21 and September 21. This is because the temple, oriented to the east, faces a range of hills whose elevation above the horizon falls on the same line of sight as the line joining the lower edge of the lintel to the inner end of the floor of the equinoctial porch. Presumably priests and nobility observed the event from the cella, while the other members of the tribe did so from the forecourt. *Joseph D. Germano*

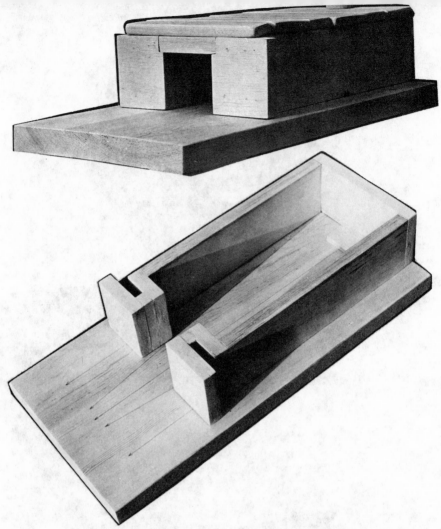

Chamber, South Woodstock, Vermont, modeled by Peter J. Garfall from sketch plans by Fell. The main chamber, or cella, is twenty feet long, and roofed by single slab lintels, each spanning the entire width of the cellas, namely 115 inches. The long axis of the temple is directed to the midwinter sunrise point, at horizon azimuth 123° which, at 43.5° N latitude, corresponds to the sun's southernmost limit of minus 23.5° declination. At sunrise on December 22 the sun is seen to rise in a notch in the distant range of hills when the viewer stands at the altar at the west end of the temple, looking out between the pillars on either side of the southeast front. Byron Dix, an astronomer investigating the orientation of these temple structures, finds that the angle subtended by the pillars to a viewer at each of the west corners of the cella yields an angular measure of the moon's 18.6 year metonic cycle, and hence could be used for predicting eclipses. The building is therefore essentially an astronomical observatory, though the dedications to various gods found on the lintels led us to refer to it as the Pantheon. The cycle of the Moon was discovered by the Greek astronomer Meto about the year 433 B.C., so this building must date from after that time. It is the largest and most sophisticated of all the Celtic stone buildings so far discovered in North America. *Joseph D. Germano*

solstice stone now stands in clear silhouette at the end of its avenue, and the sun can be observed setting behind it on December 21, when snow usually covers the ground. Byron Dix studied the Mystery Hill findings, and then began to bring to light comparable but larger calendar sites in central Vermont. One of these, which he calls Calendar Site Number 1, is located high on the hills near Elephant Valley. Another, Site Number 2, is located on a hillside at South Woodstock, near the large temple that we are calling the Pantheon.* An important contribution made by Byron in 1975 was his dicovery that the calendar used by the people who made the Vermont sites was divided into eight parts. He announced this on August 30, 1975, at the same joint meeting of interested societies at which I announced that the megalithic structures were Celtic, based on the Ogam inscriptions I had deciphered.

The next significant find was made by Daniel Leary of the site staff at Mystery Hill. On the day following the conference Bob Stone informed me that a new stone had been found with an inscription unlike any we had seen up to that time and so, with Gloria Farley of Oklahoma and John Williams, I visited the site the following evening. The inscription was partly concealed by an overlying monolith, which we then lifted to disclose a stele inscribed in Roman numerals and Ogam letters, reading in translation DAY XXXVIIII. My first comment as we examined the inscription by flashlight was to translate the writing and then immediately to ask, "Can anyone think of anything important that occurs on the thirty-ninth day?" For the time being none of us could figure the answer. Thirty-ninth day of what, or after what? So I took an aluminum peel and went back to Massachusetts to consult ancient calendars. The answer to the problem became apparent so soon as I encountered the Roman records of the calendar reforms effected by Julius Caesar. And at the same time I realized the explanation of why Byron Dix was finding an eight-part division of the year on his Vermont calendar sites. Instead of re-tracing the steps in my inquiry it will be clearer if I give here the results of it.

The purpose of the monoliths on our Celtic sites is to regulate the calendar, as Byron had already inferred even before he knew that the sites are indeed Celtic. The Celtic year was divided by the Druids into eight parts by the following system which seems originally to have been derived from a calendar used in Greece, instituted by the philosopher Hippocrates and apparently carried to Catalonia in southern Spain by the Greek colonists there. This Hippocratic year began on the day of the spring equinox, in March. Other important dates were supplied by the summer solstice (when the sun reaches its furthest northern declination,

---

* Pantheon, because the names of the several Celtic gods occur on its lintels.

+23½°, in June); then the autumn equinox, in September; and then the winter solstice, the sun being at its southernmost declination of —23½°, in December. Between these four dates, each of which marked the mid-point of the corresponding season (spring, summer, autumn, winter), there were arbitrarily selected four more dates, marking the onset of each season. Thus spring passed into summer on May 1, which the Celts called Beltane, and dedicated to the sun god Bel. The three other inter-mediate dates similarly marked the onset of autumn, winter and spring.

In 45 B.C. Julius Caesar (himself the author of a lost book on astronomy) appointed the Greek astronomer Sosigenes to advise him on how to re-form the Roman calendar, and Sosigenes recommended in effect that the Hippocratic Greek system be adopted. This system was based on the annual motions of the sun and ignored the old moon calendar because the number of moon cycles (or months) does not divide equally into the solar year. The residual odd days had always been a source of difficulty to ancient calendar makers, who found that fractions of a month were left over at the end of the solar year (based on the 365¼ days required by the Earth to complete one revolution about the sun). The new calendar of Sosigenes set the spring equinox on the 25th day of March. As this so-called Julian calendar was instituted throughout the Roman empire, the Celts of Gaul and Britannia and Hispania (Spain) were obliged to ac-cept it. The Iberian Celts, however, accustomed to starting the year on the day of the spring equinox, accepted the new calendar but continued to reckon the spring equinox as its starting point, as their religious beliefs apparently demanded. Thus May 25 now became New Year's Day. As a result, the great festival of Beltane was now found to occur 39 days after the spring equinox, counting by Latin reckoning, and so became Day Thirty-Nine.

It was now clear that the stele Danny Leary had discovered on Mys-tery Hill is the marker of Beltane in the Mystery Hill observatory. As already noted, it was found prostrate, overlain by another stone; although we do not yet know how it was employed, or whether it merely recorded an important religious festival held at the place where it lay, it is obvi-ously part of a Druidic observatory.

The fact that this stone carries Roman numerals is important as dating it to the Roman period that began for Iberia in 160 B.C. The fact that the numeral 9 is expressed as VIIII instead of IX is interesting, for that is also how 9 is written in all the calendar dates on the only other Celtic calendar inscription that has ever been found, namely the calendar of Coligny, in France. And lastly, the match with the reformed calendar of Sosigenes is also significant for it now yields the latest known date of occupation of Mystery Hill as roughly the era of the time of Christ.

You see, owing to the movement of the axis of the Earth called *precession,* the date of the equinox becomes progressively earlier and earlier, moving forward one day about every four centuries. Thus, whereas Sosigenes set the spring equinox as March 25, by about 300 A.D. it had moved forward to occur on March 24. Nowadays it occurs on March 21, by which modern reckoning the date of Beltane (May 1) has now changed to DAY XXXXIII or Day 43. So, by recognizing Day 39 as Beltane, we are in effect dating the stele to the era of the early Roman empire, after 46 B.C., but not later than about the third century A.D.

The occurrence of Roman numerals, as well as evidence of Sosigenes's calendar reform of 45 B.C., shows that the New England Celts continued to maintain a shipping connection with the Old World well into Roman times. Their acceptance of the reformed calendar is not a measure of servility to Rome, but surely an acceptance of the inevitable, namely the calendar that all their visitors and customers used. How could one have furs or other salable products at the cargo loading platform on the correct date if one party used an entirely different calendar from the other? Just as members of the Hebrew and Greek Orthodox religious communities in America today use our universal calendar, yet nonetheless reckon the beginning of the New Year at varying dates according to religious precepts, and just as the Arabic year count is hundreds of years out of kilter with the Christian reckoning, though both Arabs and Christians still employ identical annual calendars, so also could the Celts in Iberia or America conform to Caesar's edict, yet still maintain their religious festivals in accordance with ancient custom.

And now, having introduced the topic of religion, let me stress that the Celtic calendar was undoubtedly connected intimately with the Celt's religious life. There are several cogent reasons for believing this. They are:

(1) The long axes of the temples of the gods coincide with major axes of the calendar sites. This can only mean that particular religious festivals were held on days determined by the solar calendar; that is, on days when the sun was seen to be aligned with a particular dating monolith, those of the solstices and equinoxes apparently being the most important.

(2) Celtic tradition in Britain still keeps alive the names of the ancient festivals and the dates on which the festivals were held. These are seen to match the eight-part calendar of Sosigenes. Since Christian times, the function of the festivals has been assigned a Christian significance, but some pagan elements persist nonetheless, more or less glossed over.

(3) Each Celtic center in Vermont seems to have its own calendar site, as if the calendar site was itself the place at which a religious meeting was held. For otherwise it would have been enough to have had one good calendar site, from which messages could be sent out to outlying villages, setting the dates for the festivals, just as nowadays we are all content to follow the calendars determined by a few major national observatories.

To see how the calendar site was employed we have only to visit the Zuni people of New Mexico. Here certain notches and excrescences along a mountain chain are identified as places where the sun will rise (or set) on important dates, in this case the summer and winter solstices. A special magician or priest is appointed to act as the calendar-regulator or sun-priest. His job is to observe the sun regularly and to estimate some days in advance when he expects the sun to reach one of the solstice points. As soon as he has made a determination, he sends out messages summoning the subtribes to the winter solstice festival or summer solstice festival, as the case may be. This is a simple version of the Celtic system, having only two annual solar festivals. The Celtic system, employing eight festival dates, must have operated in the same way. However, studies by Byron Dix, still in progress, show that the Vermont sites have additional stones ori-ented in a manner that implies that the Vermont Druids also made a special study of the motions of the moon as well as the motions of the sun. Byron believes that his researches may eventually show that the New England Druids had a means by which eclipses could be predicted.

The Celts of Britain have never entirely forgotten the 8-part calendar of ancient time. Several academic holidays used to puzzle me when I was a student at the University of Edinburgh. For example, bonfires were lit on the second Monday of November, a relic of the old Celtic harvest festival of *Samhnag,* later Christianized to Martinmas. In February the first and second Mondays were called Candlemas and Mealie-Monday, when the students in the olden days went home to collect a bag of oat-meal; these apparently are a retention of the old pagan festival of *Imbolg.* In America the night of October 31, called Hallowe'en, is a fossil Celtic festival originally called *Samhain* (pronounced "Saven"), marking the start of the winter and the end of summer, supposedly a period of transi-tion during which the souls of the dead and certain spirits of nature were free to wander across the world. It is possible that the English phrase "Witches' Sabbath" arose from the Celtic word *Samhain* by folk etymol-ogy, and that the phallic temples on the tops of Vermont hills were frequented on the nights of Samhain. If so, then the witches of Wood-stock must have been singularly hardy to dance in the nude in so chilly a location.

As this book goes to press, Byron Dix informs me that he has just completed a computer analysis of the dates of the Vermont Celtic calendar implied by standing stones.* In the following table I have set out his computed dates for the Vermont festivals against the corresponding names and dates of the European Celtic calendar. As can be seen, the American and European calendars are essentially identical.

TABLE 6

Comparative Table of Celtic Festivals for Europe and North America in Pagan Times

Christian equivalent names given in parentheses. In ancient times the two solstices and two equinoctials occurred on the 25th day of the month, but on account of the precession of the equinoxes, these dates have now moved forward to about the 21st or 22nd day.

NAME OF FESTIVAL	DATE OF CELEBRATION BY CELTS OF EUROPE	COMPUTED DATE OF CELEBRATION BY CELTS OF NEW ENGLAND†
1 Co-thad-thrath	March equinox	March equinox
2 Bel-tuinn (Beltane)†	May 1	ca May 1 (Day XXXVIIII)
3 Grian-stad	June solstice	ca June solstice
4 Lugnasadh (Lammas)	August 1	ca August 1
5 Co-thad-thrath	September equinox	ca September equinox
6 Samhain (Hallowe'en)	October 31–November 1	ca November 1
7 An Fheill-Shlinnein (Shoulderblade)‡	December solstice	ca December solstice
8 Imbolg (Candlemas)	February 1	ca February 1

† From studies by Byron Dix. Most dates approximate.
‡ Translation or transliteration.

It is a well-known precept in education that the most important thing to do in any study is not so much to memorize facts, but rather to know what to look for and where to find it. As I mentioned earlier, not one Ogam inscription had been found at Mystery Hill before the summer solstice of 1975. Yet, after witnessing the dramatic proof of Bob Stone's conception of the monoliths as calendar markers, I now felt convinced that Celts were connected in some way with the building of the site. The similarity of the name Baal on the Phoenician dedication stone to the name of the Celtic sun god Bel recalled earlier suggestions by etymologists in Europe that the Celtic and Phoenician names of the sun god might be cognate. So, when the first Ogam inscription was uncovered nineteen days after the solstice assembly, my own reaction was more of jubilation than surprise. Our eyes were already alerted to look for Ogam and we found it, not only at Mystery Hill but all over the Vermont calendar sites as well.

* To be published in volume 3 of the *Occasional Publications of the Epigraphic Society.*

Elizabeth Sincerbeaux with equatorial adjusted by Byron Dix to point to the sunrise point on December 22, the winter solstice as seen from the metonic porch of the highest temple-observatory at South Woodstock, Vermont. Dix's researches, together with the dedication inscriptions deciphered by Fell, yield mutual confirmation that the stone slab buildings of New England were erected by Celts for calendar regulation and for religious exercises connected with the worship of the Sun God and other Celtic divinities. The building of so many substantial stone buildings (over 200 are now recorded) shows that the work was done by permanent colonists from Europe, and that New England was occupied by Celts as early as the first millennium B.C. Reiterated claims that the buildings are "root-cellars" made by colonial farmers during the seventeenth and eighteenth centuries must be dismissed, though it is true that some of the stone buildings were converted to mundane uses by those settlers who discovered them on their property. Most, unfortunately, were destroyed and their stone fabric converted to other uses. *Byron Dix*

Unlike the anonymous calendar stones of Europe, our American stones now began to yield up their Celtic names, telling of their functions. On monoliths that marked important points in the solar observatories we now recognized the faint but still legible Ogam letters that confirmed the purpose of the stone. And, as if to stress the function for people who might not be able to read Ogam, the strokes of the text were often engraved in such a manner to suggest an eye, perhaps the eye of the observer himself, or perhaps the eye of Bel, the poetic Celtic name of the sun, as we now learned from the inscriptions on the temples of Bel. From various parts, including districts miles away from Mystery Hill, finders were now recognizing the symbol of Bel, and small inscribed triangular stone plates that had hitherto baffled us we now perceived to be pilgrims' offerings, probably purchased as they entered the Mystery Hill precincts and then deposited as votive offerings at the altars. Osborn Stone and his assistants, their eyes now sensitized to the tell-tale traces of frost-worn Ogam, sent in a stream of reports of new finds. The era of mystery was now giving way to one of dawning comprehension and wonder.

Dr. Clyde Keeler came up from Georgia to examine the collection of casts of the inscriptions, familiarized himself with the Ogam alphabet and, with his artist's eye and fingers, soon found ways of perpetuating the new-found motifs in ceramic medallions and pendants whose glowing colors would have delighted the ancient Gauls. Thus it was, through the archeological interests of a medical geneticist, a national art form was created from the age-old stones of the American Celts. Some of Clyde's charming ceramics lie beside me as I write, valued mementos of memorable days and of the friends who shared them.

Byron Dix is still engaged on his analyses of the Vermont astronomical structures, but by the time this book appears in print he will have reported on his main findings in formal technical papers published by the Epigraphic Society (see Bibliography). Some of his forthcoming reports may, however, be briefly summarized here.

First, as to the manner in which he discovered the eight-part division of the New England Celtic year: this was done by computer analysis, as follows. From the central observation area on Calendar Site Number 1 he noticed the presence of distant standing stones and, making use of an astronomical instrument called an equatorial, he first determined the declination of that part of the sky that touches the horizon in the same direction as each of the standing stones. By declination is meant a sort of latitude, used in plotting the positions of stars on the celestial globe, with the celestial pole numbered 90° and the celestial equator 0°. He then programmed a computer to calculate the declination of the sun for every day of the year and compared the results with his observations of the standing stones. He found that the standing stones mark intervals of about 39 to 43 days, spread through the year. In other words, for a year that begins at the spring equinox, there is a stone to mark the position of sunset or sunrise for that date; then another stone that marks the position of sunrise or sunset some 39 days later; that is, May 1 or Beltane, then another for the June solstice, and so on. It was clear evidence of the existence in New England of a Celtic type of calendar similar to that of

Hippocrates and Sosigenes. The finding of the Beltane stone at Mystery Hill later in the season added clarification to Dix's findings, as already noted.

The second of Byron Dix's important findings concerns the orientation of the long axes of the stone temples of Vermont, as I have already reported in Chapter 10. Anyone may check Dix's findings in a simple way, by taking a magnetic compass into the Pantheon at South Woodstock and noting that the long axis of that temple does indeed lie along the intercept of the eastern horizon with the compass bearing in the southeast-by-east direction, which lies very near the celestial declination $-23\frac{1}{2}°$, the southernmost limit of the path of the sun through the sky; that is, the winter solstice sunrise point. Given this approximate correspondence, seen by only a crude instrument, I have no reason to doubt the correctness of Dix's more accurate determination made with an equatorial.

But Dix has gone further than this. He now finds that the *diagonals* of the Pantheon chamber intercept the horizon at points corresponding to the greatest and least southern limits of the moon in the course of what is called the *Metonic cycle*. The moon revolves about the earth in such a manner that its orbit sometimes carries it to a position some 5° south of the maximum southern limit of the sun, and at other times to a position 5° north of this. A period of 18.6 years is required to carry the moon into every possible position it can occupy with respect to the sun. This *Metonic cycle* of 18.6 years is the period that elapses before all possible eclipses begin to repeat in sequence, and it was discovered in 433 B.C. by the Greek astronomer Meton. There are, however, some newly found data (in Europe) suggesting a much earlier date of discovery.

So we learned how the Pantheon's dimensions are designed to register these events. From this we can infer two important things: (1) the date of construction of the Pantheon at South Woodstock is unlikely to have been earlier than the date of the discovery of the Metonic Cycle in Europe, and (2) since the Celts are unlikely to have had the mathematical ability to calculate these positions, they must have determined them empirically, that is to say, by actual experimental observation of the moon over a long period. In other words, the building of the Pantheon was probably carried out over a period of at least nineteen years. Having once constructed the Pantheon to these specifications the Druids could use it to keep watch on the motions of the sun and the moon, and they probably used them for predicting eclipses. All this information provoked astonishment when it was described to audiences or visitors.

The sophisticated science that these buildings and stone observation posts imply also argues in favor of a comparably advanced system of navigation at sea, using instruments similar to the astrolabe or to the torquetum that Dr. Sentiel Rommel and I described last year from

Libyan inscriptions found in a cave in West Irian, dated by a solar eclipse to November of the fifteenth year of the reign of Ptolemy III (232 B.C.). It is likely that the Libyan equipment, of which Rommel has now constructed replicas, very much resembled whatever corresponding equipment the Phoenicians and Celts must have used in voyages across the Atlantic.

In preparing material for this chapter I have followed the evidence of Julius Caesar in assigning to the Druids the roles of scientist and natural philosopher. But many people associate the Druids with other roles, those of priest and poet. As noted above, the geographer Strabo distributed these tasks among other officials, the Vates and the Bards. Of the Vates we know almost nothing, for their religion was virtually expunged by Roman governors who were disgusted by human sacrifice, and what the Romans left, the Christians took care to eradicate.

In the Western Isles of Scotland some traces persist of the prayers or incantations of the Vates, though usually with some Christian gloss added, so that the fisherfolk who utter these ancient words do so in the belief that they are sanctioned by the kirk or by Rome. But their similarity to the graffiti found on walls of caves frequented by ancient mariners leads me to assign them to the pagan era. Another curious point is that when Alexander Carmichael was collecting Hebridean material he reported that some of the prayers were never uttered in the presence of a stranger to the isles. The phraseology of the following prayer is, in my opinion, pre-Christian, and perhaps stems from the lips of the Vates. It is to be said upon rising in the morning:

> A Righ na gile 's na greine,
> A Righ nan reula runach,
> Agad fein tha fios ar feuma,
> A Dhe mheinnich nan dula.
>
> O King of the moonlight and of the sun,
> O King of the stars mysterious,
> Yourself aware of our needs,
> O merciful God of Nature.

The crescent of the new moon evoked prayers from hunters in ancient time, for they saw in this the symbol of Diana the Huntress. The Celts of the Hebrides are sailors, not hunters, and they have preserved an ancient mariners' invocation to the new moon as a guiding star signalling the western direction. It is certainly pre-Christian in spirit and in wording, for the Hebridean sense of the word I here translate as "lady" is actually "lady of easy virtue." Only the most innocent of priests could here suppose the prayer to be addressed to the Virgin Mary.

Failt ort fein, a gheallach ur,
Ailleagan iuil nan neul!
Failt ort fein, a gheallach ur,
Ailleagan cumh nan neamh!

Hail to thee, O new moon,
Precious beacon-of-the-clouds!
Hail to thee, O new moon,
Precious Lady-of-the-heavens!

Of the Bards we have vastly more information, in the shape of the traditional poetry, music, and epics of the Welsh and Gaelic peoples, and much also from the other Celtic lands. The music is famous especially for the plaintive airs, those of the Scots Highlands and of Ireland being especially known in English-speaking countries. The Celtic preference for stressing the first beat of a bar imparts a rhythm similar to that of the trochaic verse meter used by Longfellow in *Hiawatha*. This, however, is a topic more suitable for the spoken media.

To summarize this chapter, we find in New England some two hundred stone chambers, many of which are oriented and constructed in such manner as to make them serve as astronomical observatories for the regulation of the calendar of festivals. There are also systems of standing stones that indicate a calendar divided into eight half-seasons, all based on the annual cycle of the sun's motions in the sky. All these objects yield calendar observations to this very day for those astronomers who understand the use of ancient stone structures for this purpose, and the calendars so observed prove to match those which we know to have been Celtic. Since some of the stone structures are also labelled in Celtic script with indications of their function, we are obliged to conclude that they are the work of ancient Celts. Evidence by ancient European writers tells us that the Celtic astronomers were known as Druids. We therefore must draw the final conclusion that Druids were once active in New England. They were still practicing their astronomical craft in the time of Julius Caesar, whose reformed calendar they adopted in part, and with it the use of Roman numerals, but they retained the Celtic habit of beginning the new year on the day of the spring equinox.

One great mystery remains unsolved. When and why did the Druids of New England cease to practice their skills? Perhaps it would be fair to counter this question with another: what do we know of astronomy and calendar regulation in (say) Britain during the dark ages, after the Romans left; that 400-year blank in British history? We know almost nothing of the answers to either of these questions, so perhaps after all the American historian is not in much worse plight than his English confrère.

14

The Ritual
Phallic Monuments

BY the end of our first season's work it had become abundantly plain that the New England Celts worshipped the power of fertility in nature. It was also clear to us that the Mother Goddess, Byanu (Beanu of the European Celts) was conceived as a mighty progenitor of the human race, for her great altar in South Woodstock obviously is carved in the form of the human female genitalia, guarded apparently by the two fallen stone phallic columns we had found nearby. We were also impressed by the abundance of representations of the male organs, in relief on temple walls and lintels, on foundation stones of temples now converted into dry-stone walls, and sculptured in the round as cylindrical columns. These phalli range in size from about two inches long up to awesome erections some five feet high.

These extraordinary finds, unique in American archeology, and in total contradiction of the prevailing opinion that British colonial farmers alone were responsible for the megalithic ruins of Vermont, never ceased to arouse the wonder of visitors to our sites.

It came about that the first authority to examine our evidence was a distinguished visitor from overseas. His reaction to what he saw was in startling contrast to what we had experienced up to that juncture.

Our visitor was Dr. Ch. Chhabra, president of the Indian Epigraphical Association, Professor of Sanskrit at the University of Mysore, and for forty years epigrapher to the Archeological Service of the Government of India. India is well known for the more than 4,000 phalli that have been carved from stone and erected throughout the land these past three thousand years. Indian monuments to a belief in the divine nature of the power of reproduction and fertility are also distinguished by having engraved inscriptions, generally written along the long axis of the phallus, in the same manner as the Celtic phalli of Vermont, except that the language is Sanskrit, the ancient language of the Indian sages and kings.

Professor Chhabra's impending visit to Harvard University was therefore an event keenly anticipated by us, for we knew that in him we might expect to find a highly competent and experienced archeologist, long familiar with an analogous fertility worship in another context. We also knew, from the linguistic studies of our colleagues in Britain, that the Celtic languages are closely related to the common Indo-European tongue from which Sanskrit and the Aryan languages of Europe all descend. His long experience as an epigrapher further meant that he could look at our inscriptions with that penetrating gaze and comprehending inner eye that is the mark of an expert.

At last we had found an authority who had the knowledge to assess our finds. Our expectations were more than amply realized. This quiet-spoken scientist and his charming wife Sheila, with their editor son Vinod, in the space of a day's discussion and examination of the inscriptions not only vindicated our work, but added a whole new dimension to it by setting the objects we had found into the broad context of Bronze Age fertility cults.

We of the Western World have until now had almost no relics to study of the phallic beliefs of our remote Celtic predecessors. The earliest Christian missionaries to the Celts made it their business to see to the eradication of the fertility cult and the near total destruction of the phallic columns so offensive to Christianity. In India, on the other hand, the ancient Aryan beliefs were tolerated or even espoused by the various winds of religious thought that have swept across that land since classical times.

Under Dr. Chhabra's tutelage, we now began to realize that Celtic scholars have till now overlooked a linguistic aspect of the names written on the phallic columns and the images of the female organs. As we now learned, the phallus (or *linga* as it is called in Sanskrit) is most commonly represented in India in company, or actually in physical contact, with the female organs, which are termed in Sanskrit the *yoni*. It is true that John Williams and I had been struck by the occurrence of two fallen phalli near the female pelvis in Woodstock, but it was now apparent that the connection was closer than we had then realized.

You will recall that when we found the giant female stone, the inscriptions occurring with it had told us that this altar was dedicated to a divinity whose name was expressed, in the sequence of consonants given in the Ogam script, as

M-H   M-B   B-Y-N

an inscription which I had read, in accordance with what our colleagues in Europe have found, as requiring vowel points to give

Ma-hair Ma-bon, Byanu

meaning "Mother of Heroes, Beanu." In Gaelic spelling, *ea* and *eo* represent the sound of *ya* or *yo*. The name *Byanu* (or Beanu) has been taken by European students of the ancient Celts as representing the old Gaulish pronunciation of a word *beann,* meaning "woman," and nowadays commonly spelled *ban*. Hence the name of the Mother Goddess has been taken to be *Woman*—with a capital "W," to parallel the Hebrew *Adam,* meaning *Man*—with a capital "M." As Man is to be taken as the father of all men, so it was supposed, Woman is the mother of all men.

But Dr. Chhabra's conversation and insights now threw new light on this matter, as he cited the corresponding fertility images of India, and their Sanskrit or Prakrit inscriptions.

We first of all examined the actual inscriptions in Ogam on the phalli, together with the inferences I had drawn as to the Celtic words that the consonants were intended to represent. To summarize in tabular form, we have:

TABLE 7

Representative Ogam Inscriptions Found on Phalli in Vermont

OGAM LETTERS FOUND	INFERRED GOIDELIC WORDS INTENDED	MODERN GAELIC WORDS MOST CLOSELY SIMILAR	INFERRED MEANING OF THE GOIDELIC INSCRIPTION
B-G	Bog	Bog (to swell)	Let it swell
B-B	Bab	Pab (tassel)	Penis
B-G B-B	Bog Bab	Bog pab (-)	Penis erectus

Dr. Chhabra, a Sanskrit scholar, was not familiar with the Ogam script, but as I vocalized the letters for him it became evident that the ancient Celtic words I was attempting to rebuild from the consonantal framework were roots already familiar to him from India. He first assured me that the sense of the inscriptions, as I had deduced it, matched the sense of corresponding inscriptions on phalli in India. Next he drew direct parallels with the corresponding words in ancient Sanskrit. This, in turn, led me to consult Professor Calvert Watkins's instructive article "Indo-European and the Indo-Europeans" in the recently published *American Heritage Dictionary*. Putting together the three sets of information (from the Celtic phalli, from Sanskrit, and from comparative linguistics) we can now construct a new table giving the most ancient words known to us for male sexuality in the Indo-European tongues. These are:

TABLE 8

Words Relating to Male Sexuality in Bronze Age and Iron Age Tongues of the Indo-European Family

INFERRED ANCIENT INDO-EUROPEAN ROOT	INFERRED ORIGINAL MEANING	ANCIENT SANSKRIT EQUIVALENT AND ITS MEANING	ANCIENT CELTIC EQUIVALENT AND ITS MEANING
bheug (1)	"to have pleasure"	*bhoga,* "have sexual enjoyment"	*boch,* "ecstasy," "joy"
bheug (2)	"to swell"	(uncertain)	*bog,* "to swell"
bozd	"penis"	*bodh,* "excite," "expand"	*bod,* "penis"
pap, pu	"to swell"	(uncertain)	*pab, bab,* "penis," "tassel"
(uncertain)		*linga,* "phallus" (penis erectus)	*leam, blade* (cf. Old English *waepon,* "penis")
men	"to protrude"	*mehana,* "penis"	*mian,* "libido" (cf. Latin *mentula,* "penis")
mari-to	"bride-provided"	*mariya,* "rites of god of love"	*maraist,* "copulation" (cf. Latin *maritus,* "husband")
spor	"seed," "inseminate"	*spris,* "sprinkle"	*por,* "seed," "semen" (cf. Greek *spora,* Latin *sperma*)

For the sake of brevity I have included in the table the modern Gaelic word *bod* (penis) which does not in fact occur on the New England phalli; it should be listed, however, for *bod* is known to range back at least to the period from 1200 to 1550 A.D., when manuscripts such as the *Book of Lismore* were composed. Also the rare British phallic stones (found in the remoter districts of Ireland) are known to the local people by this name, an example being the so-called *Bod-Fearghus* (Penis-of-Fergus) at Tara, seat of the ancient Irish kings.

The principal sources of old Gaelic words available to us now were compiled a century or more ago, mainly through the well-meaning efforts of learned Presbyterian ministers and Irish monks. These clergymen were prone to gloss over words with sexual connotations. Thus Neil Mac-Alpine, whose dictionary was first published in 1832, sometimes records a sexual word but gives a printed dash as its translation; or alternatively he may offer a slang substitute word such as *tassle* (for "penis," apparently), or refer vaguely to a "member." Alexander MacBain, whose learned dictionary appeared seventy years later, contented himself with giving Latin or Greek meanings for words he considered improper, but omitted many others, probably only because he could not explain their etymology to his own satisfaction.

Having examined the vocabulary of the New England phallic monuments, Dr. Chhabra and I turned to the known role of such monuments in the religious beliefs of India. Here it became apparent that, whatever the more philosophical and priestly significance of these objects might be, the chief role they play in the daily life of the peasants is more directly related to sexual and marital problems, particularly of women.

Thus we would be mistaken in thinking that phallic monuments are primarily connected with the male ethos of masculinity. Dr. Chhabra also drew attention to the parallel of the Indian phalli to the once-famous phallic rocks of the Hawaiian island of Molokai, on the hill overlooking Father Damien's leper colony. These ancient fertility symbols used to be visited by barren Hawaiian women who would be directed by the *kahuna* (priest) to recite certain prayers to encourage the latent potency of the stone penis to enter her uterus; the age-old and harmless rite was abruptly terminated, so he told us, when the local park authorities erased the inscriptions. (Mahair-Mabon forbid that any Vermont town council attempt a like sacrilege!)

I think, and Dr. Chhabra agrees with me, that the Vermont phalli must have served a similar role. In support of this view I would cite the remarkable series of engravings found by us under the base of one of the phalli at the summit of an 1,800-foot eminence near South Woodstock. Here we have an unmistakable sequence of necessities for the production of a child (page 225). These are four in number: (1) an erect penis with the testicles indicated, showing that their role in male fertility was understood; (2) a succeeding diagram in which penetration of the female is indicated; (3) a carving of what appears to represent the swelling uterus, following a successful mating; and (4) the developing fetus, attached by its umbilical cord to the circular placenta.

In the same hilltop area we found libation bowls cut into the bedrock (and partially filled by rainwater), the adjacent portion of the exposed bedrock cut into what has the semblance of a ritual copulation table, the stone excavated into a negative mould of the buttocks of the two marital partners, seated side by side. This sanctuary, for as such it evidently is to be regarded, we had at first called Phallus Hill, but after considering all the relevant facts we could elicit from the surviving relics, Peter and John and I felt that a more appropriate name might be *Hill of the Wedding Rite*, and so we marked it on the map, where no name had stood before.

When considered in the light of the foregoing discussion one is filled with awe at the survival for these two thousand years and more of such ancient relics of profound mystical importance to those Celtic wanderers from Europe who made their home in this far-off country. The phalli now lose their comic aspect, and can be seen as objects of religious venera-

Fertility Cult, series of engravings on the base of a carved stone phallus, four feet high, Temple of the Marriage Rite, South Woodstock. Upper row, from left: (1) erect phallus, (2) intromission, (3) the swelling uterus, (4) the growing embryo attached by the umbilical cord to the circular placenta. *Joseph D. Germano*

Several large phallic stones are associated with ruins of a fertility temple on a hilltop near South Woodstock, Vermont. Some of the stones carry traces of Ogam inscriptions relating to fertility rites, and other bas reliefs depicting the formation of an embryo. Large quartz testicle stones, one of which is seen in the foreground, occur also in association with sun temples and other ruins. These Celtiberian phallic stones may be compared with similar objects seen in Portugal and Brittany. *Peter J. Garfall*

The giant phallus of Kerdef, Brittany, exceeding in size all known European and American megalithic monoliths. For long attributed to a supposedly unknown neolithic or Bronze Age culture, current opinion is now growing that this and similar megalithic structures of Carnac were in fact the work of Celts before they acquired the art of writing. *Dechelette, 1908*

Giant phallus, originally standing seven feet high on its base (right end in picture), now forming part of a colonial wall at South Pomfret, Vermont. The Ogam inscription, seen upside down in this view, reads from the base upwards, L-Ia-G B-L (T-N), Beltane Stone, the last two letters damaged. The Celtic festival of Beltane, held on May Day, originally in pagan times included revels danced around an erect phallus. In Europe, after Christianity was introduced, the phallus was replaced by a maypole. This phallus was discovered by John Williams. *Joseph D. Germano*

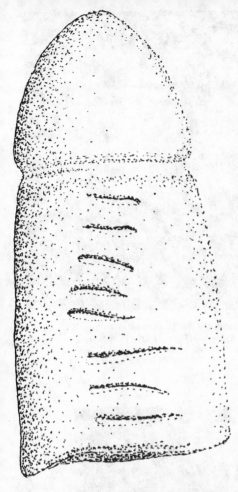

Phallic claystone talisman from Algeria, after Rossello-Bordoy (1969). The engraved strokes appear to be North African Ogam script, spelling the Punic word Q-F, presumably matching modern Arabic *qaf*, and meaning "stand erect." Although phallic stones occur in the Iberian region, this inscribed form from northwest Africa seems most closely to parallel the Ogamic Celtic phalli of Vermont. Uninscribed phalli have been considered neolithic, but this example should probably be referred to the late Bronze Age or early Iron Age. Numerous table knives with phallic handles have been found in ruins of houses and military barracks of Romano-Celtic sites.

Phallus from open-air precincts of Byanu, found near the large yoni altar at South Woodstock, Vermont. The Ogam characters read from left to right, Ya-S-G L-Y, apparently meaning "To inseminate the (Mother Goddess's) birth passage." *John Williams and Joseph D. Germano*

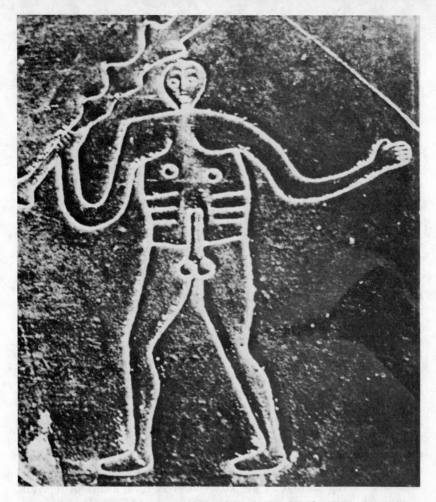

Bronze Age fertility cult in Britain. This figure, known as the Cerne Giant, is cut into the chalk bedrock of a hillside. Its outlines have been kept free from overgrowth by vegetation through the care of the local villagers through the centuries since it was first created, probably in the first millennium B.C. The giant is 180 feet high, the phallus 35 feet, thus the largest phallic monument in Britain. These figures, dependent largely upon the chalk bedrock for their production, are apparently lacking from the Celtic areas of America and Iberia.

Fertility cult, South Pomfret, Vermont. The phallus shown middle left is engraved on the lower side of a now recumbent 6-foot phallus built into a colonial wall. Beside the engraving is the Ogam inscription shown in the lower photo, reading B-G, corresponding to modern Gaelic Boc, and meaning "Let it swell." *Joseph D. Germano*

tion, evoking the prayers of hopeful young parents, or of disappointed couples who longed for children, and who doubtless carried out ritual acts in accordance with the advice of the Druids of the clan. May these historic relics escape the onslaught of vandals! Probably they should be transferred as soon as possible to a museum, where they can be seen by all but kept safe from desecration.

Following Dr. Chhabra's visit I researched what is known of phallic stones among the Celts of Britain and learned some facts that support the inferences we had drawn from the Indian and Hawaiian parallels.

From Dr. Richard Brash's work on Gaelic Ogam monuments I learned that there had once been a phallic stone of almost identical proportions to the larger phalli of Vermont, located in the churchyard of St. Olan's at Aghabulloghe, near Coolineagh in County Cork, Ireland. It is no longer intact, for the *glans* was deliberately destroyed ("made away with" is the term used) by the clergyman of the church some time before 1876. This outrage, in the name of Victorian prudery, was committed because the phallus was the object of ancient veneration among the parishioners for the cure of certain illnesses and for the promotion of successful child-bearing. The phallus, now deprived of its *coppeen* (as the amputated portion was called) stands 5 feet high, with a girth around the base of 42 inches. In former times the *coppeen* was much in demand as a medical aid, and was often borrowed for temporary use in one of the crofts. If the borrower failed to return it, the *coppeen* was said to have the miraculous power of returning unaided to the tip of its columnar counterpart. A recipe for headache was to take the *coppeen* from the phallus and to place it on one's head, at the same time walking solemnly round the church three circuits, repeating the *Pater noster* at every turn, a curious survival of early Christian concessions to pagan beliefs. In addition to promoting childbirth, it was efficacious in the treatment of what Dr. Brash called female complaints.

What the Gaelic villagers thought of the outrage committed by their ignorant pastor is sufficiently shown by the fact that a replacement *coppeen* was surreptitiously manufactured and placed where the ancient one had been; it was crudely carved, however, and Brash refers to it as an unshapely lump, with little of the reputation formerly enjoyed by its ancient predecessor. The cylindrical body of the penis carries an Ogam inscription along the vertical axis, as in the American examples. Apart from the word *maq,* however, the letters are damaged or incomplete, and a decipherment has not been possible. It would appear that the phallus may have had an earlier pagan inscription erased, to be replaced by a funeral inscription of some important personage in early Christian times who chose to employ it as his tombstone. It is currently known as St.

Olan's Stone but, as Brash shows, the puzzling inscription has nothing to do with the saint.

Village people have long memories. That is to say, they perpetuate beliefs held by their forefathers from generation to generation. In this case there can be little doubt that, through all its vicissitudes, the phallus of St. Olan's, and its movable *coppeen,* was remembered for powers it was reputed to have long before St. Patrick began the destruction of the ancient monuments of the Irish Celts.

Taking now what evidence we have gleaned from the available Indo-European sources, including the pathetic Irish remnants, some conclusions may be hazarded as to the role the New England phallic stones may have played in the pagan Celtic society of this country 2,500 years ago.

As mentioned above, Dr. Chhabra stresses the association of Indian phalli with corresponding stone representations of the female organs, or *yoni.* Consider also that in Vermont we have found two large stone phalli lying prostrate a short distance from the two-ton female stone of South Woodstock. John Williams further reports that he has noticed other, smaller stones with the same carved similitude to the female organs.*

Are these male-female juxtapositions merely an accident of ruin, their scattered distribution a reflection of no more than the random disintegration of temples under the combined attack of time and the wall-building colonists of the late eighteenth century? This matter can now be examined.

*In 1980 Professor Warren Cook and some of his students gathered up the various phallic stones in the Woodstock area and transferred them for safekeeping to the Library of Castleton College, Vermont, where they now can be seen.

15

Mother-of-Heroes, Lady Goddess Byanu

O F the two great divinities of the ancient Celts, Bel and the great Mother Goddess, the goddess may not be the second but the first. Many archeologists who have examined the evidence yielded by the famous ruins of the early Mediterranean civilizations such as those of Greece, Crete, Italy, and parts of Asia Minor have concluded that worship of the powers of nature in the guise of a Mother Goddess represents perhaps the earliest organized religion of the human species.

The argument adduced to justify such a belief is twofold: (1) in the lowest, and hence earliest, levels of the accumulated debris left on this planet by our predecessors we find many carvings, paintings, and complete sculptures of women in situations such that we can only conclude that they represent a major divinity, whereas male figures are apparently reduced to a secondary role; and (2) images or carvings of pregnant females ranging back even into the paleolithic age suggest that the one event that aroused the greatest wonder and admiration of ancient people was the mystery of birth, the means by which the human family was kept in existence.

In view of the self-evident fact that the earliest human beings cannot have had a deeper understanding of their sexual behavior than of any other instinctive action such as eating or urinating or foraging for food, it is clear that the purpose of copulation was a mystery that had to be pondered upon and eventually explained by some mastermind of remote times. Thus many archeologists have come to the conclusion that probably the predominance of divine females in the religious records of early civilizations reflects an early feeling of wonder and admiration that all people, men and women alike, felt for a pregnant woman. Somehow women became pregnant and this was a measure of their essential role in perpetuating the tribe.

Male chauvinism, by this argument, was born when it was first discovered that no woman ever became pregnant unless a man had previously mated with her. Once this discovery had been attested by experiment and repetition, the potency of the male was recognized. From this it was a step to recognizing the penis as the source of fertility and, as chance injury or wounds would soon disclose, that the penis is useless unless accompanied by the intact testicles. Thus the notion of the phallus became the symbol of natural fecundity. Male gods of hunting and warfare were added to produce a pantheon of father-like divinities, divine youths and cunning wonder-workers, smiths, guardians of the home, ships and the like, divine inspirers of song and dance, and so on. These, with their assorted wives and children, now became the extensive pantheon of gods and goddesses who replaced the original Mother Goddess. Among the ruder, less civilized peoples, such as the Celts, the power of the Mother Goddess lingered longest, shared now with her divine spouse, the sun god Bel. For the youth, the hope of the tribe, a youthful figure was granted divinity in guise of Mabo-Mabon, Youth-of-the-Youth or Hero-of-Heroes, sometimes equated with Apollo of the Greeks.

Julius Caesar, when he wrote his account of Gaul in the sixth decade before the birth of Christ, listed the divinities worshipped by the Celts as he knew them. Many others have been added by European archeologists who have read the numerous, though fragmentary, inscriptions found in Celtic excavations. So far, in the New England Celtic ruins, we have not found definite evidence for more than the three divinities mentioned above. It seems likely, then, that the ancient Celts had fewer gods than their descendants of Roman times, for our New England Celts would bring to America a religious system corresponding to that of Celtic Europe in about 800 B.C., always provided that we are dating the New England inscriptions correctly.

If I am correct in assigning the era of the Celtic incursion into America to around 800 B.C., then we must admit that by this period the European Celts had transferred to the male of the human species the honor that had formerly been accorded the female. It is on the phallic monuments that we find the inscriptions relating to sexuality. The stages in the creation of a human infant are depicted not on the altars of the Mother Goddess, but in separate Phallic Precincts apparently frequented by women who had difficulties in producing a child and probably also by newly married couples or couples carrying out the ritual copulation that was part of the Druidic wedding ceremony, as we may judge from corresponding petroglyphs found in Scandinavia, where Celtic influence is apparent during the Bronze Age.

If, therefore, the human male had now assumed the mantle of glory as the producer of the magic fluid that somehow caused women to become pregnant, what was the role of the great Mother Goddess in this male-oriented hunting society? This question is not easy to answer on the rather scant evidence so far uncovered in our preliminary survey, not yet one year old. But several facts seem important to me at this juncture.

Examine again the table of Ogam inscriptions found on the New England phalli as set out on page 221. Next compare it with the table of Bronze Age words relating to male sexuality given on page 222. I think we have here indications of a transitional phase in the evolution of our forefathers' conception of the function of sex. The root *bheug*, for example, is instructive. On the one hand it conveys a sense "to have pleasure" and on the other hand it has a second sense "to swell"; that is, become erect. I think this linguistic twin reflects man's original notion of sex as purely an avocational act of play, a pastime that gave enjoyment—and no more than that. The second sense, on the other hand, is related, I guess, to the realization that copulation is also a serious business, and can bring about the birth of a baby.

It is this second sense that relates to the transfer of supremacy in the religious sense to the male of the species, to the origin of the concept of fatherhood. By discovering the potency of semen, humans now discovered a new mystical power within the male, and soon after began to devise initiation ceremonies for the young males, requiring a proof of their seminal capacity. Similar hints of a former view of sex as merely an enjoyable pastime are conveyed, I think, by the root *mari-to*, "bride-provided," and the cognate Sanskrit sense of pertaining to the rites of the god of love. In contrast, the root *spor*, "to sprinkle," "to inseminate," and "seed," in these various senses again betokens realization of the role of the male as father and producer of the magic fertilizing fluid.

Perhaps it would be natural, in this changing view of the role of the female, for a new sense of devotion and affection of the male for the female to develop. Woman is no longer the dominant power who alone regenerates the species. Instead she has become man's-wife (as the word *woman* indeed means), his object of love, the mother of *his* children (as opposed to her former role as the mother of *her* children). Woman is the human partner who brings up the infants while the father is hunting. She is the expression of the presiding genius of the rude hovel that he calls home. As Caesar and other Roman writers noted, she accompanies him to battle, cheers him on and shares with him his every fortune, good and bad. In her new role the Celtic woman came to exercise a power over the men so great that the Romans, in order to quell the martial spirit of the Britons, were compelled to kill the women instead of enslaving them. Perhaps this interpretation may help us understand why the New England Celt found it expedient to erect major temples to the Mother Goddess, for in his concept of woman lay the breath of life, his personal honor, and the respected and beloved bearer of his children.

This, then, is probably the origin of the primary title of the Celtic Mother Goddess, *Mahair-Mabon*, "Mother-of-Heroes." As woman is to man, so is *Mahair-Mabon* to Bel, the father god whose symbol is the sun itself.

What, then, of the secondary title accorded to the Mother Goddess in her New England inscriptions? As I first read it, this *Byanu*, matching *Beanu* or *Beann*, of the European Celts, meant "Woman"—Woman the personification of all women. My conversations with Dr. Chhabra, however, caused me to reexamine this interpretation, and I would now prefer to substitute a different explanation of the etymology and sense of this secondary title, *Byanu*.

The cross-shaped Ogam symbol which the *Book of Ballymote* tells us stands for *ya* (*ea* in Gaelic spelling for the sound "ya") can also stand for the sound "yo," as for example in the proper name *Yo-g-h-an*, which we have found on a New England gravestone, and which we know (from British sources of evidence) is the earlier form of the modern Celtic names Ewan and Evan. Thus *Byanu*, the name of the Mother Goddess, might once have been pronounced "Byonu," or even "Byoni" for that matter.

This is more than mere academic hair-splitting. Suppose the Ogam letters of the goddess's name, "B-Y-N" in the form in which we find it spelled on the New England monuments in her honor, were indeed intended to be pronounced "Byonu" or "Byoni." In that case we could scarcely fail to draw a direct parallel between the name and the Sanskrit name of the female organs of generation, *yoni*. The etymology, too, would be consistent, for the Celtic root *yann* (or *iann*) means "that which is internal," and this also is the root sense of the Sanskrit word for the female genitalia, the inner organ, as opposed to the phallus or *linga*, which is the outer sign or manifestation of sex. The ancient Romans had a similar concept in that maleness in a newborn baby was indicated by the "witnesses," as the word *testes* in fact means, the outer witness of sex that determines maleness.

Added to this etymological argument is the fact well attested by the Indian phallic monuments; that in most cases the phallus is depicted with, or enclosed by, the yoni. The concept of sexuality as a means of pleasurable activity is, as is well known, deeply ingrained in Sanskrit writings. Much of the *Kama Sutra* is devoted to the discussion of how to maximize these aspects by insuring that the phallus and the yoni are mutually concordant by selecting mating couples on the basis of the proper dimensions of these parts.

I suggest, therefore, in the light of the evident parallels between the phallic and female elements of New England Celtic monuments on the one hand, and the Indian linga and yoni on the other, that it is not improbable that the secondary name of the Celtic Mother Goddess, "B-Y-N," should rather be read as something like *B'i-iannu,* meaning *She-of-the-Yoni,* or as a phrased epithet in apposition to her primary title, *Mother-of-Heroes, being She-of-the-Yoni.* By this suggested interpretation we would have, in effect, the aspect of the Mother Goddess that relates to the first sense of the root *bheug,* namely the pleasurable aspect of sex, as it was understood before the true role of the male had been discovered. But to the Celt of 800 B.C. with his religious thoughts stabilized once he had deserted the shores of Europe, the primary title of the Mother Goddess would be her first one, that expresses her motherly role.

Although the Celts of Britain and France have left us many sculptures depicting their gods as they envisaged them under the influence of Rome, we have very little from the earlier period before the *Pax Romana* came to the people of Gaul. Much the same comment may be made of the Celts of Spain, except that under Phoenician tutelage, numbers of rather crude or unintentionally humorous statues and paintings have come down to us from Iberian populations that may have been predominantly Celtic, though imitative in some degree of the higher civilization they perceived among their Punic neighbors. These Iberian Celts have given us Picassoesque pictures of themselves, but seemingly little in the way of visual realizations of their ideas on the gods of their pantheon.

This being so, it is astonishing to find that after only one season's activity in Vermont we have been able to identify at least one ceiling painting of Byanu. The goddess can be identified with absolute certainty because the painting was found in a medium-sized temple whose portals proclaimed (when John excavated them at my request) in very large, clear Ogam script, the word B-Y-N. But the very first glance at the ceiling figure (drawn to my attention by our Oklahoma colleague Gloria Farley, who was visiting the New England sites) disclosed that the divinity depicted is in fact none other than the Carthaginian goddess Tanith! Comparison of the illustrations (page 238) will make this clear. Tanith, in her strangely stylized and doll-like posture, is found wherever Punic influence penetrated. She is the Punic concept of the spouse of Baal, the Semitic sun god. Here we have clear evidence that the Celts of Iberia had

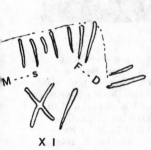

A critical clue whose decipherment led us to the Precincts of the Gods of Iargalon. Two portions of a three-part Celtic milestone found at South Woodstock, Vermont. In the upper photo the stem-line bisects the single stroke of the M to the left, then lies above the following staves till it curves down at the right-hand angle, so that the last two staves lie above the line. The inscription therefore reads M-S F-D, with XI on the button-shaped stone below. Interpreting this as *Mios fad, XI*, "Measure of distance, eleven (Celtic leagues or Roman miles?)", we instituted a search for another settlement at the indicated radial distance. Eventually John Williams located the ruined temples at the place apparently intended, lying at a distance of 10 miles (i.e., 11 Roman miles) from the milestone. From this area we went on to discover the Beltane Phallus, inscriptions to the Mother-Goddess, and ultimately to find the fallen statue of the Mother-Goddess herself. *Fell and Joseph D. Germano*

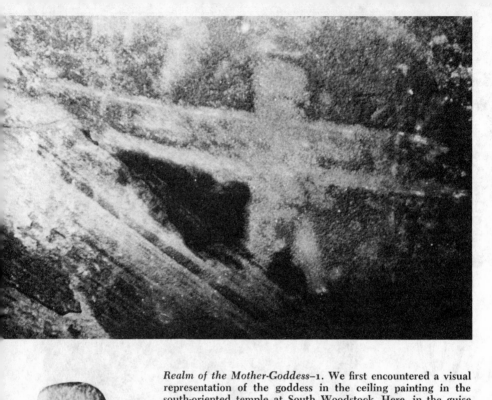

Realm of the Mother-Goddess–1. We first encountered a visual representation of the goddess in the ceiling painting in the south-oriented temple at South Woodstock. Here, in the guise of the doll-like Phoenician Tanith (as in the Iberian figurine, left), she spreads her arms like wings. On a buried portal of the same temple, John Williams and I uncovered her dedication in Celtic Ogam, reading (below, left to right) B-Ya-N, or Byanu. Ten miles further north we found ruins of another temple to the Mother-Goddess, again with Phoenician symbols and this time with her name expressed in Phoenician language, though in Ogam letters. *Top photo by Fell and Peter J. Garfall; bottom photo by Fell and Joseph D. Germano*

Realm of the Mother Goddess—2. Ten miles north of the temple of Byanu at South Woodstock, Vermont, signs of the Mother-Goddess reappeared on ruins of masonry, this time represented by a stylized Phoenician symbol of Tanith (above), and also her name T-N-D written in Ogam characters (below), both inscriptions on stones built into a dry-stone farm wall. Other inscriptions nearby gave the goddess's name in its Celtic form, Byanu, while a flat milestone informed us that we had now entered Ya-N-D D-Ya-D Ya-R-G-L-N, "The precincts of the Gods of Iargalon." *John Williams and Joseph D. Germano*

Realm of the Mother Goddess–3. At South Woodstock we found, on a hillside under birch and maples, a giant 2-ton female stone or yoni, carved in the form of the pelvic region of a woman. The inscription on a fallen phallus nearby told us that this object was known as "The Loins of Byanu." On various stones built into dry-stone farm walls within a few yards of the great yoni we found Ogam inscriptions that read (1) M-H M-B (Mahair-Mabona, or Mother of Heroes), shown above, left. (2) B-Ya-N (Byanu, or She-of-the-Yoni, Beanu, or Woman of European inscriptions, shown above, right. (3) S-Ya-M-M-Ya-M (in dedication), middle row. The part of the yoni stone where the female genital cleft is carved is shown in the lowest photograph. It appears from the presence of large phallic stones at this site that it was an open-air fertility precinct. No temple ruins occur nearby. *All photographs were taken by Peter J. Garfall, the inscriptions cast from materials collected on the site by Williams and Fell.*

Realm of the Mother Goddess—4. The appearance of sacred beasts, carved after the manner of the Iberian Celts, was a sign of the proximity of sacred precincts. The Sacred Boar (lower photo) was found by Fell near the Woodstock site. Some months later John Williams reached the Grotto of Venus, to find it guarded by a seated bull weighing about 160 pounds (top). *Peter J. Garfall and Fell*

Realm of the Mother Goddess–5. John led me to the new site to see the sitting bull he had found on the ledge, apparently unmoved since some hands placed it there over 2000 years ago. But before I had more than glimpsed the beast above, my eyes fell upon the sight we had never dared to expect—the torso of the great goddess herself lay stretched out among the pine needles, dappled by the play of autumn sunshine from the west. She lies there still, now buried beneath the snow of winter, carved from native New England schist by some unknown Celtic sculptor, now shattered in part by the frosts of centuries, discolored and overgrown by lichen, but beautiful despite the ravages of time. *Joseph D. Germano*

already absorbed much Carthaginian religion, having not only indulged in that favorite Greek habit of equating foreign gods and goddesses with native-grown divinities, but also accepted the foreign notion of how the divinity appeared.

When account is taken of the foregoing arguments, it is not to be wondered at that the Tanith of South Woodstock shares her ceiling with a conspicuous but lightly engraved phallus, with the usual exaggeration of the length of the penis that characterizes many of the Vermont phalli.

Tanith appears in two guises on the Punic monuments of Carthage and the Mediterranean areas where the Carthaginians penetrated. In one form she has her arms spread outwards as if flying, and the South Woodstock version shows her thus, the arms looking like angel's wings. Since the temple inscription is Celtic, and declares the structure to be dedicated to Byanu, I suppose we should call the ceiling figure *Byanu-Tanith,* and infer that this temple was visited by both Celts and Phoenician visitors from Tarshish who had sailed up the Connecticut River to trade in the Woodstock area. Curiously, Gloria Farley, who first set eyes on the Woodstock painting, is also the discoverer of another American Tanith, one

Realm of the Mother Goddess–6. We returned once more, with Joe Germano to record the find on film, and then left the goddess to sleep undisturbed. We called her Venus of the Snows. Next year, if our research resources should permit it, we plan to return with gear and manpower to bring her back to whatever museum may grant her shelter. It is our hope that the citizens of Vermont will establish a museum at South Woodstock, where these national treasures may be seen by all. *Fell, Joseph D. Germano, and John Williams*

carved on the Cimarron cliffs of the Oklahoma Panhandle. This southern example, identified in Iberian Punic script, is evidently not the work of Celts. It conforms to the second variety of Tanith figures, in which the arms are not wing-like, and some ritual objects are held in the right hand.

There remains another cult object that may be related to the worship of the Mother Goddess in her role as She-of-the-Yoni. This is a class of rock slab in which a circular opening has been cut, rather like the porthole of a ship. One of these strange holed-stones was dug up recently in the town of Derry, New Hampshire. The town fathers, deciding it was an object of local historic interest, have erected it in a conspicuous position on the town square.

In Chapter 14 I mentioned that there are two large phallic stones associated with the yoni-altar of Byanu at Woodstock, in the woods that now cover the lower slopes of the hill opposite the Stag Court. Each of these phalli carries an inscription directly related to the altar of Byanu, and therefore differing in character from the phalli described in the preceding chapter. One of these (page 224) is relatively long and slender, and carries an Ogam inscription that may be read as meaning "For the loins of Byanu." The other (page 228), shorter and with an exaggerated glans region, adds the words "To inseminate her vagina." Apart from the inscriptions they carry, whatever esoteric significance these may have is at present obscure.

Late in the 1975 season when I withdrew temporarily from field work to write this book, John Williams carried out exploration in the Royalton and Pomfret areas of Vermont, finding a number of interesting new sites to which he subsequently led me. One of these proved to be a secluded grotto on a steep hillside now covered by pine woods. The grotto, seemingly constructed originally in the form of a shelf dolmen, is now partly collapsed. On a ledge stands a petromantic beast weighing (we guess) about 160 pounds. By *petromantic* I mean a partly sculpted stone object evidently inspired by a natural free form that suggested an animal to the Celt who improved upon nature by reshaping the contours a little, though not so much as to make the resultant carving precisely identifiable. It remains innominate, a sacred beast, on guard, head thrust into the air, apparently unmoved since some unknown hands placed it there.

Fallen from the chamber of the grotto is a half-ton slab of stone, partly carved as a recumbent female torso, again petromantic, a form suggested by a natural stone that some early sculptor's hand has retouched to indicate the breasts, trunk and thighs of a reclining woman, now headless. This, we suppose, is also a representation of Byanu, not in her role as Mother of Heroes, but rather as the seductive bride of man. So we have called her dolmen the *Grotto of Venus*. Vandals have not as yet discovered her secluded bower, and we hope she may rest yet awhile longer in the forest, undisturbed until some museum may offer her safe refuge.

One day, during the Indian summer, we returned with Joseph Germano, who brought cameras to record the scene, and then withdrew, leaving her and her guardian beast to sleep on. So far as we can tell we three are the only visitors to the shrine in modern times. Filled with misgivings following vandalism of the Running Deer at Mystery Hill only a week before, we have felt constrained to withhold information on the position of the grotto.

Similar cult objects, sacred beasts and half-sculpted free-form petromanteia of Bel and unnamed gods are gathered into the safety of national museums in Portugal and Spain. There is an unfortunate dogma pervading some American museums, that no Europeans settled America prior to the Norsemen or Columbus, and this has deprived us of the means of rescuing the Celtic inheritance of this country.

We have asked Vermont citizens interested in the Celtic finds to form a committee to try to establish a museum for the safe repository of such objects. Until some action eventuates, it seems that they must be left to fend for themselves, as indeed they have these past twenty-five centuries.

LW

16

New England's Celtic Place Names

BY early October the fall was well advanced in the Green Mountains and the opening of the hunting season meant that it would no longer be safe to venture far from the beaten tracks, since any movement we might make in the underbrush would be likely to attract a rifle shot. I also had writing commitments to attend to, so John and I agreed to separate our efforts for the time being, he to roam the back-country roads to check on promising areas we had been considering for some time, myself to pound the typewriter.

However, we were pleased to receive a most cordial invitation from Professor Warren L. Cook of the Department of History and Anthropology at Castleton State College, inviting John and Peter and me to meet with his students for lectures and seminars on our finds. Several of his students had in fact called me or telephoned to offer their assistance as voluntary field parties, or in any other capacity in their power. Nothing could be more appropriate than to give the first college lectures on our work at Castleton, in the heart of the Celtic country. One beautiful fall day, therefore, we made the trip.

Our audience was enthusiastic and well prepared, asking many apposite questions and holding us until late in the afternoon. Jim Whittall and Bob Stone came too, and some of the local landowners were there. This chapter covers material included in one of the Castleton meetings, where I pointed out to my audience that they already knew many Celtic words.

When as a stranger to the land I first began, some twelve years past, to travel the country roads of New England, I was frequently amazed and amused by the extraordinary barbarity of such Amerindian place names as had somehow survived the onslaught of the colonists (who renamed almost every part they settled after some British hometown). Words such as *Umbagog* or *Squunq* conjured images of Neanderthal uncouthness, totally out of kilter with my own Polynesian background of euphonious words, often with a romantic connotation. What exiled Umbagogian could shed tears for Umbagog?

But I was mistaken. Modern Gaelic, preserving as it does many spelled letters that are no longer pronounced, looks considerably different if converted to a phonetic manner of writing. If, further, one allows for the ancient spelling or pronunciation of Gaulish, the ancestral tongue of the Celts, then many New England names assume a new aspect despite the quaint manner of transliteration used by the colonists in the days before Webster introduced a standard form of matching spelling to the spoken sound.

Take the name of the Amoskeag River, for example, where important archeological remains exist. When I first visited the site the name meant nothing to me and I assumed it to be Algonquian, but never thought to inquire if the name had a meaning. Indeed it has, as J. Almus Russell has pointed out in an article (1972) recently brought to my attention by my friend Gertrude Johnson. According to Russell, competent scholarship shows that the Algonquian sense of *Amoskeag* is "one who takes small fish." But no sooner had I seen this translation than I immediately recognized the word as the Celtic *Ammo-iasgag,* which means "small-fish stream." The Gaelic word for fish is *iasg* and the suffix *-ag* is the sign of the diminutive, giving the sense "small-fish." Evidently the main purport of the name was imparted to the Algonquian Indians by the Celts, but some details of the sense as well as the precise pronunciation have been blurred by the passage of time.

Alerted by this surprising coincidence of meaning and sound, I began to look at New England place names with a new and more critical eye, as often as not perceiving familiar Celtic words and phrases where formerly I had not. There was a time, not so long ago, when my heart leaped whenever John Williams took me across the border into Vermont, and I sensed the Celts all about me. But now I perceive their unseen presence all along the Merrimack valley, and the geographical names of New Hampshire and the other parts of New England are strung like a rosary whose beads tell of times long past. The Celtic presence is all-embracing, by no means confined within the borders of the Green Mountain state. Let me give just a short list by way of examples.

Look at the river names first, since we have already cited the Amoskeag. Bear in mind also that in Britain nearly all the river names are Celtic, even though now flowing through regions where Saxons have usurped the land these past fifteen hundred years. Here, as also there, Celtic names have a strangely enduring quality, and rivers, it would seem, tend to keep their old names despite the invasions of foreign conquerors.

Russell tells us that the Algonquian meaning of the river name *Ammonoosuc* is "small fishing river." But read it as *Am'-min-a-sugh* and you have the old Celtic roots that mean "small-river-for-taking-out-(fish)." Surely no coincidence! "Cohas Brook" and "Coos County" are both said to take their names from an Algonquian word meaning "pine tree." But *Cohas* is nearly the sound of the redundantly spelled Gaelic word *ghiuthas,* meaning "pine tree."

The Merrimack River has more than one Indian name. One of them is *Kaskaashadi,* which looks (and sounds) very much like the Gaelic phrase *'g-uisge-siadi,* meaning "with slow-flowing waters." No one now seems to remember the meaning of the Algonquian name, but I put my money on the inference that the Gaelic is the true explanation. And as for the other name of the same river, *Merrimack,* this sounds like the Gaelic words *mor-riomach,* meaning "of great depth," a pretty good match for Russell's Algonquian translation, which reads "deep fishing." The *Nashaway* River is recorded by Russell as meaning "land between." Could this not be a rather illiterate rendering of the Gaelic *naisg-uir,* meaning "land-connected"?

Then there is the *Piscataqua* River, said to mean "white stone." It seems very similar to the Gaelic *Pios-cata'-cua,* meaning "pieces of snow-white stone," presumably with reference to the white quartz abounding in the region. Then there is the *Seminenal* River, said to mean "grains of rock"; but *semen-aill* in Celtic would have the same meaning. And so we come to the *Umbagog* River—said by Russell to mean (rather cryptically) "shallow great waters near another." Here I admit defeat, finding no Celtic roots in any way related to such a sense. So we assign that name to another nation and another tongue. Who knows, perhaps the Celts, too, found the name endearingly ridiculous, and carefully preserved it as an antique curiosity from Stone Age times.

Earlier in this book I have noted that the name *Quechee* matches the Gaelic *Cuithe,* meaning "pit" or "chasm," a feature for which Quechee is famed, some 162 feet deep; and the river *Ottauquechee* flowing through the gorge may be read as *Otha-Cuithe,* "the Waters-of-the-Gorge" (and probably pronounced in ancient times more like the Algonquian version than is the modern Gaelic with its aspirated t's suppressed).

The *Cabassauk* River is said to mean in Algonquian "place-of-sturgeon." The sturgeon, unfortunately, has fallen victim to environmental deterioration, but those few readers who may be familiar with the fish will recognize the epithet "gap-toothed" as being appropriate to the appearance of the large tooth-like scales in several rows, separated by large gaps. In Gaelic *Cabach* means "gap-toothed," and the residual *-sauk* of the Algonquian name parallels the Gaelic *-sugh,* meaning "a place-for-taking-out"—thus, fishing for sturgeon.

The names of mountains in Britain frequently are corruptions of old Celtic names, and the same is true of New England. *Attilah* Mountain is said to mean "blueberries"; this seems to be meant for *aiteal,* a Gaelic word nowadays used for "juniper (berries)." *Munt* Hill is said to mean "people" (Indians) and the Gaelic word *muintear* means "people" also. *Monad,* which is Algonquian, and *monadh,* which is Gaelic, both mean "mountain," and appear in mountain names therefore. So does *Kan-* (matching the British *Kin-,* and the Gaelic *Ceann-*), all of them prefixed to names of peaks and headlands. *Cnoc,* a Gaelic word for "hill" or rocky outcrop, seems to be matched by the New England suffix *-nock,* found in the names of hills and mountains. Another Algonquian name used for mountains is *Wadjak,* though its real meaning is "on top"; but that is also the meaning of the Gaelic *uachdar,* seemingly the same or a related word.

In Scotland and in the Hebrides, conical hills (especially if paired) are frequently known by English names such as the Paps (of whatever), seemingly a relic of Bronze Age times when such features were attributed to the Earth Mother. In New Hampshire we have the mountains called *Uncanoonucks,* translated from the Algonquian as meaning "Woman's breasts." The equivalent in Gaelic would be Uchd-nan-Ugan, of which the geographical name appears to be a corruption. Our forefathers also attributed to tall cylindrical rocks a comparable name, such as the Phallus-of-Kupe, but I have not as yet noticed any Celtic equivalent in New England, though it is doubtless to be found.

Cowissewaschook is an Algonquian mountain name in New Hampshire said to mean "proud peak"; it is evidently derived from *Cuiseach-stuc,* which is Gaelic for the same meaning. Similarly the name *Kearsage,* also used for this peak, means "sharp-pointed," matching the Gaelic *Cuimsich* with the same meaning.

Then there are the names of places that do not always relate to the geography. For example, *Saco,* meaning "south side," matched by the Gaelic *seach* and the Latin *siccus,* both meaning "dry," a quality appropriate to a district where the rain and the snow commonly sweep in on the north wind. *Ponemah* is an Algonquian place name meaning "resting-place"; it seems to derive from the Gaelic *bonn-a-muigh,* meaning a "permanent resting place."

Monomonock Lake is said to mean "island" or "lookout place." It seems to match the Gaelic *Moine-manadh-ach,* meaning a "boggy-lookout-place." *Pontanipo* Pond is said to mean "cold water" in Algonquian, but the same sense is given by the Gaelic *Punntaine-pol* (literally, "numbing-cold-pool"). The Algonquian name *Natukko* is said by Russell to mean "cleared place," and the same sense is given by the Gaelic *Neo-tugha*, meaning "not-covered" (by vegetation). *Asquam* Lake is said to mean "pleasant-watering-place," and if this corresponds to Gaelic *Uisge-amail*, then the sense would be "seasonable-waters."

Enough has been given here to illustrate the subject, and to continue indefinitely would become tedious. If you would like to study the subject of geographical place names further, in this Celtic context, you might find the following books useful: *Macalpine's Pronouncing Gaelic Dictionary* and one of the Algonquian dictionaries published by the U.S. Bureau of Ethnology. A member of the Epigraphic Society, John Philip Cohane, is preparing materials for *Maps of Prehistoric Place-Names*. Another worker in this field is Professor Norman Totten, Bentley College, Waltham, Massachusetts, who will be glad to learn of studies in progress or completed.

17

The Egyptian Presence

THIS chapter sets out newly recognized evidence showing clearly that ancient Egyptians once visited North America and, while here, imparted a detailed knowledge of their complicated hieroglyphic writing to the people who lived in Canada and the United States at that era. The evidence is extraordinarily rich in variety and amount, and perhaps one of the more surprising things is that no one until now seems to have noticed it.

My opportunity to study it came about mainly through sleuthing by John Williams. After the ground froze in New England, John began a lengthy search of the documents stored in the great Widener Library of Harvard College. He was seeking out references in earlier reports of excavations that might lead us to find new sites to explore, or to museums where material of significance to our studies might be stored. In the course of this inquiry he consulted works in the Indian languages. One day John brought me a copy of a curious document printed in New York in 1866, and included in a book on the Wabanaki Indians of Maine written by Eugene Vetromile, a priest who ministered to the Indians. This document, comprising a single sheet, was headed *The Lord's Prayer in Micmac Hieroglyphs*. At first glance I perceived that about half (at least) of the hieroglyphic signs were remarkably similar to Egyptian hieroglyphs as rendered in the simpler cursive form called *hieratic*. But what was more surprising, indeed mystifying, was that the meanings of these signs in Egyptian matched the meaning assigned to them in the English transcript of the Micmac text given on the document. Now, I had read in standard works on the American Indians that certain tribes in the northeast make use of a hieroglyphic writing system "invented by missionary priests who found it easier to teach the Indians by using hieroglyphic signs." But that did not accord with the evidence now before me, for this seemed to show that someone familiar with the Egyptian hieroglyphic system had contrived the Micmac writing.

a. Micmac:

b. Egyptian:

The Exalted One (God) | Heaven | his dwelling | is. | Anything at all | he can create.

a.

b.

Foreign-men's | idols | of silver | and | gold | by | men | are created.

a.

b.

Mouths they have, | not | speaking. | They have | eyes, | not | seeing.

a.

b.

Ears they have, | not | hearing. (experiencing) | Noses ("breathers") | they have, | not | for the air.

Parallel versions of part of Psalm 116, *Non nobis Domine*. Micmac hieroglyphs in the upper lines, as composed by the Abbé Maillard circa 1738; and an Egyptian rendering in the lower lines.

Meaning	Micmac	Ancient Egyptian		Meaning	Micmac	Ancient Egyptian
name				men		
mountains				ram, sheep		
metal				mouth		
silver				1. to walk, go 2. det. for motion		
gold				flowing		
stone				to become		
sand, dust				and, also		
sea, lake				out of, from		
river				them, their to them		
to be like				I, my, me		
idols				thou, thee		

Examples of Micmac and ancient Egyptian hieroglyphs of similar form and meaning. Whereas the Micmac hieroglyphs were already in use before 1738, when the Abbé Maillard adopted them for his *Manuel Hieroglyphique Micmac*, the ancient Egyptian equivalent signs were not deciphered until 1823, when Champollion published his first paper on the Rosetta stone. Ideograms in the above table include evidence that the ancestors of the Micmac people were familiar with metals, and employed the same hieroglyphs for silver and for gold as were used by the ancient Egyptians.

Meaning	Micmac	Ancient Egyptian	Meaning	Micmac	Ancient Egyptian
reed, grass			today, now		
to keep safe, preserve			water, rain		
Greetings! Hi!			dwelling, sanctuary		
shining, glory			Earth, lower world		
rock-slab			heaven		
not			burn to ashes		
make an offering			fire		
tremble, earthquake			to skip about, leap		
come in haste			faults, sins		
full, all			fruit		

Some more examples of closely comparable Micmac and Ancient Egyptain hieroglyphs, the former all taken from the Micmac manuscript begun by the Abbé Maillard in 1738 and continued until his death in Nova Scotia in 1762. A preliminary study suggests that several thousand of the Micmac hieroglyphs are derived from Egyptian models. As the modern decipherment of Egyptian began only in 1797, when Zoega deduced the meaning "name" for the cartouche sign, it is evident that the Micmac hieroglyphs must already have been transmitted to North America more than 2000 years ago, when they were still in use in Egypt.

The Micmac are a tribe of Algonquian Indians inhabiting Acadia, the eastern provinces of Canada, and they are closely related to various tribes of Maine commonly called the Wabanaki, or *Men-of-the-East*. Reference to Schoolcraft's great work on the American Indians showed that he reported to Congress in 1851 that "reading and writing are altogether unknown to them" (i.e., to the Algonquian Indians). This statement, combined with a recorded claim by an eighteenth-century French priest, Pierre Maillard, that he personally invented the Micmac hieroglyphs, seemed to establish the reputed modernity of the writing system. Had Maillard, then, studied Egyptian hieroglyphs in order to invent his Micmac system? A check on dates soon showed that this would be impossible, for Maillard died in 1762, 61 years before Champollion published his first decipherment of the Egyptian hieroglyphics. Any resemblance between his system and that of the Egyptians would have to be due to pure chance. So I asked John to look for more examples of Micmac writing, if these could be located in the Widener Library or elsewhere. He soon came upon a copy of a 450-page book in Micmac hieroglyphs, the work of Father Maillard, containing much of the Catholic order of the Mass, a catechism, a religious history, and translations of psalms and hymns. This was printed in Vienna during the years 1863–1866 from original manuscripts bequeathed by Father Maillard to the Micmac Indians at the time of his death in 1762. It proved to contain hundreds of different hieroglyphic signs, a considerable proportion of which are clearly derived from, or even identical with, ancient Egyptian hieroglyphs or their hieratic equivalents. Examples of the writing and its Egyptian counterpart are shown in the tables accompanying this chapter.

As was now quite obvious, the Micmac writing system (and also part of their language) is derived from ancient Egyptian. But how could this be? Surely Maillard could not have secretly deciphered the Egyptian language himself; besides, he is not known ever to have traveled to Egypt or to have been involved in any activity beyond that of the devoted care of his Indian flock, who lovingly preserved his manuscripts for 120 years. So we now had the makings of another first-class mystery. At John's earnest request on my behalf, the librarians at Harvard began to make available to us all relevant books on the Micmac and Wabanaki Indians. From some of these (listed in the bibliography at the end of this book) I now learned the truth of the matter.

It turns out (on the evidence of Father Maillard's contemporaries and successors) that he did not really invent the writing system but, instead, he borrowed and adapted a system of writing *already in use* among the Indians at the time when Cardinal Richelieu first dispatched French missionaries to work among the Canadian Indians. From various deposi-

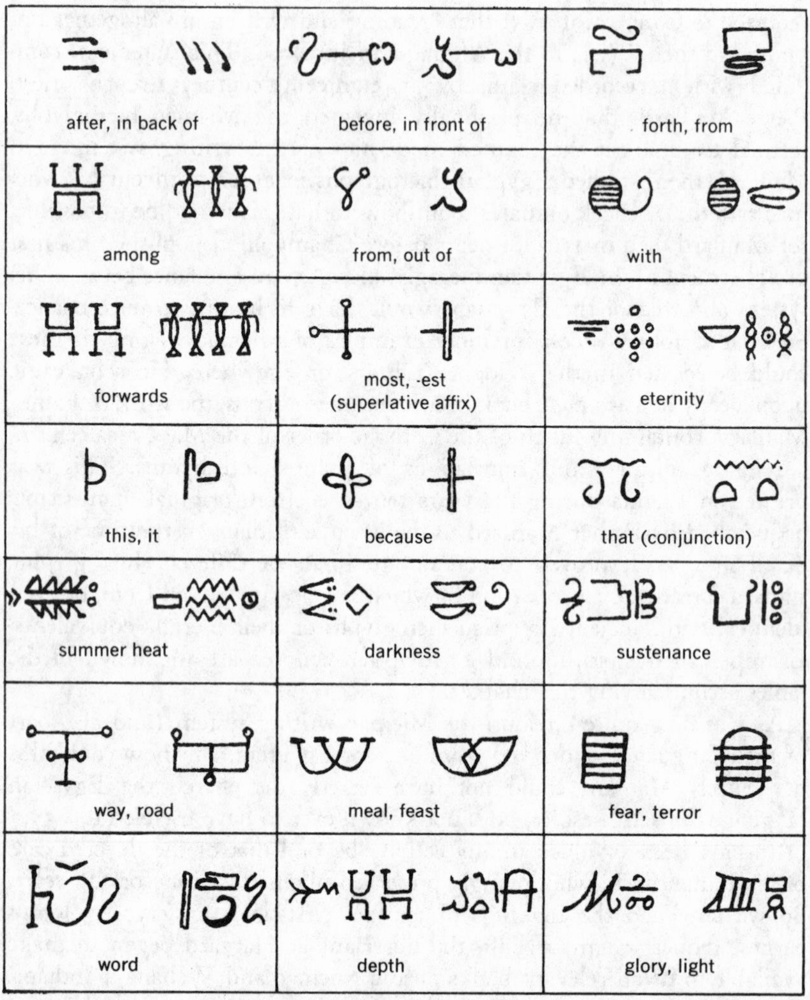

after, in back of	before, in front of	forth, from
among	from, out of	with
forwards	most, -est (superlative affix)	eternity
this, it	because	that (conjunction)
summer heat	darkness	sustenance
way, road	meal, feast	fear, terror
word	depth	glory, light

Words such as prepositions, adverbs, conjunctions, and other words that have no obvious representation by natural objects can only be rendered by purely arbitrary ideograms. The striking parallels between the Micmac and the Ancient Egyptian signs for these add convincing proof that the North American and Egyptian writing systems are directly related. In the above pairs, the Micmac sign is shown to the left, and the Egyptian to the right, both signs of every pair having the same meaning. Other unremarkable parallels are seen in the cross-signs, which share the identical yet unrelated meanings *because* and *most*.

tions made by authorities listed in the bibliography (section 9, page 304) it is clear that when the first Christian instruction was given to the Micmacs, the French priests noticed that some children appeared to be making signs on birchbark while the priests were preaching. When questioned later, the children explained that they were recording some of the statements. They explained that a five-pointed star represents heaven, and a circle represents the earth, and so forth.

Father Eugene Vetromile (1866) relates the same of the Wabanaki Indians among whom he worked in Maine, and his account, the most illuminating, may be taken as applying evidently to the Micmacs. It is as follows, and his statements are supported by other missionaries, notably by the Rt. Rev. Bishop Colin F. MacKinnon, Bishop of Arichat, and a leading authority on the Micmac Indians.

When the French first arrived in Acadia, the Indians used to write on bark, trees, and stones, engraving signs with arrows, sharp stones, or other instruments. They were accustomed to send pieces of bark, marked with these signs, to other Indians of other tribes, and to receive back answers written in the same manner, just as we do with letters and notes. Their chiefs used to send circulars, made in the same manner, to all their men in time of war to ask their advice, and to give directions.

From this evidence it is clear that we have for long been mistaken in thinking of the Micmac writing system as a modern invention, and hence unworthy of serious study by any epigrapher interested in the history of writing systems in ancient times. Father Vetromile goes on to say that he has in his personal possession three manuscripts in the Micmac hieroglyphic style. This was, of course, in 1866, and so far I have been unable to trace the present whereabouts of his manuscripts, two of which, he says, were written by Indians. Vetromile also states:

Several Indians possessed (in the time of the first French missions) in their wigwams a kind of library, composed of stones and of pieces of bark, and the medicine men had large manuscripts of these peculiar characters, which they read over the sick persons. . . . The Indians assert that by these signs they could express any idea with every modification, just as we do with our writings. When the French missionaries arrived in this country they made use of these signs, as they found them, in order to instruct the Indians. Fathers Mainard [sic, Maillard is doubtless intended] and Le Loutre improved them, and others were added in order to express the doctrine and mysteries of the Christian religion.

Father Vetromile records that similar writing was employed by all the northern Algonquian tribes, the Micmacs, the Wabanakis, and the Etchemis of northern New England included. He says that he has met older people among the Indians at Oldtown, Maine, who remember a time when the writing was inscribed vertically, and also horizontally (as today) but in either direction. He adds:

I hope that this kind of writing will not be suffered to be buried in silence amongst the ruins of time, but that the memory of this kind of scripture shall be transmitted to future ages, to show the antiquity and education of the noble and gentle but ill-fated Abnaki.

Thanks to the resilience of the Indians of Acadia, the Micmacs in particular, and thanks also to the actions taken by the French missionaries, Father Vetromile's wish has been fulfilled. It is now our task to investigate the probable manner in which Egyptian writing came to the northern Algonquian tribes.

The first question that occurs is: "Are the Micmac and related Algonquians the descendants of ancient settlers from Egypt?" The answer is certainly "No." For their language is Algonquian. However, a limited but recognizable Egyptian vocabulary is present, suggestive of contacts with Egyptian or Libyan speakers from whom these words could have been acquired as loan elements, at the same time as the writing system was acquired.

Is the writing system an ancient acquisition of the Algonquians? Here the answer is apparently yes; for the various Algonquian tongues, especially those of the northern tribes, are rich in vocabulary connected with writing and writing implements and materials. These words are dissimilar to French and English words for writing, but sometimes quite similar to Egyptian words for these ideas. An extensive list of words of this category appears in the oldest Wabanaki dictionary, that prepared in Maine by Father Sebastien Rasles (whose missionary work began in 1690). The original manuscript of Rasles' *Dictionnaire* is preserved in Harvard College Library, its opening passage showing that he began to compile it in 1691; he was still working on it when he was killed by British soldiers in 1724, during the attack on Oldtown, Maine, where his monument now stands. Rasles, too, was familiar with the hieroglyphic writing system, though he did not make use of it.

While pondering how to determine the antiquity of Egyptian writing in the Americas I naturally spoke of these remarkable facts to my various colleagues. One of them, James Whittall, learned from another archeologist that there are relics of Father Rasles in private ownership in Massachusetts, these including bronze artifacts of the Wabanaki, and also that some birchbark manuscripts are in existence in at least one collection. These facts we have not yet had time to investigate, but luckily John Williams came upon one telling piece of evidence reported in the scien-

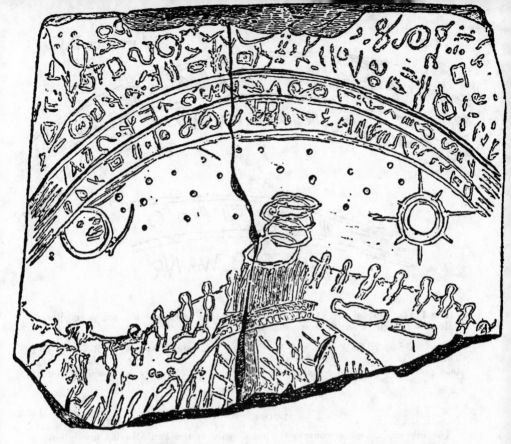

The Davenport Calendar stele, found in a burial mound in Iowa in 1874 by the Reverend M. Gass, together with numerous other artifacts of North African and Iberian origin or relationship. This inscription is written in three languages, Egyptian hieroglyphs at the top, then Iberan-Punic from right to left along the upper arc, and Libyan from right to left along the lower arc. The Libyan and Iberian-Punic inscriptions say the same thing, namely that the upper hieroglyphs contain the secret of how to regulate the calendar. The hieroglyphs give this information by indicating that a ray of light falls upon a stone called the "Watcher" at the moment of sunrise on New Year's Day, which is defined as the spring equinox in March, when the sun passes the first point of Aries. This stele, for long condemned as a meaningless forgery, is in fact one of the most important steles ever discovered, for it is the only one on which occurs a trilingual text in the Egyptian, Iberian-Punic, and Libyan languages. It is in the Putnam Museum, Davenport, Iowa, the repository of other pricless national treasures found by Gass. (From S. D. Peet, *The Mound Builders*, 1892.)

tific literature of the 1870s. This evidence comes from a distance of some 1,500 miles from New England, from the prairies of Iowa.

One day in 1874 a Reverend M. Gass, assisted by two students, was engaged in opening a small burial mound near Davenport, Iowa. Near the surface they found an intrusive Indian burial of obviously modern date but, as they descended deeper into the mound they began to uncover

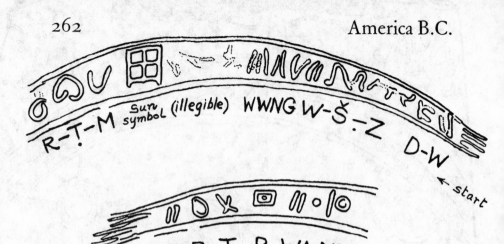

The Libyan text of the Davenport stele from the Iowa mounds, see page 261. Read from right to left the inscription is as follows:

W-D	Z-S	W-W	G-N-W-T	....	Sun sign	M-T-R	R-N	W-A
The	is	around	with a	(illeg-		It	the	the
stone	inscribed		record	ible)		reveals	naming,	length,

		B	T-R-W	
		the	of the	
		placing	seasons.	

The Libyan inscription conveys the same sense as the Punic-Iberian inscription that occupies the other arc, immediately above the Libyan arc. Vowels are omitted from ancient inscriptions. A fuller account of the decipherment, with dictionary references to the words, may be found in the *Occasional Publications* of the Epigraphic Society, vol. 3, 1976. The checkerboard sun symbol is the same as is seen on the equinoctial calendar temple near South Royalton, Vermont (see page 55), and it is possible, therefore, that this symbol has a special reference to the use of the sun as a calendar regulator. On one of the inscriptions at Cachão da Rapa, in Portugal, the same sun symbol is set beside Ogam letters that spell the Libyan word Ra (Sun), see page 70.

the skeletons of the persons for whom the mound had initially been raised. There were two adult skeletons, and a third skeleton of a child placed between them. Nearby they found an engraved tablet, now known as the Davenport Calendar Stele. This was extensively engraved with strange signs (page 261) and came into the ownership of the Davenport Academy of Science, now the Putnam Museum. It aroused much interest at the time. Later it was all but forgotten, for scholars at Harvard and the Smithsonian Institution declared it to be a forgery. The main grounds for this opinion were that the writing could not be·read by anyone, that it contained some letters resembling the letter O, and the numeral 8, together

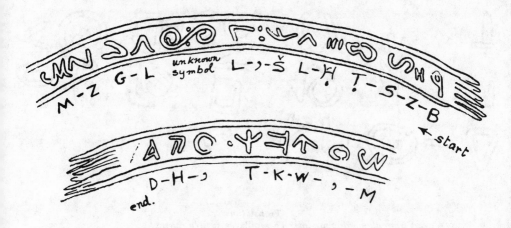

The Punic-Iberian text of the Davenport stele from the Iowa mounds, see page 261. Read from right to left the inscription is as follows:

B-Z-S-Ṭ	Ḥ-L	S-i-L	(sign)	L-G	Z-M	(M)-i-W-K-T	i-H-D
Set out	Around (this)	(is) a secret	(secret sign)	text	defining	the seasons'	delimiting.

The Punic-Iberian inscription conveys the same sense as the Libyan inscription placed beside it (see page 262). Neither the Libyan nor the Punic-Iberian scripts had been deciphered at the time when the Davenport stele was unearthed in 1874, yet both texts yield intelligible and mutually consistent readings, the words being all found in standard dictionaries (see *Occasional Publications*, vol. 3, Epigraphic Society, for details). These facts show that the stele cannot possibly be a forgery as has mistakenly been believed since 1890, when an archeologist at the Smithsonian Institution declared the inscriptions to be a meaningless jumble of signs based on the English alphabet. No one appears to have noticed the Egyptian part of the inscription which could have been translated at that date. Fortunately the Davenport Academy preserved the stele, together with the associated artifacts, now seen to be of North African and Iberian provenance.

with at least one N and one F, and some signs resembling Hebrew and others resembling Phoenician. For these reasons the stone was considered to be a worthless and meaningless fake! Luckily the Davenport Academy preserved the stone, in spite of various claims that it is a forgery.

I give in this chapter and in the diagrams (pages 262-265) the various parts of the inscription and their decipherment. They are based on my study of the published illustration of one face, which John found in one of the contemporary reports held in the Harvard Library. Our colleagues of the Early Site Research Society, now that they are apprised of its importance are taking steps to have photographs of it and of

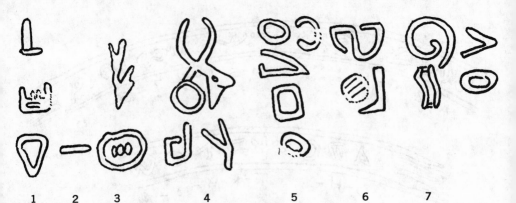

1   2   3   4   5   6   7

Translation

1. *Read from above downwards:* To a pillar/attach/a mirror/
2. /so that/
3. *Read from above downwards:* /at New/Year/
4. *Read from above downwards:* /the sun being in conjunction with the Ram/ in its house (i.e., zodiacal constellation)/
5. *Read from above downwards:* /at the tilting of the balance (i.e., of night and day, the equinox)/in the Spring/
6. /the Festival/
7. /of celebration of the First of the Year/

Phonetic rendering

1. t-h-n m-n-i o-n-h   2. r   3. r-n-p w-p-t-r-n-p-t
4. Re-S-b-i p-r S-b-i   5. r-kh-w P-r   6. h-b   7. w-p-pt.

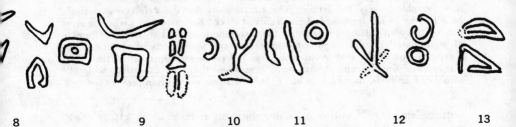

8   9   10   11   12   13

Translation

8. /and religious rites of the New Year/
9. /are to take place/
10. /(when) The Watcher/
11. /stone/
12. /at sunrise/
13. /is illuminated/

Phonetic rendering

8. Rn-n-pt   9. kh-pr   10. w-rs   11. i-n-r   12. dw-w   13. t-k.

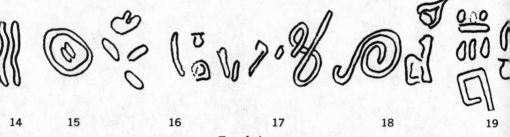

14   15   16   17   18   19

Translation

14. /by/
15. /the sun./
16. /(signed) Star-watcher/
17. /Priest/
18. /of Osiris/
19. /of the Libyan region/.

Phonetic rendering

14. i-n   15. Re   16. w-n-t-y   17. ntr-nmh
18. W-sir   19. Th-n-w w.

other inscribed stones sent to us for study. So far as can be determined at present, one side of the Davenport stele gives the following remarkable information.

In the middle of the stele is an engraved scene, and around it are inscriptions in three languages, namely Egyptian, Iberian Punic, and Libyan, each in its appropriate alphabet or hieroglyphic character. The Iberian and Libyan texts, written on engraved scrolls, each report that the stone carries an inscription that gives the secret of regulating the calendar. These parts of the inscription and their alphabets are shown on pages 262 and 263. The remainder of the inscription is in Egyptian hieratic hieroglyphs, and the details of the decipherment are shown here and on the opposite page. The Egyptian text, given literally in the captions, may be rendered into English as follows:

To a pillar attach a mirror in such manner that when the sun rises on New Year's day it will cast a reflection on to the stone called "The Watcher." New Year's day occurs when the sun is in conjunction with the zodiacal constellation Aries, in the House of the Ram, the balance of night and day being about to reverse. At this time (the spring equinox) hold the Festival of the New Year, and the Religious Rite of the New Year.

The tablet carries an engraving which depicts the Egyptian celebration of the New Year on the morning of the March equinox (corresponding to the modern date March 21, but later in March in ancient times). This

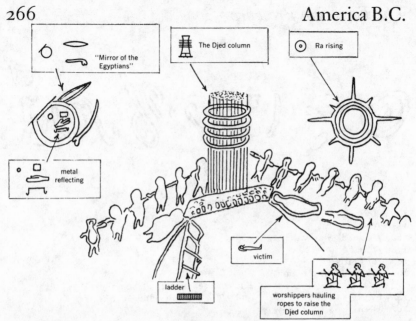

The Djed Festival of Osiris as celebrated in Iowa around 700 B.C. Explanation of
the scene depicted on the Davenport stele, the hieroglyphs incorporated into the
picture being here translated, and also rendered in the formal Palace style. The
Djed column, made of bundles of reeds encircled at the top by rings, represents
the backbone of Osiris, in whose honor the Djed column was erected each year
on the day of the spring equinox. This information, originally obtained by Adolf
Erman from a tomb inscription of the XVIII Dynasty in Thebes, Egypt, is here
completely confirmed by the inscription and illustration on the Davenport stele of
Iowa. The mirror of reflecting metal, shown to the left of the picture, relates to
the Egyptian text of the stele, which instructs the reader to attach a mirror to a
column in such a way that the rays of the rising sun, on the morning of the spring
equinox, will be reflected onto a signal stone called the "Watcher."

festival consists in the ceremonial erection, by parties of worshippers
pulling on ropes, of a special New Year Pillar called the Djed. It is made
of bundles of reeds, surmounted by four or five rings. It represents the
backbone of the god Osiris.

To the left is seen a carving of the mirror, and beside it are hieroglyphs
that read "Mirror of the Egyptians." On the mirror are hieroglyphs that
read "reflecting metal." To the right is the rising sun, with the hieroglyph
Ra (*Sun god* or *Sun*) written on the disk of the sun. Stars as seen in the
morning sky are above. As the caption on the illustration shows, the
Iowa stele confirms what we already know from evidence yielded by a
tomb in Thebes, about the ceremony of the Djed column on New Year's
day. The Egyptian record tells us that the ceremony occurred in *Koiakh,*
a word meaning the month of March, again confirming the statements on
the Iowa stele. The Egyptian text of the Davenport stele goes on to say

A recent photograph of the Djed Festival tablet, courtesy of the Putnam Museum, Davenport. The detail, here shown photographically enhanced by Malcolm Pearson, presents certain discrepancies from the original published engraving shown on page 261. In particular some letters appear to have been abraded from the area of the mirror, on the left. The suggested decipherment, given on page 266, is based on the engraving; it is possible that the inferred reading "Mirror of the Egyptians" and "Metal reflecting" may have to be discarded, but they are left on page 266 as a plausible interpretation of the now-lost signs.

that it is the work of *Wnty* (Star-watcher), a priest of Osiris in the Libyan regions.

How did this extraordinary document come to be in a mound burial in Iowa? Is it genuine? Certainly it is genuine, for neither the Libyan nor the Iberian scripts had been deciphered at the time Gass found the stone. The Libyan and Iberian texts are consistent with each other and with the hieroglyphic text. As to how it came to be in Iowa, some speculations may be made.

The stele appears to be of local American manufacture. Perhaps made by a Libyan or an Iberian astronomer who copied an older model brought from Egypt or more likely from Libya, hence probably brought on a Libyan ship. The Priest of Osiris may have issued the stone originally as a means of regulating the calendar in far distant lands. The date is unlikely to be earlier than about 800 B.C., for we do not know of Iberian or Libyan inscriptions earlier than that date. The Egyptian text, as stated above, may merely be a local American copy of some original. That original could be as old as about 1400 B.C., to judge by the writing style.

More, I think, should not be said at this time, for the subject is still under active study, and not all of the inscribed material from Davenport has yet been seen. But it seems clear that Iberian and Punic speakers were living in Iowa in the 9th century B.C., making use of a stone calendar regulator whose Egyptian hieroglyphs could apparently be read. The settlers had presumably sailed up the Mississippi River to colonize the Davenport area.

I would hazard the guess that the colonists first came on board ships commanded by a Libyan skipper of the Egyptian navy, during the 22nd or Libyan Dynasty, the pharaohs of which were energetic men who favored overseas exploration. With them probably came an Egyptian astronomer-priest. Either he, or his successors, engraved the Davenport Calendar Stele.

Probably around this time came other Egyptian astronomer-priests, accompanying other expeditions, such as that to Long Island, New York (page 270), and the Libyan voyagers who reached Quebec, to leave there the inscription found two years ago by Professor Thomas Lee of Laval University. These voyagers may well be the people who settled New England, teaching the ancestors of the Micmac and Wabanaki how to write Egyptian hieroglyphs. Since hieroglyphs are ideograms, and can be read (as ideas, not sounds) in any language, it would not be difficult for the learned Libyans or Egyptians to teach their fellow colonists and native Indians how to read and write hieroglyphs. With the passage of time the modern Algonquian language would come into existence (Chapter 18), and then the hieroglyphs would be pronounced as Algonquian.

As I close this chapter, then, my colleagues and I are actively seeking

meaning	formal or Palace style of Egypt	informal or hieratic style of Egypt	hieratic style of Iowa
the god Osiris			
the New Year Festival			
sunrise			
stone			
illuminated			
priest			
Star-watcher			

Examples illustrating the script styles employed in the formal hieroglyphic inscriptions of public monuments in ancient Egypt, the hieratic or informal script of ancient Egypt, and the hieratic style of the Davenport stele of Iowa. Use of the spiral sign in place of the chicken symbol for the sound W points to a date later than about 1400 B.C., and the presence of Iberian and Libyan script on the same stele probably brings the date to about 800–700 B.C. This would correspond to the XXII (Libyan) Dynasty of Egypt, at which epoch it is likely that Libyan Pharaohs would encourage distant voyages. The priest who inscribed the tablet, whose name seems to have been Star-watcher, probably accompanied a mainly Libyan expedition that established a colony in Iowa by sailing up the Mississippi River.

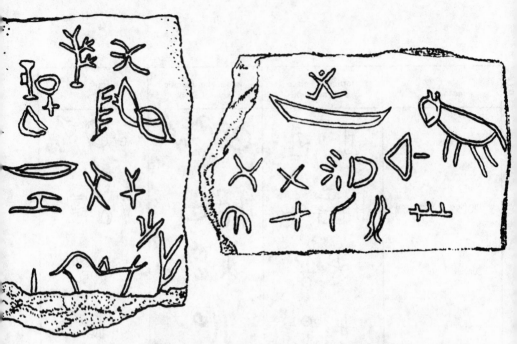

Bilingual Egypto-Libyan inscribed tablet in the Museum of the American Indian, New York, originally discovered about 1888 in a shell midden at Eagle Neck, Orient, at the eastern tip of Long Island. Until now it has been supposed to be an Indian petroglyph recording a hunting trip. It has never been considered spurious and, indeed, the Libyan inscription (right) which matches the Egyptian (left) could not have been forged, for Libyan was not deciphered until 1973. The tables on pages 271 and 272 give the comparative analysis of the elements of the script, which probably dates from about the ninth century B.C., though the actual tablet itself may be an Algonquian copy of the original (some of the Egyptian signs are written in the Micmac manner). The Egyptian text may be translated as "A ship's crew from Upper Egypt made this stele with respect to their Expedition." The Libyan text may be rendered as: "This ship is a vessel from the Egyptian Dominions," and is notable for employing one Egyptian hieroglyph (as the table on p. 272 explains). Details of the decipherment are given in the *Occasional Publications* vol. 3 of the Epigraphic Society. Features of the script suggest a connection with the Micmac hieroglyphic script, a fact which, taken together with the recent recognition of Egyptian vocabulary in the Micmac language, suggests that early visitors from Egypt during the Libyan (XXII) Dynasty may have traded with the Algonquians and taught these Indians how to use ideograms to express their own language in writing. *Drawn by Daniel A. Young, Heye Foundation, New York.*

Sound	Style of Tunisia and Numidia	Style of Libyan visitors to Long Island	Style of Libyan voyagers in Pacific (Ancient Maori)
d, ṭ	Ⴃ	Ո	Ⴖ
p	⊗	⊗	⊗
(e) t	+	+	+
t (a)	×	×	×
m	U ,)	く	C , U
h (i)	☰ , ||||	⋗	||| , Ⴭ , ✳
r	O , D , D	D	O , □
w	= , ||	ЛL	= , ||
3 (= a)	◁ , ▷	◁	unknown
s, z	—	—	—
Egyptian hieroglyph Dominions	𓏤𓏤𓏤𓏤	𓏤𓏤𓏤	unknown

Libyan alphabetic signs appearing on the tablet from Orient, New York, compared with other Libyan alphabets. The Libyan text of the tablet is given on page 270, with a translation. The phonetic rendering of the lower section of the tablet, left to right, is "ḍ-p-t T-m-i-r W-à-s" (vessel from Egyptian Dominions), and the top line reads "Ta d-p-ṭ" (this ship).

meaning	formal or palace style of Egypt	informal or hieratic style of Egypt	hieratic style of Long Island
crew isw – w – t			
South-Land (i.e., Upper Egypt) Rsw – t			
stele, engraved stone oho			
made i – iri			
relating to r – m			
expedition mso			

Explanation of the Egyptian words on the Orient, Long Island, tablet from New York, illustrated on page 270. The sign in the Long Island rendering of the second figure of a seated man in the word *expedition* differs from that of hieratic of Egypt, but matches the hieroglyph still used in modern Micmac hieroglyphic writing. This fact, together with the incongruous presence of two representations of animals (sea fowl and bear) on the tablet, suggests that this tablet is not the original stele, but rather an Algonquian Indian's copy of the original. The phonetic rendering of the hieroglyphs in the Egyptian language is given in the column on the left, but it is possible that the tablet was read as Micmac, for which the same Egyptian hieroglyphs can serve as a writing system.

This tablet, no. AR15339 in the Putnam Museum, Davenport, is the reverse face of the slate slab depicting the Djed Festival. The slate separated afterwards by cleavage, and each side has been imbedded in plaster, the writing delineated with talcum. A decipherment of the Micmac inscription is given separately on page 274. The scene depicted is the corresponding equinoctial Hunting Festival, held in September, six months after the Djed Festival, and marking the second half of the Celtic year. As the Egyptians did not divide the year in this manner, the tablet implies that Celtic characters were probably retained by the Algonquian culture even after their partial Egyptianization and replacement of Ogam script by Hieratic, which in turn became the Micmac script. As the inscription explains, the hunting scene in the foreground deals with the September butchery and smoking of young wildstock, including waterfowl and fish. The conserved portion of the wild fauna, labeled "Herds of the Lord," is shown left unmolested in the upper part of the picture. This engraving, by its writing style seen to be an American original, dating little earlier than 500 B.C. (and possibly as late as 100 A.D.), implies in turn that the Djed Festival scene on the March equinox face must also be an American production, probably by the same engraver; but the Djed scene, incorporating three different scripts, none of them Micmac, must have been imitated from an older original, probably brought to North America from Libya. *Putnam Museum, detail photographically intensified by Malcolm Pearson.*

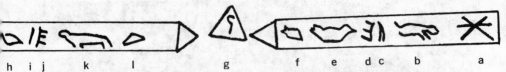

h　i　j　　　k　　l　　　　　　　g　　　　f　　e　　d c　　b　　　　　a

EARLIEST KNOWN EXAMPLE OF MICMAC SCRIPT. The inscription on tablet AR15339
in the Putnam Museum, Davenport, Iowa (The September Hunt), being the now-
separated reverse face of the slab depicting the Djed Festival of Osiris. Unlike
the Djed-Festival face, which is an Indian copy of an Egyptian original, this
reverse face is the original work of an Algonquian Indian, perhaps dating to about
2000 years ago. The inscription retains Egyptian features no longer exhibited by
modern Micmac writing for, as common on Egyptian decorative inscriptions, there
is a central item of interest, marked g above, and the reading direction is from
either side toward the center. Another Egyptian feature is that the animals face
into the reading direction, so the hieroglyphs of the two halves each face toward
the nearest edge, and appear as mirror images. The approximate translation is:
"Hunting (a) of beasts (b) and (c) their young (d), waterfowl (e) and fishes (f)."
"The herds of the Lord" (g, relating to the upper part of the tablet), "(h illegible) and (i) their young (j), the beasts (k) of the Lord (l)." See the illustration
of the tablet (page 273) for further explanation, and also compare the writing
with the modern example of Micmac shown below, where some similar hieroglyphs occur.

a　　　　　b　　　　c　　　　d　　　　e

f　　g　　　h　　　i　　　　j　　　　k

MODERN MICMAC FOR COMPARISON WITH THE DAVENPORT HUNT TABLET. This is a
facsimile of verse 4 of Psalm 113, In exitu Israel, as rendered in the Austrian edition of the Abbé Maillard's translation. It deals with the rolling back of the Red
Sea "when the mountains skipped like rams, and the little hills like young sheep."
It is here chosen for comparison with the Davenport Micmac text, as certain
features of the Davenport style are retained, while new features are introduced.
The literal translation is: "The mountains (a) skipped (b), likewise (c) the sea
(d) as beasts do (e), also (f) (g, untranslatable particle) the hills (h) as do (i) the
beasts' (j) young (k)." Note conversion of reading direction to L-R, though the
heads of the animals are now wrongly oriented by Egyptian rules; old Indian
residents of Maine in 1866 could still recall when the script was written both
vertically and horizontally in any direction. Note the retention of the characteristic Algonquian E-shaped sign meaning "young," an adaptation from a hieratic
form in which 3 horizontal signs represented the word "child" in Egyptian. The
duplication of the Child-sign here, the upward slope of the central bar of the E,
and reversal of the second E are merely idiosyncratic, the Austrian engravers
being quite inconsistent, and in most passages the sign is rendered with all bars
horizontal. The duplication is a sign of the plural (as in Egyptian), but here again
the texts are inconsistent. The general correspondence of the Micmac signs to
their Egyptian hieratic originals is obvious (see tables on pages 254–256).

(1)

(2)

LATER EVOLUTION OF THE MICMAC SCRIPT. The Vienna engravers produced a formalized, though often inaccurate, version of the manuscripts left by the Abbé Maillard. The upper text (1) is a facsimile of two lines of an isolated leaf of manuscript, *B.N. Américain 34,* collected in Nova Scotia from Micmac Indians, and now in the National Library of France, in Paris. Hitherto undeciphered, it may be identified as a portion of a homily on the eucharist written in the early eighteenth century by Maillard. The lower text (2) is a transcription of the same passage in the style of the Vienna engravers, and corresponding to lines 5 to 7 of page 37 of the 1921 edition of the *Sapeoig Oigatigen,* a Canadian reissue of the Vienna plates. Comparison of the two texts discloses that the Austrian engravers, often unable to formalize some cursive signs, would resort to using a somewhat similar but different sign. Thus in the modern texts we often find the same ideogram used for signs of widely different meaning. Conversely, in different versions of the same psalm or prayer an ideogram occasionally will be found with a totally incongruous meaning.

all relevant clues as to how the Egyptian language came to America. Our special quarries are old birchbark documents, engraved stones, and bronze artifacts from New England's suspected Egyptian and Libyan visitors, as well as further examples of ancient engraved steles from Iowa and neighboring regions.

We can now set the wonderful stone carvings of African animals, found in Iowa many years ago, in this developing picture, as the work of sculptors who came to America from North Africa. That carvings of elephants occur in the fields of Davenport need no longer be a mystery—they *must* be the work of the same people as those whose remarkable Calendar Stele we have just described.

Similarly the terra cotta and stone portraits of people with North African, Nubian, Phoenician, and Iberian features or clothing, now fall into place; for the states where they occur, such as Tennessee and Kentucky, are lands that border the Mississippi, where ancient colonists were accustomed to sail. There are still many pieces missing from the jigsaw puzzle, but at least now we perceive its nature and the manner of its ultimate solution. As the mound burials and the urns give up their honored dead I find no disrespect in such disinterments. For out of the dust of our remote predecessors there is now emerging a grand historical vista in which we perceive the wide range of ethnic stocks that contributed to the ancestry of the Amerindian peoples, and brought art and science to the New World. Now Egypt too is added to the tally.

18

The Algonquians

THE Algonquian nation comprises the most numerous and most widely dispersed linguistic group among the North American Amerindians. From the Montaignais of southern Labrador in the northeast they range Canada so far west as the Rocky Mountains. In the United States they once occupied the coastal Atlantic lands so far south as North Carolina, inland to Kentucky, skirting the Iroquois salient to the east as far north as Maine and Nova Scotia, and on the west as far north as Minnesota, where they join the Canadian Algonquian belt. Some fifty tribal dialects occur.

In the east of the country the Algonquians no longer occupy their old tribal territories, though large numbers must have intermarried with modern colonial settlers. Such integration was inevitable, for the old paintings show that the eastern Algonquians closely resemble southern European and Mediterranean people, and that when they donned European dress, they were scarcely to be distinguished from other settlers. Towards the west of their range a more Mongolian aspect is evident, and were we oblivious of every other detail of their history, we might well suppose that the western Algonquian tribes have a higher proportion of Asiatic ancestry. This is consistent with their proximity to the region from which Asiatic immigration might be expected to occur; and by the same tokens we might suppose that the eastern Algonquians have somehow acquired a European cast of features by some ancient immigration from Europe.

In this chapter I discuss the origin of the Algonquians in the light of three main sources of evidence, namely (1) What their own traditions have to say on their origin and ancestry, (2) What evidence is provided by the archeological remains so far explored, and (3) What evidence is yielded by the modern spoken dialects of Algonquian.

Meaning	Micmac	Egyptian
sun-grid (sign found on lintels of sun temples of New England)	Atna-kuna "checkerboard"	i – tn k – n "chessboard of the Aton"
sun, same word also used for moon	kisus	k-o-h-w s-s-w "radiant disk"
to rise (used of the sun)	waban	w-b-n
eclipse, to be eclipsed	sokwet	s-k-t-t "night-bark of the sun"
sky, vault of heaven	muskun	m-s-kh-n "abode of the gods"
Heaven, abode of God	Wajok	W-a-dj-y-t "Abode of Amen-Ra"
east, sunrise	abn	i-a-b
circle	oweaoo	O-w-o-w
copper artifact	soom-alke	soom-alikt (Coptic)
numeral prefix	tan-	t-n-w-
star	wata	(Libyan w-t, Maori whetu)
elapsed time, the past	sak	s-k-i
midpoint, balanced midway	akta	a-k-a-y-t
half full, to mid capacity	akta-bak	a-k-a-y-t b-a-kh
summer, summer heat	nipk	n-b-i-b-i
midsummer	akta – nipk	a-k-a-y-t n-b-i-b-i

The Micmac language has evidently acquired much of its technical and astronomical vocabulary from ancient Egyptian, as this comparative table illustrates. The ideas listed in the left-hand column in the English language are expressed in the Micmac language by the words given in the middle column (compiled from vocabularies given by Chief Sozap Lolo Kizitogw in 1884 and by Dr. Silas T. Rand in 1902). In the right-hand column are the matching words in ancient Egyptian, taken from Professor Raymond O. Faulkner's Dictionary, 1972. Some of the Egyptian words require explanation. The checkerboard sign is part of the hieroglyphic rendering (called the determinative) of the expression "checkerboard of the Aton," the Aton being the deified disk of the sun. Why a checkerboard should be associated with the Aton is not clear, but the Micmac word atnakuna implies this connection, as also has been inferred (chapter 6) from other evidence. The "night-bark of the sun" in Egyptian religion was supposed to carry the sun at night, when the sun was invisible, hence the association with an eclipse is logical. Amen-Ra, the Sun-god himself, was assigned to the highest heaven during periods in Egyptian history when sun worship was predominant (as during the Libyan XXII Dynasty, when visits to North America evidently occurred). The root *wata* for star is at present known only from Libyan and Polynesian contexts. Officers of the Egyptian navy were required to be skilled scribes, the highest ranks being reserved for holders of the degree of First Class Scribe; hence the transfer of Egyptian and Libyan hieroglyphic skills, as well as actual vocabulary, could be expected during voyages of exploration along the North American coasts.

I. TRADITIONS

It is both common sense and courtesy to listen first to what the Algonquian peoples themselves have reported to early investigators. These seem first to have been made public by John Johnston, an agent of the Shawnee tribe, in the year 1819 in a letter dated July 7 and subsequently reprinted in the first volume of *Archaeologia Americana* (page 273), and later still reprinted by Schoolcraft in 1851 in his *Indian Tribes of North America*. Johnston wrote:

The people of this nation have a tradition that their ancestors crossed the sea. They are the only tribe with which I am acquainted which admit to a foreign origin. Until lately [i.e., 1819] they kept yearly sacrifices for their safe arrival in this country. From where they came, or at what period they arrived in America, they do not know.

It is perhaps also significant that the Algonquians had retained a tradition, still alive when Johnston made his written report, that there were other foreign people in America too, in former times. Johnston says, on this point, that the Algonquians informed him as follows:

It is a prevailing opinion among them that Florida had been inhabited by white people, who had the use of iron tools. Blackhoof [a celebrated chief] affirms that he has often heard it spoken of by old people, that stumps of trees, covered with earth, were frequently found, which had been cut down by edged tools.

These traditions of the Algonquian people deserve serious consideration.

Also warranting careful consideration is another tradition concerning the names assigned to certain stars. The constellation of the Great Bear was distinguished by various Mediterranean peoples of the Bronze Age, among them the Greeks, who called it by the name *Arctos,* and the Romans, who called it *Ursa Major,* both names signifying Bear, though there is nothing about the stars of the group to suggest why they were given that name. Whether Celts or Iberians or any other European or Mediterranean nation may have carried this traditional designation to America we cannot at present tell, but it is a fact that when Cotton Mather inquired of the Natick Indians in Boston as to what knowledge they had of the motions of the stars, he wrote (in a letter addressed to the Royal Society, London, in 1696): "It has been surprising unto me to find that they have always called Charles' Wain by the name *Paukunnawaw,* or The Bear, which is the name whereby Europeans also have distinguished it."

In the Micmac dialect of Algonquian the word used for bear is *mooeen,*

Antiphona.

Psalm. In exitu Israël.

What can now be seen to have been the greatest cultural achievement of the French Missions Etrangères of the seventeenth and eighteenth centuries in northeastern North America was the preservation of the Ancient Micmac hieroglyphic writing system. In this edition of the Maillard manuscripts based on Austrian plates engraved from Maillard's papers in 1865, more than 600 signs are employed. The page opening gives Maillard's translation of Psalm 115, *In exitu Israel*. This text is also referred to on page 274.

and in 1884 Dr. Silas Rand noticed and recorded the fact that the Micmac name of the constellation is also *Mooeen*. This fact, taken with the observation by Cotton Mather, where a different word is involved, shows that a definite transmission of an astronomical idea occurred between the Old World and New England and Nova Scotia, and that the matter cannot be explained away as merely a coincidental similarity of names. To my mind the facts show that ancient mariners brought to the New World a knowledge of old Mediterranean beliefs about constellations, and in particular about the mariners' direction-finder and clock, *Ursa major*.

These traditions, scanty though they be, seem to imply a former cultural connection, to say the least, with peoples of the Mediterranean lands and Europe.

2. ARCHEOLOGICAL EVIDENCE

As the material in this book shows, there is abundant epigraphic evidence in the form of inscribed stones and buildings to show that New England was either visited, or in some cases, settled, by European and Mediterranean peoples who employed the Celtic, Basque, Phoenician and Egyptian languages. This evidence is consistent, therefore, with Algonquian tradition if we suppose that the visitors were in fact ancestors who remained in America, presumably intermarrying with preexisting inhabitants of an original Mongolian stock. On this interpretation, the Algonquian people would be of mixed ancestry, with a higher proportion of Mongolian blood in the west, and a higher proportion of European on the eastern seaboard. The inference may be tested against linguistic evidence next discussed.

3. LINGUISTIC EVIDENCE

Russian investigators (see Bibliography, section 10) have assembled vocabularies amounting to some 25,000 words from the many nomadic tribes that inhabit the northeastern extremity of Siberia, and the adjacent islands. These, together with studies of the grammatical structure of the languages, exhibit very clear affinities with tongues spoken in the northwest of the North American continent. It is clear that communication and even migration has occurred between Asia and North America in quite recent times. It is highly probable that similar communication and migration has occurred for thousands of years.

We can extend these studies to the Algonquian languages, and work now in progress shows that substantial numbers of Siberian roots occur in the western dialects of Algonquian, the proportion diminishing as one passes eastward into the New England region, and into Nova Scotia. The facts can be illustrated by referring to particular words, and tracing their distribution along the track I have indicated. For example, the word *matsu,* and similar forms, designates "tree" in the northeast Siberian tongues, the root element being the syllable *ma-.* As one passes into the Americas, words very similar to *matsu* are used for tree all across the Algonquian belt until one reaches New England. There an abrupt change occurs, and the word for tree in the Wabanaki dialect of Maine becomes *abassi.* Now *abassi* means "foeman" in the Siberian tongues, so why does it designate tree in New England? The answer is simple, it is not a Siberian word at all, but instead a well-known Semitic word, meaning "tree" and still in use to this very day among the Hebrew-speaking people of Israel, the language of which is related to Phoenician.

Evidently in this case, as in others that need not be listed here, the older Siberian word of the Algonquians has been displaced in the east by a word introduced from the Mediterranean lands. Similar evidence is provided by many hundreds of other words of clearly Semitic origin, found in the modern Wabanaki language, but lacking from the western dialects of Algonquian, where apparently the Phoenicians did not penetrate.

Celtic words are far fewer in the east Algonquian dialects, and most of them relate to topographic features, as discussed in a previous chapter. The following table lists some other words of probable Celtic origin that are still in use in the northeastern Algonquian dialects.

TABLE 9

MEANING	N.E. ALGONQUIAN	GAELIC
woman	bhanem	ban
immigrant	alnoba*	allaban
netting	lhab	lion-obhair
town	odana	dun
everywhere	na'lwiwi	na h-uile
frost, snowflake	kladen	cladan
boat	pados	bata
mountain	monaden	monadh
height	aden	ard
gorge	cuiche	cuithe

* literally, person

That there were substantial injections of Egyptian vocabulary, also, is apparent from the hundreds of roots in Wabanaki and Micmac that have now been identified: and in the case of the Micmac tribe, the writing system is also one derived from Egypt. Following are examples of Egyptian roots still in use.

TABLE 10

MEANING	N.E. ALGONQUIAN	EGYPTIAN
sun, sun god	Nepauz	N-b-w
moon, moon goddess	Nepauz-had	N-b-w h-ḏ
thunder	neem	n-h-m-h-m
foul	nish	n-š-w
erect, be erect	nepau, nepattu	n-b-w, n-b-i-t
child	neechnw	n-kh-n-w
plus (with numerals)	nab	n-b
bring back	nayew	n-w-y
feed and protect	nadt-uppo	n-d o-b
inquire for news of	nadtow-wompu	n-d w-p-w-t
hence, because	na	n
water, wet	neip	n-p-a
a piece, one	nequet	n-k-t
see, look	na	n
to be weak	nauw	n-w

That Norse visitors came to America is attested by archeological remains in eastern Canada. We might reasonably expect some trace of these visits in the languages of the region, such as Micmac, and as the following table shows, there is such linguistic evidence.

TABLE 11

MEANING	N.E. ALGONQUIAN	NORSE
bay	bookt	bukt
boat	pados	bata (or Celtic)
the wind is blowing	wejoo-suk	vejret sukker
I am well	wel-ae	vel äro
it is (getting) hot	weksa-dek	vaeckser hedt
bob up and down (fig.)	weksit-paktesk	fiske efter torsk
rope	lab-	reb
must	mos	maa

This chapter has done no more than sample an area of linguistic inquiry that is still very poorly understood. Whatever the uncertainties, I think we must prepare ourselves for one more jolt to our conception of the Atlantic as a barrier impassable to man until Viking times. Far from serving as an impassable barrier between the European and American worlds, it may actually have been a challenging highway, one free from the opposition of hostile tribes, demanding not brute strength for its passage but ingenuity and tenacity. If Neolithic man of Europe had the courage and skill of Neolithic man in Polynesia, then we may well find that the first great Atlantic navigators were among the earliest ancestors of the Algonquians.

Whether or not any Atlantic crossings were made in Neolithic times, it now seems indisputable that numerous crossings took place during Bronze-Age times, including trading ventures year by year, as well as voyages to carry out permanent settlement. The voyages and colonizations during the Bronze Age were performed by the European and Mediterranean peoples whose vocabulary has given rise to that of the modern dialects of the eastern Algonquians, and the eastern Algonquians themselves are for the greater part descended from these early visitors.

Postscript

THE first reports from James Whittall of his new expedition to visit sites in Portugal speak of the charm of the Iberian countryside in autumn and of the rich harvest of inscriptions in Iberian script, some also in Ogam. The photographic records will come later when he himself returns. Thus so far have we progressed this summer; and on the basis of inscriptions analyzed in New England we can now pinpoint the expected matches in Iberia and find them. No longer is Ogam a peculiar script found only in the British Isles.

Nor is that all. Jim's notes read as a continuing diary.

Yesterday I photographed standing stones with libation holes in the rocks nearby. I also photographed bronze points exactly like the one found on Monhegan Island in the shell midden.

There are grinding stones exactly like that found at Mystery Hill. I can also state that some Amerindian points are identical to those found here.

He also sends sketches of a crude standing-stone image reminiscent of the fallen monolithic image of Bel that John Williams found at South Royalton, Vermont, after Jim had already departed for Portugal. The familiar checkerboard symbol is on the Iberian example, the sign of Bel that also occurs at South Royalton. Later letters speak of the cordial reception Portuguese archeologists have extended to him, and of their keen interest in his photographs of New England sites.

As if by some divine ordinance Portugal has chosen this time to issue new postage stamps featuring an ancient dolmen of the Iberian Bronze Age, so the Whittall reports come appropriately decorated both without and within.

Here in New England the last warm days of the Indian Summer entice us out upon the mountains, only to find that we have left the warmth

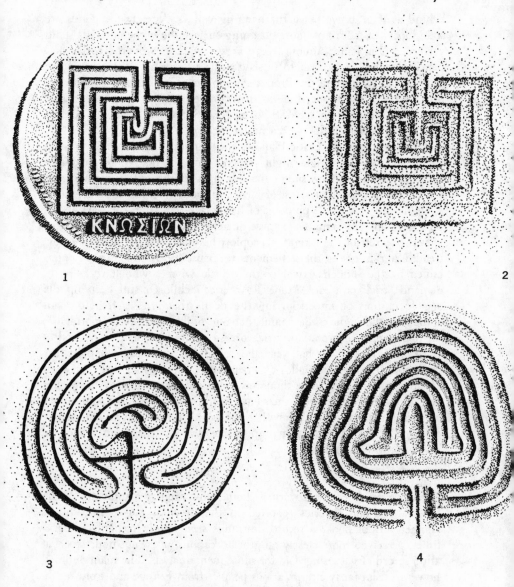

1

2

3

4

Knowledge of the ancient labyrinth of Knossos, Crete, was brought to the Americas by voyagers who carved these Arizona examples (2) and (4), drawn from photographs made by the late William Coxon. Matching examples from the Old World are given on the left, (1) an ancient coin from Knossos, and (3) an engraving from India.

behind as soon as we reach the hanging valleys. Already the ponds are solid blocks of ice from whose gleaming surface the withered reeds stand yet erect. Our hands almost freeze as we work among the rocks, and pencil sketching is a task to be laid aside till spring. I wonder if the climate was warmer in the Bronze Age in New England, as we know it to have been in Europe; but no firm answer can yet be given to that question by experts in the U.S. Geological Survey. If it was as cold as now, those ancient Celts were a hardy race!

Samhain comes, the Celtic Hallowe'en. John and I, determined to tread Celtic soil on the magic night, set out on yet one more mountain excursion to study a new site he has found. As darkness falls we find ourselves gazing upon that rarest of scenes in modern times, an entire landscape devoid of a single pinpoint of light, save that from the stars above. So lonely and mysterious are these ancient hills that have preserved for ages the secrets of the forgotten people who once trod the paths we now tread. Later, at one of the settlements we pause for a meal. We are entertained by the sudden arrival of three little witches who have come to demand "trick or treat." Modern American children still keep up the age-old custom of impersonating the devils that are set free to roam abroad on the night of Samhain, that one night when every mortal has the opportunity of propitiating the forces of evil by an offering of food to ward off ill luck in the half-year ahead. It is an astonishing thought that the modern customs of Hallowe'en perpetuate ancient rites that the Green Mountains witnessed three thousand years ago, performed by the young people of what must surely then have been the most isolated community of Celts in the world. And with these occult reflections we collect our day's gleanings of aluminum impressions and sketches, and make our way back to Cambridge.

If this were a technical work, I should now prepare a summary of the observations and theories reported in the previous pages. But this is another sort of book, a record of things seen, dimly recognized sometimes, perceived more clearly on other occasions, often not understood at all; a record of gathering data for subsequent analysis. The main outlines, however, seem fairly clear. Various peoples from Europe and from northwest Africa sailed to America three thousand years ago and established colonies here. The primary evidence rests in the structures they built and in the inscriptions they wrote in letters that we now can identify as spelling phrases and sentences whose meaning we can grasp. Like Vallancey and his pioneer associates in eighteenth-century Ireland, we are surely making many errors that only time will reveal and correct. Like Vallancey we are probably in touch with the basic truths of the situation, though still fumbling with the details.

The decipherments point to Iberia as the principal homeland of most of the wanderers who found their way to America in the millennium before Christ. Inductive prediction (the final test of any scientific hypothesis) led us to search for evidence of writing like that of the American inscriptions in the ancient sites of Portugal and Spain; and as we are now learning, Ogam inscriptions of the American type—devoid of vowels—are being located in the Iberian lands as predicted.

The obvious steps to take next year will be the closer examination of the Vermont sites and a wider exploration of the adjacent areas in the neighboring states. Sites already known in Connecticut, Massachusetts, and New Hampshire will come under more searching study.

Most urgent is our need to find a museum to house our finds, now so vulnerable to the destructive onslaught of vandals. Already some of our earlier discoveries have been stolen or damaged. Without the support of a research society or organization we are obliged to leave irreplaceable objects lying on the hillside where we found them. Next year must surely bring forth some solution to what has now become our greatest worry.

Professional archeologists will be welcome colleagues when the time is ripe to undertake formal digs. But the role of the amateur is now surely established, and it is a role that he will continue to fill with distinction. And so it is to the amateur archeologists of America that this book is dedicated.

Nor should we forget that several distinguished professional archeologists are to be numbered among those who have pondered the meaning of the mysterious stone chambers of New England. Hugh O'Neill Hencken and Hallam L. Movius Jr., both professors at the Peabody Museum of Archeology at Harvard University, paid attention to the facts brought to their notice by William Goodwin, and although they believed he had not established a case for Irish monastic builders, this did not lead them to dismiss Goodwin's work. Far from it, they recognized that here was a sincere and industrious investigator, and that many unexplained facts required such investigators to solve them.

During the mid-1950s another distinguished Harvard man began to examine the problem of the New England stone chambers. This was the polar explorer Dr. Vilhjalmur Stefansson, who during his polar expeditions discovered a race of blonde "Eskimo." He saw evidence of stone chambers in the Canadian arctic lands similar to what a New Zealand colleague, Diamond Jenness, had also seen. Stefansson, along with other colleagues at Dartmouth College, notably Professor Hugh Morrison, established the Early Sites Research group for the study of the Vermont

Vilhjalmur Stefansson (1879–1962), polar explorer and anthropologist, who was one of the founders of the Early Sites Research Society, devoted to solving the problem of the origin of the stone chambers of New England. Stefansson believed that these were built by people from Europe or Phoenicia, as his letters (now in the Harvard Library) make plain. *New York Times*

stone chambers. This was the origin of the present Early Sites Research Society. In the archives of Harvard College Library I have deposited copies of letters exchanged by these men, showing that they believed Europeans or Phoenicians had built the New England chambers at some time long antecedent to Columbus.

Some thirty-five years ago Professor Hugh Hencken wrote, "if pre-Columbian European remains are to be found on our coasts, it will be through the energy and perseverance of such investigators as Mr. Goodwin." William Goodwin and Malcolm Pearson, with their few amateur assistants, have now been succeeded by hundreds of interested and well-informed amateur archeologists organized in several active societies that record new finds in regularly published bulletins. As Professor Hencken foresaw, it has indeed been through the energy and perseverance of amateurs that the evidence was eventually uncovered.

Now the amateur is returning to the campus, this time as invited guest with specialist knowledge, to lecture to general courses of archeology and history. As I write these words John Williams is already conducting field excursions for students of Castleton State College, where Professor Warren Cook had been the first New England academic to voice public support. John's and my lecture engagement schedules, once all but blank, are now fast becoming so busy as to interfere with research plans. But the time spent on such duties proves rewarding, as many letters from young inquirers show. "Thank you for showing us your collection of inscribed stones, it is reassuring to know that these precious relics are in good hands," writes one graduate student, who also encloses some parts of his forthcoming thesis. To meet the many requests for visits to campuses I have had to call upon my field colleagues and other associates to undertake more of this work, which is assuming something of a ministry; for it is plain that the word we bring is something that many young people have longed to hear, namely that America is a part of the great Western World whose roots lie in the Mediterranean and whose branches lie on far-flung continents. Later, when studies are more advanced on the Pacific seaboard, we shall doubtless find the corresponding oriental branches, and so eventually come to perceive the synthesis of West and East that arose in the Americas.

Until then, California and British Columbia and Arizona keep many of their ancient secrets. The tantalizing lines of mysterious script of the Flora Vista tablet, with its elephant figures, remain unsolved, to challenge us to yet further decipherments. In Mexico that great humanist Alexander Wuthenau brings forth a parade of hundreds of sculpted Amerindian portraits from ancient times, telling in unmistakable language of the many races that long ago entered Central America and found haven there. How little we know of all this, yet how much do our modest New England studies warn us is yet to be learned!

So take heart, young Americans, there are challenges aplenty for you to meet and if I am still around when you succeed, I shall surely rejoice with you as Harold Gladwin has been spared to do with us. Good hunting!

But an inquiring mind is not, thank God, the prerogative of youth. If it is true that young people have provided most of the voluntary field explorers and laboratory photographers for our studies, it is equally true that thoughtful elders have guided us to important sites and participated

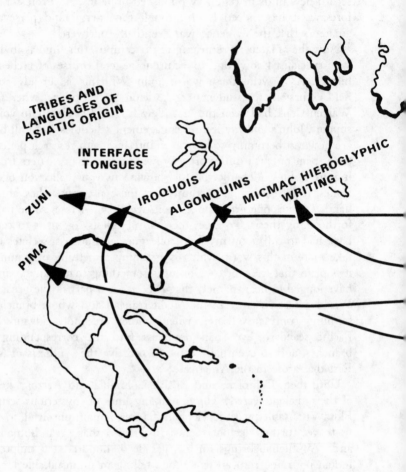

TRIBES AND
LANGUAGES OF
ASIATIC ORIGIN

INTERFACE
TONGUES

ZUNI

IROQUOIS

ALGONQUINS

MICMAC HIEROGLYPHIC
WRITING

PIMA

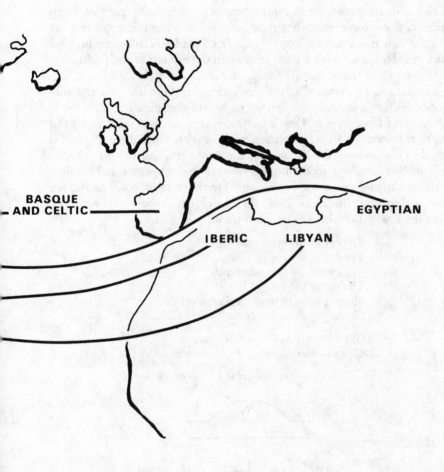

BASQUE
AND CELTIC

EGYPTIAN

IBERIC   LIBYAN

The cultural heritage of the Amerindian peoples is reflected in the complex linguistic relationships of the spoken languages today. Only a few of many facets are illustrated above. The earliest languages came from Asia, via the west coast, and there has been a continuing input of Asiatic words from the Pacific as repeated incursions have taken place. On the Atlantic side ancient Libyan, Egyptian, Phoenician, Celtic, and Basque colonists brought dialects of which some descendant tongues can still be recognized. Incursions from the south added Iroquois, while some Norse speech entered the Algonquian area from the northeast. Interfaces between the various language areas generated new languages of mixed origins.

with enthusiasm in seminars and other study groups. Men and women with young families could yet find time to catalog stones or sketch inscriptions, and others who are grandparents have shared in our work.

Nor is interest confined to North America. From many parts of Latin America have come eager letters of inquiry, and from Europe and the Middle East many others. For the people of the homelands of our most ancient colonists preserve a lively interest in the exploits of their ancestors. One letter came from a family having the surname of Hanno!

The catalog of names that we are finding on America's oldest tombstones disclose a lineage that reaches back into the mists of antiquity. If Hanno and Ham sing of Dido's Carthage, then so also Galba and Saliq evoke memories of Iberian Romans and Frankish kings. Our Yoghan is but the older form of the Ewans, MacEwans, Evans, and Bevans of Celtic Britain. So to all these modern descendants of ancient heroes and heroines who crossed the great waters we send greetings, *ceud mille faillte,* ten thousand greetings from Iargalon, the "Land-that-lies-beyond-the-sunset." May the eye of Bel look kindly upon us all.

> The eye of the great god,
> The eye of the god of glory,
> The eye of the king of hosts,
> The eye of the king of life,
> Shining upon us through time and tide,
> Shining upon us gently and without stint.
>
> Glory be to thee, O splendid Sun,
> Glory to thee O Sun, face of the god of life.
>
> —*Ancient Celtic Hymn to the Sun*

Appendix
Cracking the Code

WHEN we found the first American inscription in the Ogam alphabet none of us was really surprised, for the character of the stone chambers and the astronomical alignment of the calendar stones at Mystery Hill had already suggested some relationship with the Celtic civilization of ancient Britain. What did surprise me, however, was the peculiar character of the inscriptions we encountered. They consisted only of consonant signs, having none of the smaller interposed points that mark the vowels in British inscriptions. There was also a total lack of crosses or other Christian symbols that distinguish most of the Irish and Scottish Ogam monuments and, because of the lack of vowels, the signs spelled out unfamiliar and seemingly barbarous words. The inscriptions simply did not look like the British ones I had studied in Scotland—and yet, despite their strange aspect, the signs were apparently arranged in accordance with principles quite like those governing the British Ogam inscriptions.

Added to these obvious differences was the fact that no indisputable evidence of a Celtic presence in North America had ever been adduced before. It was clear that we could not assume that the inscriptions were directly comparable to the Ogam of Britain and Ireland, and that until I could give a rigorous proof of their direct relationship to a known writing system, many archeologists would not even admit that the inscriptions comprised any kind of writing at all.

There are, of course, no medieval manuscripts to search out in America, as Vallancey had been able to do in Ireland, so that method of decipherment was unavailable. However, the experience of epigraphers in certain Old World lands that the ancients regarded as remote from civilization, such as Arabia and India, led us to hope that we would eventually uncover bilingual inscriptions. Luckily that hope was realized and now, as the work begins to assume a broader coverage in North America, there is a steady flow of bilingual texts as the river cliffs are examined for ancient engravings by explorers of classical times, from localities so far

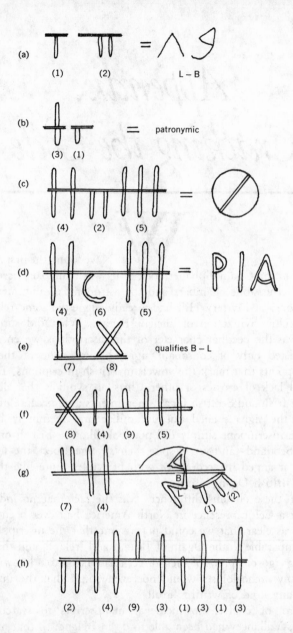

Cracking the Code. Eight equations and expressions by means of which the phonetic values of American Ogam letters were determined. The final solution proved to be nearly identical with known sound values for British Ogam, based on the traditional values in the Book of Ballymote. Vowel points are lacking from American (and Iberian) Ogam, and the symbol for NG in British Ogam is employed in American Ogam for the sound of N. New England Ogam uses the same sign for both L and R, whereas Caribbean and Oklahoman Ogam distinguishes these two letters by the same signs as are used in British Ogam.

away as Oklahoma and the other states whose territory is traversed by the Mississippi or one of its several great tributaries. For it is now plain that the great rivers of America were the highways of ancient visitors and explorers, who penetrated far into the interior of the continent.

Not content merely with carving their names as evidence of their visits, these old-time explorers would often add a brief transcription in a different alphabet, so as to increase the chances that some other, later visitor would be in no doubt as to who had been there before him. Thus it was, for example, that some ancient Celtic river navigator named Gwynn who ascended the Arkansas River so far as its Cimarron branch, not only cut his name in Ogam letters, but also explained in Iberian Punic script that his name means "White." Thanks to these early bilingual writers, some of whom also cut temple dedications in both Ogam and Iberian letters, we have been able to perform an independent decipherment, on our own American materials, and so demonstrate a satisfactory concordance between the American Ogam letters and the corresponding letters of other alphabets. And when the American Ogam inscriptions are deciphered in this way, the language revealed is found to be a very ancient form of Celtic. The following analysis shows how the sound values may be determined for the individual signs appearing in the equations and expressions on page 296. These relate to 8 of the 15 Ogam signs that occur in American inscriptions; the remaining 7 signs may be solved by similar substitution methods. The entire alphabet is set out on page 47.

ANALYSIS

I. In equation (a), found on the lintel of the buried chamber near White River, Vermont, sign (1) must either equal Iberian **L** or **B**, and sign (2) equals whichever of the two Iberian letters that sign (1) does not equal. Which of these two alternatives is correct depends on whether the unknown signs are read from left to right, or from right to left.

II. In equation (b) we have a pair of signs that invariably occur in the middle part of sign-sequences found on isolated stones that are evidently memorial headstones. It is inferred therefore that this pair of signs is a patronymic, and that the general formula for any name on a gravestone is either "X son-of Y," or else "X whose-father-was Y." The second of these possibilities is the usual formula for any Semitic memorial stone, in which case the word represented is **B-N**. The inferred patronymic includes the sign (1), which was deduced to have the value **B** in I above. If this is so, then sign (3) in expression (b) must have the sound value of **N**. However, that deduction is improbable, for it would require that sign (1) in equation (a) have the value of **B**, in which case the letters in equation (a) read from left to right, while those of equation (b) read from right to left. Therefore we must discard the inference that expression (b) represents the Semitic patronymic **B-N**.

III.   The only other Iberian language known to employ a biconsonantal patronymic placed in the middle of a name is Celtic. If the patronymic is Celtic then it should either represent the letters **M-Q** (as in Celtic tongues of the Q-group), or else the letters **M-B** (as in P-Celtic). But **M-Q** is excluded as a possible solution, because sign (1) occurs in equation (a) also, and must therefore have the sound value of either **B** or **L**. Therefore the correct solution of equation (b) is probably **M-B**, to read from left to right. In that case the signs of equation (a) also read from left to right, and in both equations sign (1) will have the value of **B**.

IV.   From the foregoing, therefore, it follows that:

   sign (1) = **B**
   sign (2) = **L**
   sign (3) = **M**

and the language appears to be Celtic.

V.   Equation (c) occurs beside a painting of the solar disk bearing the equinoctial line on a rock-shelter wall at Cachão da Rapa, Portugal, where we have identified inscriptions that conform to the American type of Ogam, lacking vowel signs, and accompanied by Iberian Punic letters. It is to be assumed that the Ogam letters identify the solar disk, because an associated Punic Iberian inscription similarly identifies the solar disk in Punic language (**T-R-S**). The Celtic name for the solar disk can either be **H-W-L** or **G-L-N**. However, the first of these two possibilities is excluded by the fact that sign (2) occurs as the middle letter of the Ogam group, and has been shown to have the probable sound value of **L**. Therefore the second alternative **G-L-N** is the one that is acceptable.

VI.   From the foregoing it follows that this sign sequence also reads from left to right, and is therefore consistent with equations (1) and (2), and that the following additional sound values may now be assigned:

   sign (4) = **G**
   sign (5) = **N**

and the language still appears to be Celtic.

VII. Proceeding now to equation (d), found by Gloria Farley in a cliff cave at Turkey Mountain, Oklahoma, the Iberian Punic letters spell the word **P-Y-'** (meaning in Punic "white"). This is equated with Ogam letters that spell a word with 3 consonants, of which the first is **G** and the last is **N**, the middle letter being unknown. The word "white" may be rendered in Celtic by the consonants **G-W-N,** corresponding to the name Gwyn or Guin. From this result it may be inferred that

sign (6) = **W** (or **UI**)

and that the contained language is Celtic.

VIII. The expression (e) occurs on an inscription near a stone chamber at Danbury, Connecticut, explored by John Williams, and it is associated with the Iberian Punic letters **B-L**. Since the signs cannot represent the name **B-L** (the sun-god Bel), they must instead signify some qualifying epithet applied to Bel. The most likely word would be "god," which in Celtic would be represented by the consonants **D-Y**, where **Y** has the sound of ya, as in the equivalent Punic letter. It is tentatively inferred, then, that the word is indeed **D-Ya** (Dia), and that therefore

sign (7) = **D**

sign (8) = **Y** (or **Ya**)

and the contained language is Celtic.

IX. Expression (f), cut on a headstone in a necropolis near the White River temple chamber, Vermont, can now be read without difficulty as the well-known Celtic name **Y-G-H-N** (Eoghan, modern Ewan, etc.), the one new letter, sign (9) = **H**, therefore.

X. Expression (g), a lintel inscription of Vermont, reads, by using the solutions, as **D-G** followed by **B-L** in Iberian and Ogam script. The word **D-G** evidently spells the old Celtic *degos* (tegos), meaning a building or temple. The Punic Iberian and Ogam signs are combined to form an Egyptian eye-hieroglyph which, in Ptolemaic times, also had the pronunciation Bel, and signified "eye" as well as the name of the god Bel.

XI. Expression (h), a headstone inscription from Vermont, is evidently to be read as **L-G-H M-B M-B M**, "To Lugh, son of Mabo the Elder." Numerous similar transliterations and translations can be made, all yielding apparent Celtic language, while the sound values of the remaining signs can be inferred from their contexts. The alphabet is given on page 47. Except for the semi-vowels Y and W, all American and Iberian Ogam letters represent consonants, thus precisely matching Punic in this regard.

Epilogue—1989

$\mathbf{I}$N the early 1970s, a group of us who were interested in ancient scripts used to meet occasionally at Harvard University to discuss the decipherment of what we believed to be ancient inscriptions. Out of these beginnings came the Epigraphic Society, formally inaugurated in 1974. Once our publications began to appear the membership grew till now there are a dozen chapters in the Americas and overseas. In this epilogue some of the more interesting results of the Society's work are presented.

The cup-and-ring is a man-made stereotype motif engraved or pecked into rock, and it is composed of a central cup surrounded by one or more concentric rings. Petroglyphs of this type occur in many parts of the Old World as well as in both North and South America, and on various oceanic islands. Although their meaning has been discussed since 1859, when Sir J. Gardner Wilkinson drew attention to British examples, no certain conclusions have been reached. Their occasional association with megaliths and stone circles has been held to imply a religious significance, and it has also been suggested that they may have served as markers for early mining activities, since large numbers of examples are known from regions where metallic ores occur; and a calendric use has also been suggested. The example illustrated (opposite, upper illustration) was originally found near Canton, Georgia, but has since been removed for safer conservation to the campus of Reinhardt College, Waleska, Georgia. An article on the American examples, written by the British authority on the subject Ronald W. B. Morris, appears in volume 17 (1988) of the Epigraphic Society's *Occasional Publications*. The age of American examples cannot as yet be determined, but Morris states that the oldest example in the British Isles is believed to be at New Grange in Ireland, occurring in a megalithic tomb built around 3200 B.C. The Reinhardt College example was photographed by Bart B. Henson. Petroglyphs of this kind may be among America's oldest legacies of visits by people from the Old World. Most archeologists have sought to explain the petroglyphs as merely examples of independent invention. That explanation, if such it is to be termed, cannot apply to the next case, illustrated in the lower photograph opposite.

Cuneiform tablets of baked clay and of Mesopotamian origin have from time to time turned up in America and have been explained as being specimens brought here in modern times by collectors who supposedly then lost them. However, in an article published in volume 15 of the Epigraphic Society's *Occasional Publications* (hereafter referred to by the acronym ESOP), Dr. Alberto Marini recorded a late Sumerian cuneiform inscription from Bolivia, cut on a stone bowl found near Lake Titicaca. It is a religious invocation addressed to the Supreme Deity, praying for blessings and guidance in growing grain and herding farm animals. It is associated with archaic Aymara hieroglyphic signs incorporating some cuneiform letters, and thus is a native American product, not an import from abroad. Dr. Marini holds degrees in Sumeriology, including honorary doctorates from both U.S. and Latin American institutions, and is at present a professor at John Kennedy University in Buenos Aires. He finds the grammar and vocabulary and letter forms of the Titicaca inscription to imply a date of about 2000 B.C., and he deduces that persons who used the Sumerian language (presumably Sumerians) were present in the Altiplano at that era. This important inscription is now in the Museo Murillo in Ciudad de La Paz, where it may now be seen. Full details of the text appear in succeeding volumes of ESOP.

The Tifinag alphabet, shown below, occurs in Bronze Age Norse petroglyphs where it is used to render Old Norse words, omitting most of the vowels. A related form of Tifinag is used to this day by some Berber tribes in North Africa, whose ancestors may have acquired it

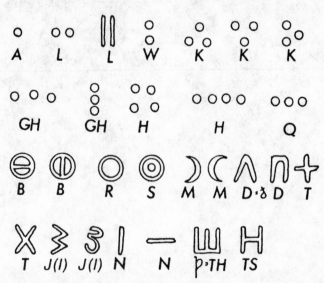

Letters of the Tifinag alphabet as employed in Bronze Age petroglyphs in Scandinavia.

from Norse raiders in Bronze Age times, when Norse elements may have been included in the general term "Sea Peoples." Well-known sites where such Norse inscriptions occur are those in Bohuslän, Sweden, where fleets of ancient ships are depicted (see below).

In 1954 Canadian field geologists discovered a richly varied petroglyph site near Peterborough, Ontario, in which are featured ancient ships resembling those of the Scandinavian sites, interspersed with human and animal figures, with numerous Tifinag letters between the pictorial elements. It was at first supposed that the site had been created by Algonquian artists, though the local Indian people could throw no light on the subject matter of the carved pictures and the archeologists did not recognize the Tifinag letters. In 1982 in my book *Bronze Age America* I deciphered the greater part of the inscriptions, and showed that they are written in archaic Norse and relate to a religious

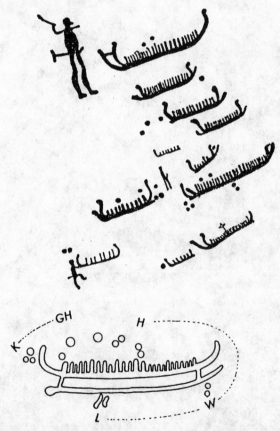

Part of a Bronze Age petroglyph at Lökeberget, Foss, Bohuslän in Sweden depicting a fleet of ancient seagoing vessels. Interspersed among the vessels are the dot-formed letters of the Tifinag alphabet naming the ships. Below, details of a single ship, the letters reading K-GH H-W-L, to be understood as Old Norse Kogge Hval, i.e., the trading vessel "Sea Monster."

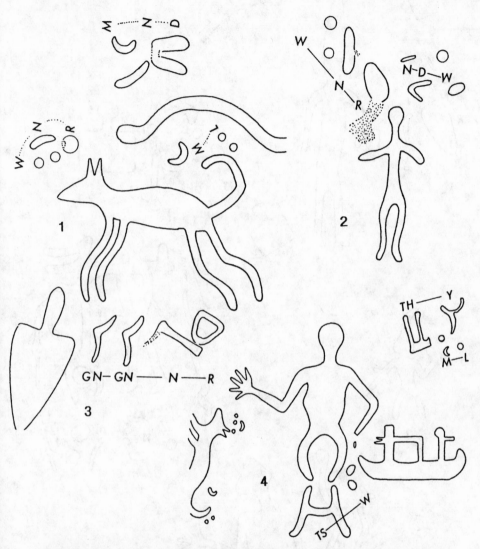

Old Norse mythology as depicted at the Peterborough site, Ontario. 1. The Fenrir wolf that bit off the hand of the war god Tsiw. Tifinag text translates as Wenri (= Fenrir) Crunch-Hand. 2. Odin, here rendered in Tifinag as Wanir Woden, but the word Wanir (Earth gods) apparently refers to some adjacent figures not here reproduced. 3. Woden's magic spear Gungnir. 4. The war god Tsiw, after the attack by the Fenrir wolf, the Tifinag text reading Tsiw lymth, "Tsiw maimed."

OPPOSITE PAGE:
Bronze Age Scandinavian petroglyphs at Peterborough, Ontario. Uppermost, the sun-ship that supposedly carries the sun across the sky in Old World mythology. Below, various vessels that apparently were sailing between Scandinavia and Canada around 1700 B.C.

Old Norse mythology as depicted at the Peterborough site (continued). 1. Thunor the Thunderer (later Thor). The Tifinag text reads from right to left, Nema Thunor Molnir, "Thor grasps his hammer, Molnir." 2. Thor using his giant glove, Glofi, to defeat serpent dragons. The Tifinag text reads Molnir, Glofi, ve maki orm rittit, "Molnir and Glofi, woe is their power to the serpent writhing." 3. Thor holding Molnir. 4. Thor wearing Glofi, at left two serpents of Middle Earth.

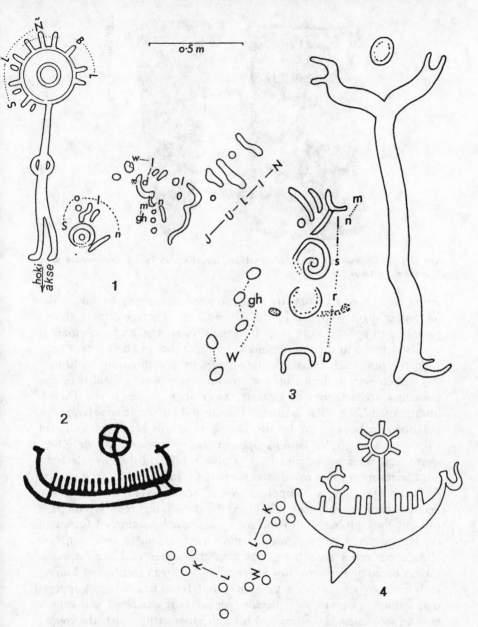

Old Norse mythology as depicted at the Peterborough site, Ontario (continued). 1. The Sun God, the Disk Ogam apparently reading Solen-bal, "blazing Sun." The other letters are Tifinag Hwild gaman oll, Julen, "Holiday for rest and games for all, Yule," relating to the mid-December pagan rites. 2. Sun-ship as depicted in a petroglyph at Bohuslän, Sweden. 3. Ugdrasil, the forked two-branched World-tree of Norse myth. The Tifinag letters read in Old Norse Ugha drasil nama, "Ugdrasil by name." 4. The Sun-ship at the Peterborough site (compare with the Swedish example, number 2). The Tifinag letters read Keol we loki, Old Norse Kjol ve logi, "Ship of the Blazing Standard." These, and the preceding mythological figures, are from *Bronze Age America*, Barry Fell, 1982.

Axe of Late Bronze Age Scandinavian type, found on an Indian reservation near Brantford, Ontario.

center established by Norse traders who were exchanging woven textiles for copper ingots supplied by the Algonquians. The age of the site was estimated to be such as to place it in the Bronze Age, and astronomical details included in the inscriptions suggested a date of about 1700 B.C.

At the time such trans-Atlantic voyages by Scandinavians in Bronze Age vessels were unheard of, and my inferences were ridiculed by the Canadian archeologists of Ontario. Since then, however, the Danish historian Jon Galster has examined the site and his conclusions have been published in book form by the Dansk Historisk Håndbogsforlag in Copenhagen (1987). Galster's opinion totally supports my decipherments and conclusions, and he was able to add further details from Scandinavian sites that match and support the inferences.

The copper "ingots" supplied to the Scandinavian traders of the Peterborough site may have resembled the natural ingots shown on page 96 and they probably also included man-made hammered lumps of copper extracted by the ancient miners of Michigan. Some 5,000 abandoned mines have been found on the shores of Lake Superior, carbon-dated by Professor Roy Drier of the Michigan Institute of Mining and Technology to between 2000 B.C. and 1000 B.C., while it appears that millions of pounds of metallic copper were extracted and cannot now be accounted for. Drier and his colleagues surmise that the copper must have been shipped overseas, and now the discovery of the Peterborough site seems to confirm that. For Drier's account of the matter, see *Prehistoric Copper Mining in the Lake Superior Region* by Drier and du Temple (1965).

In 1977 Professor Gad Rausing suggested that Scandinavian Bronze Age voyages may have occurred, his evidence being the bronze axe shown on this page, and now located in the Museum of the American Indian, New York. Significantly the axe was found in Ontario.

Above right: Plan of stone circle at Big Basin, Santa Cruz Mountains, California, some 15 meters in diameter, comprising 13 stones, with the meridional axis as shown. On the southeast bearing two larger stones mark the direction of the winter solstice sunrise. Drawn by Jerry McMillan.

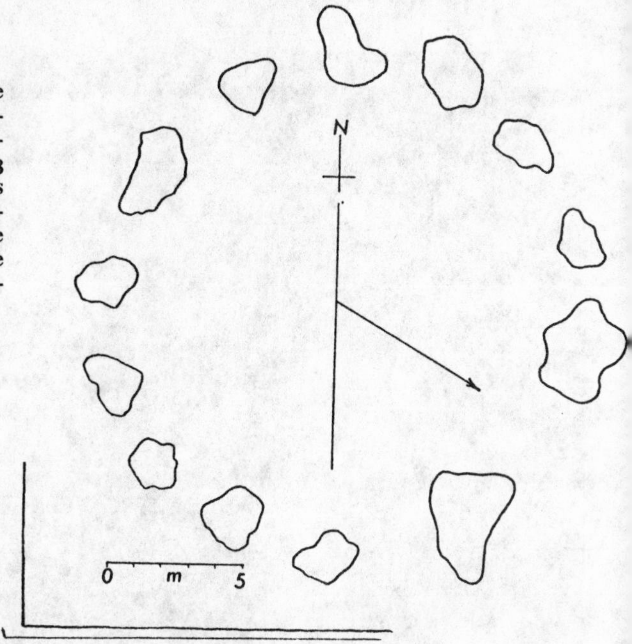

N

0   m   5

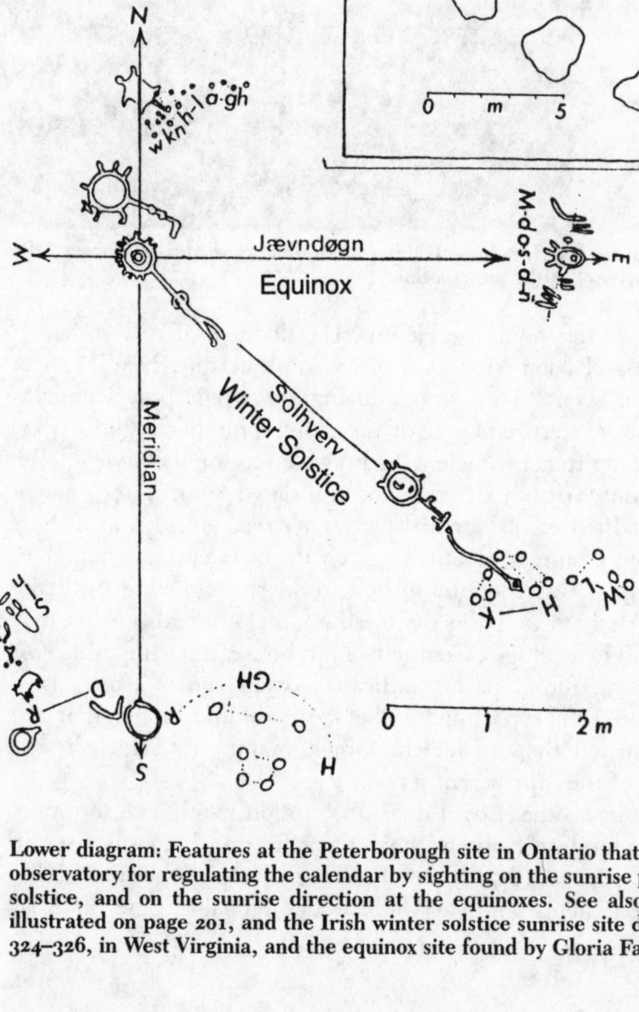

w knh-lå·gh

N

M-dos-d-n'

Jævndøgn

Equinox

E

W

Meridian

Solhverv
Winter Solstice

K   H   Mo

CH

S

R

H

0   1   2 m

Lower diagram: Features at the Peterborough site in Ontario that suggest a possible observatory for regulating the calendar by sighting on the sunrise point at the winter solstice, and on the sunrise direction at the equinoxes. See also the stone circles illustrated on page 201, and the Irish winter solstice sunrise site described on pages 324–326, in West Virginia, and the equinox site found by Gloria Farley, on page 323.

© Ida Jane Gallagher

The famous Los Lunas inscription on Hidden Mountain, New Mexico. Lower left, Fell, who reported (1985) on the punctuation.

This remarkable version of the Hebrew Decalogue or Ten Commandments, located on Hidden Mountain, near Albuquerque, New Mexico, became the main focus of attention during the Epigraphic Congress sponsored by the Western Chapter of the Epigraphic Society in 1984. The inscription, written in ancient Hebrew letters of the style of the Moab stone, about 1000 B.C., was not translated until 1949, when Professor Robert Pfeiffer of Harvard University recognized it as a short version of the Ten Commandments as given in the twentieth chapter of Exodus. For long it was thought to be a modern engraving until the examination carried out in 1984 disclosed anomalous features that may imply antiquity. The geologist George E. Morehouse, reporting in ESOP volume 13 (1985), found patina indicative of an age of from 500–2,000 years, and Fell, reporting in the same volume, noted that the punctuation matched that of ancient Greek manuscripts, such as the *Codex Sinaiticus* of the fourth century A.D.

A full account of the Los Lunas inscription, with transcription, transliteration to modern Hebrew characters, and translation, is given in ESOP vol. 10, part 1 (1982), by Professor Joseph Naveh, Hebrew University of Jerusalem, L. Lyle Underwood, Donald Cline, and Jay Stonebraker.

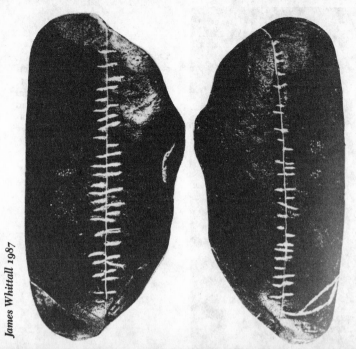

Marian Fagn 1900

Ogam consaine inscriptions occur on prostrate monoliths in New England and Quebec. The example shown in the lower picture is at Blanchard, near Cavendish, Vermont. Warren Dexter, who stands behind, has given much attention to these, and has also visited corresponding sites in Ireland (see page 155). The lack of vowels and occasional severe weathering make the decipherment difficult and uncertain. The weathered aspect and patina imply considerable antiquity, perhaps comparable with the Epimegalithic of Ireland (about 1200 B.C. onward), when Gaelic-speaking people occupied Ireland, according to the interpretation of Professor R. A. S. MacAlister (1972). Above: This small stone, on its two surfaces, carries a pagan invocation for protection against sickness and the Evil Eye: David P. Barron reported it from Connecticut (see ESOP vol. 16, 1987).

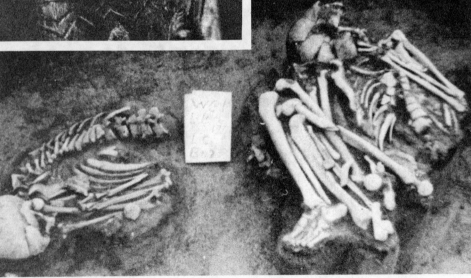

LEFT: Portion of a bone imprint stamp for pottery, bearing letters of the Celtiberian alphabet. BELOW: Skeletons of the burial site where the stamp was found in east Tennessee, yielding a radio-carbon date of third century B.C.

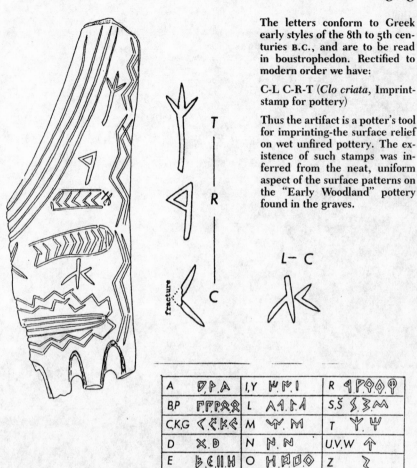

The letters conform to Greek early styles of the 8th to 5th centuries B.C., and are to be read in boustrophedon. Rectified to modern order we have:

C-L C-R-T (*Clo criata*, Imprint-stamp for pottery)

Thus the artifact is a potter's tool for imprinting-the surface relief on wet unfired pottery. The existence of such stamps was inferred from the neat, uniform aspect of the surface patterns on the "Early Woodland" pottery found in the graves.

In 1979 Dr. William P. Grigsby of Kingsport, Tennessee, noticed engraved letters on a supposed bone comb that had been excavated by members of the Tennessee Archaeological Society from an Early Woodland period burial site at Snapps Bridge. He submitted the object to me for study and, as shown in the illustrations above, the script is Celtiberian, and identifies the object as a stamp for marking designs on pottery. Pottery found at the site carried just such marks as the artifact would produce. The skeletal material found at the site yielded a radio-carbon date of 2160 ± 135 C-14 years B.P. (i.e., about the third century B.C.). This result gave us the first firm dating for the presence of Celtiberian people in North America, and it was published in my book *Bronze Age America* (1982), where fuller details can be found.

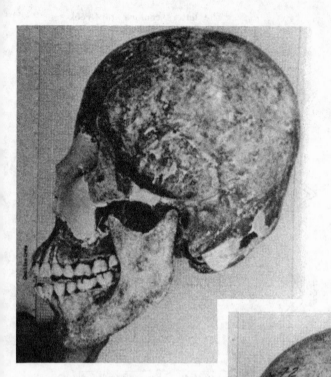

Skulls from Holiston Mills, near Snapps Bridge, east Tennessee, excavated by the Archaeological Society of Tennessee, and exhibiting two markedly different racial types, though found in associated burials. See comments on the facing page. Photos by Walter T. Eitel.

Hebrew inscription, Bat Creek, Tennessee, now dated by radiocarbon to the Middle Woodland period, about 1605 years B.P. ± 170.

Skeletons excavated from Early Woodland sites in east Tennessee show great diversity of skull types. Some, as exemplified by the upper photograph on the facing page, are pygmy types with round (brachycephalic) heads and very conspicuously projecting jaws (prognathous). These must represent an ancient type derived from the Oriental region, where similar people are still found today in the mountains of Malaya and the Philippines. A contrasted type, illustrated in the lower photograph, resembles European and Mediterranean races, and probably is derived from immigrants who crossed the Atlantic from the Old World and settled among the Tennessee Indians.

Six years after the carbon dating of the Celtiberian inscription from east Tennessee another radio-carbon date was obtained for a Tennessee inscribed object, namely the stone bearing eight Hebrew characters excavated by William Emmert of the Smithsonian Institution in 1889 from an unrifled burial mound at Bat Creek. The stone was found with nine skeletons, wooden earspools, and metal bracelets. Cyrus Thomas, curator of ethnology at the Smithsonian, supposed that the mound was one made in historic times by the Indians, and that the inscription is in Cherokee syllabic script, and hence not older than the early nineteenth century. In 1964 Dr. Henriette Mertz recognized Phoenician letters in the inscription, and independently it was found by Dr. Joseph B. Mahan that the letters read LYHWD in Hebrew if the stone is inverted from the orientation adopted by Thomas. In 1972 Dr. Cyrus Gordon, the Hebrew scholar at Brandeis University, recognized that the letters belong to Hebrew styles of the Roman period, and was able to translate the text as "A comet for the Jews," a standard formula dating from the revolt of 125 A.D., when Bar-Kochbar was associated with prophecy regarding a comet. The inscription of the Bat Creek stone was accordingly assigned to that date. A full explanation of the decipherment is given in Professor

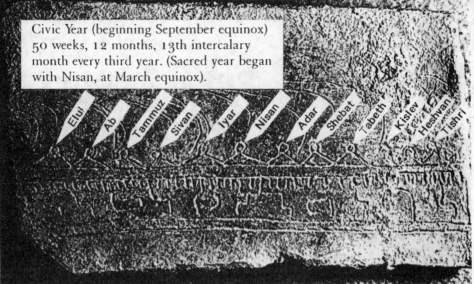

Civic Year (beginning September equinox) 50 weeks, 12 months, 13th intercalary month every third year. (Sacred year began with Nisan, at March equinox).

Elul · Ab · Tammuz · Sivan · Iyar · Nisan · Adar · Shebat · Tabeth · Kislev · Heshvan · Tishri

Neopunic calendar, 1st–3rd century A.D., excavated at Comalcalco Mayan ruins, by archeologists of the Mexican National Institute of Anthropology and History.

Cyrus Gordon's book *Before Columbus* (1971). See also *The Secret* by Joseph B. Mahan (1983).

At the Epigraphic Society's San Francisco Congress in June 1988, Professor Huston McCulloch, Ohio State University, made known the result of an age determination based on Accelerator Mass Spectrometry of a 30 mg wood sample taken from one of the earspools found with the inscribed stone in the Bat Creek mound. The test was performed in Zurich, Switzerland, with the cooperation of the Smithsonian Laboratory of Anthropology and funded by the Institute for the Study of American Cultures. The result showed that the date of the Bat Creek burial is 1605 ± 160 years B.P., thus far earlier than Cyrus Thomas had supposed, and within the range of dates postulated by Professor Gordon's epigraphic analysis.

Details of Professor McCulloch's report can be found in the *Tennessee Anthropologist,* Fall 1988.

Evidence of trans-Atlantic crossings from North Africa to southern Mexico has been uncovered in the excavations at the ancient Mayan city of Comalcalco, located on the coast of Tabasco. Here, on account of the absence of rock formations (as the district comprises muddy lagoons), the only available building material was clay, fired to make bricks. In the 1960s Tulane University made a site survey, in the course of which two of the bricks were found to carry inscriptions. From 1976 to 1978 the archeologist Pancio Salazar carried out excavations under the control of the National Institute of Anthropology and History of Mexico. At that time some 4,000 inscribed bricks were discovered. The Institute, together with some other interested learned bodies, has control of these

Another of the inscribed ceramic tablets excavated at Comalcalco by the Mexican National Institute of Anthropology and History. The Libyan cartouche at upper left reads Yašwa Hamin (Jesus, Protector).

Neil Steede 1988

finds, and after Salazar's death in 1980, Neil Steede, President of the Sociedad de Epigrafia de Mexico, catalogued the collection, and submitted a collection of photographs to me for identification and translation of the inscriptions. Most of the inscribed markings prove to be Mayan glyphs, but a small proportion carry inscriptions in scripts and languages of the Old World. Two examples are shown here, above and on the facing page.

Most notable is a calendar (p. 316) lettered in Neopunic script, the very debased last phase of the Phoenician script that was used at Carthage in Tunisia around the time of Christ and perhaps as late as the 3rd century A.D. The calendar exhibits 12 successive full moons, each of the moons matching 4 subdivisions, evidently weeks of 7 days. The match is not absolute, so that instead of 48 weeks there are 50. Each month, reading from right to left, is designated by a Neopunic letter which is the initial letter of the name of the month. The sequence is such as to show that the calendar is the one used for business and civic affairs, beginning with the month Tishri at the September equinox. I infer that the maker was either a Carthaginian trader or a Mayan pupil who had learned it from a visiting Carthaginian trading ship.

The other tablet selected for mention here is shown above, and was evidently the work of a North African Berber who used the Libyan

Roman amphorae of the 3rd century A.D. brought up from the seabed at Guanabara Bay, Brazil.

alphabet. In ancient times the name Libya was applied to all of North Africa west of Egypt, so the scribe may have come from Morocco, or from as far away as Cyrenaica. He was evidently a Christian for the tablet bears a crude representation of a man who is identified in the Libyan script as Yašwa Hamin, "Jesus, Protector." Perhaps the maker of this inscription was a sailor held in captivity by the Mayans.

Fuller details of these discoveries are given in a series of articles by Steede and by Fell, appearing in volumes of ESOP from 1985 onward. The Catalog by Steede is also available (see Bibliography) but does not contain translations or identifications.

There is much other evidence to support the belief that Roman ships were crossing the Atlantic from Moroccan ports during the third century A.D. Most impressive are the finds of ancient amphorae lying on the seabed and evidently marking the sites of ancient shipwrecks. Punic amphorae were discovered in 1972 off the Caribbean coast of Honduras. Museum officials in Honduras have stated that a permit to investigate the wreck was refused because the Honduran government wished to have no investigation that might be an affront to the reputation of Columbus. Archeologist Robert F. Marx in a series of reports in ESOP (vols. 10, 11, and 14, 1982–1985) has diving investigations on the

Roman coins believed to have been washed ashore from a vessel thought to have sunk around 375 A.D. off the coast of Beverly, Massachusetts.

seabed of Guanabara Bay, 15 miles from Rio de Janeiro, where two
groups of amphorae are lying on underwater reefs. The amphorae have
been dated to the third century A.D. by Dr. Elizabeth Will, Department
of Classics, University of Massachusetts, and she and Dr. Michael Ponsich
both concur that the amphorae were manufactured at the Moroccan port
of Zilis. Permits to investigate the inferred wreck were withdrawn by
the Brazilian authorities after Dr. Harold Edgerton conducted a sonar
survey to locate buried wrecks, and found two likely targets, each
associated with tumbled Roman amphorae. Grounds for denying the
permit were the same as in the case of Honduras, save only that it was
the reputation of the Portuguese navigator Cabral that was considered to
be at stake.

Underwater treasure has been successfully located using clues provided by coins that are washed ashore from sunken wrecks. Examples
are the vessels of the Spanish Armada, now being located and explored
on the Irish coast, and the Spanish treasure ship found off the coast of
Florida. In each case the vessel's whereabouts are disclosed approximately by the fact that the coins washing ashore are all of roughly the
same date—i.e., were in circulation at the time of the wreck. On the
other hand, when isolated coins of widely differing dates are found on
beaches, this merely indicates that random losses have occurred, and the
coins are not coming from a sunken treasure chest.

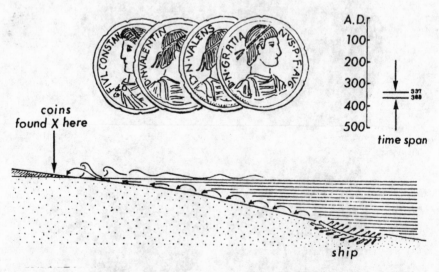

Evidence of this kind tells us that in all probability a Roman wreck
sank around the year 375 A.D. offshore from Beverly, Massachusetts.
All the coins shown on page 319 were found within one square yard of
sand on the beach, with the aid of a metal detector. They comprise

examples only of late fourth century issues, belonging to the reigns of four consecutive emperors. These are Constantius II (337–361 A.D.), Valentinianus I (364–375 A.D.), his younger brother Valens (364–378 A.D.), and Gratianus (367–383 A.D.), the nephew of Valens. As there were 58 emperors of Rome, who issued some 3,000 kinds of coins commonly found in Europe, the chances of a single find-site yielding coins of consecutive rulers spanning only four decades can be estimated as roughly one in 100,000.

Thus the coins are not being found as a result of accidental losses by collectors but are strongly correlated with some factor linked to a short time-span of 337–383 A.D., and linked also to a single very restricted find-site. The only reasonable explanation is that these coins are coming from the money chest of a merchant ship carrying current coin in use around 375 A.D. Over the past 1,600 years the coins have gradually drifted inshore on the bottom current, and are now being thrown up by waves in heavy weather. The coins illustrated on page 319 are now in the collection of James P. Whittall of the Early Sites Research Society.

Desciframiento por Fell del silabario vasco.

THE CREE SYLLABIC ALPHABET.

Related systems of syllabic writing used by the Basques of pre-Roman times and continuing in use into the Middle Ages (left), and a variant form used by the Cree, Ojibway, and other Amerind tribes, as far south as Puerto Rico. Long supposed to be the "invention of missionaries in modern times," in all probability the system was brought to America by Basque navigators.

Evidence of early Basque contacts with America is not new. A century ago the German zoologist Brehm drew attention to the fact that dated specimens and information relating to the North American narwhal occur in European collections dating to pre-Columbian times. Whale products are also referred to in letters from the Vatican addressed to the bishops of Greenland, antedating Columbus. In 1981 I drew attention to the evident match of the so-called Cree syllabary (actually shared by other tribes) and the pre-Roman and medieval Basque inscriptions of Spain. (*Bronze Age America,* 1982). Since then, Professor dos Santos Junior, president of the Portuguese Anthropological and Ethnological Society, and Dr. Imanol Agire, the Basque philologist, have given evidence of the truth of this inference (ESOP vols. 13, 15, 1985–6).

Chapter 13 gives the archeoastronomy of the New England sites so far as we had been able to interpret it up to the year 1976, when the first edition of *America B.C.* was published. The one disappointment had been our inability to discover any Ogam inscriptions that relate to the inferred archeoastronomy. It seemed obvious from the orientations of the chambers, and the plan layout of the stones of the Calendar Circle at Mystery Hill (page 206), that the makers of these structures had one major object in mind, the observation of the sun's motions by which the calendar could be regulated precisely. Yet not a hint of this could be found in any of the Ogam texts we had discovered.

In 1979 there came the first indication that all this was about to change. In that year I received from Gloria Farley in Oklahoma a latex peel of a cave inscription in Ogam letters (page 323) that at first puzzled me, for the letter H, a single stroke above the stemline, was repeated 6 times. The decipherment indicated that the sun is the subject of the inscription, and that a numeral would be appropriate in the place where the six H's occur—and so I made the obvious inference that the number 6 is intended (none of the Irish guides to Ogam had made any reference to numerals). The inscription could now be read as making the statement "The sun is six months in the north, and sinks south for an equal space of months." On December 8, 1980, I wrote to inform Gloria Farley of this reading.

Dr. Jon Polansky, of the San Francisco Chapter of the Epigraphic Society, was visiting Gloria at the time, and when he saw my decipherment he immediately suspected that the cave might be an archeoastronomical site for observing the equinoxes. Visits to the cave at the times of the vernal and autumnal equinoxes showed that the setting sun casts a shadow of a pointed projection of rock onto a series of inscriptions, and that therefore further investigation would be justified.

Meantime other developments were taking place. In March 1982 I was gratified to receive a message from Professor Alexander Thom of

Oxford University, sent to me by his son Dr. A. S. Thom of the University of Glasgow. The letter read, in part, "Having read your book *America B.C.* soon after it was published, and having recently read *Saga America,* I write to express my hope that you will continue with the good work. To my expression of goodwill I add the good wishes of my father, Alexander Thom, Emeritus Professor of Engineering Science, Oxford University. He has a strong fellow feeling for you, in that for decades he has experienced the cold shoulder from archaeologists of the establishment. For years nobody would publish his accurate surveys of stone rings and alignments, nor would they accept his analysis of the geometry of Megalithic man, and his carefully expressed exposition of stone age man's conception of mathematics and astronomy." A few months later I received an invitation from Ida Jane Gallagher and Arnout Hyde, editor of the state magazine of West Virginia, to study some long rock-cut inscriptions of that state which, Ida Jane suggested, appeared to be a form of Ogam.

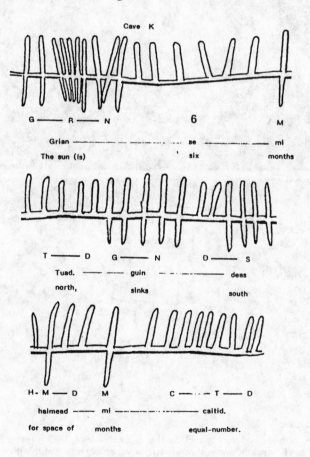

Cave K

| G | R | N | | 6 | | M |

| Grian | | | se | | mi |

| The sun (is) | | six | | months |

| T | D | G | N | D | S |

| Tuad. | | guin | | deas |

| north, | | sinks | | south |

| H - M | D | M | | C | T | D |

| haimead | mi | | caitid. |

| for space of | months | | equal-number. |

Top: The Ogam-inscribed rock panel on the mountain ledge in Wyoming County, West Virginia. The decipherment was made from an enlargement of this photograph. Middle: The same panel as illuminated by the rising sun on Christmas Day, the rays from the left casting shadows of trees on the panel. Below: Related inscription at Horse Creek, deciphered on page 328.

One of the inscriptions was cut on a rock face on a mountain in Wyoming County in West Virginia. According to my decipherment of the photographs of the inscription the text read: "At the time of sunrise a ray grazes the notch on the left side on Christmas Day, a Feast-day of the Church, the first season of the (Christian) year, the season of the blessed Advent of the Savior, Lord Christ (Salvatoris Domini Christi), Behold, He is born of Mary, a woman." If my reading was correct, the statement about the sun should be demonstrably true. So I called Arnout to ask if a party of observers could ascend the mountain on Christmas morning before dawn, to see what happened. On December 25, 1982, seven observers were at the site, and their account of what transpired was published in the March 1983 issue of *Wonderful West Virginia*. At sunrise, as predicted by the inscription, a ray of light penetrated a notch in the rock face and illuminated the sunburst and the left-hand end of the inscription (see page 324).

Thus, as was now for the first time demonstrated, we had identified an Ogam site as serving for calendar regulation at the winter solstice (originally December 25) and, furthermore, had predicted the event that was observed. Yet, in spite of that, some archeologists continued to claim that the Ogam strokes, Chi-Rho signs and all, were merely "random marks made by Indians sharpening their spears."

Six months later, June 6, 1983, Professor Robert Meyer, an authority on Old Irish, and Professor of Celtic Studies at the Catholic University

© Nick Crettier 1988

Professor Robert T. Meyer of the Chair of Celtic Studies at the Catholic University of America.

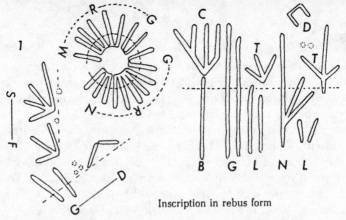

Inscription in rebus form

Converting to a uniform stem line, and supplying vowel points,
the inscription reads:

S-i-ſ g-a-d a-m e-r—i-g g-r-e-n cab gl-e-t D. Natal.

1. At the time of sunrise a ray grazes the notch on the left side on Christmas Day.

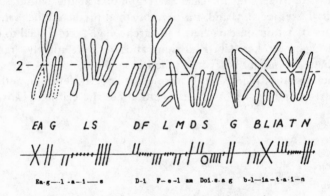

EA G   LS   DF L M D S   G BLIA T N

Ea·g—·l -a--i — s   D-i F--e--l am Doi·e·a g b-l—ia—t-a·i—n

2. A Feast-day of the Church, the first season of the (Christian) year.

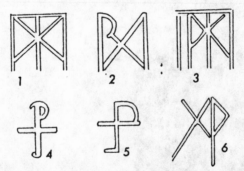

ABOVE, AND OPPOSITE PAGE: Decipherment of the Wyoming County inscription.
Bottom: Examples of Chi-Rho sacred monograms: 1, as on coins of Gratian (367–375): 2, late Anglo-Saxon version as on coins of Wulfred (805–833): 3, matching version at Wyoming site: 4, of Justinian I (527–565): and 5, 6, versions at Wyoming site.

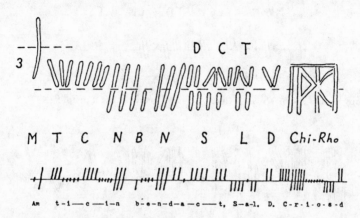

3. The season of the Blessed Advent of the Savior, Lord Christ (Salvatoris Domini Christi).

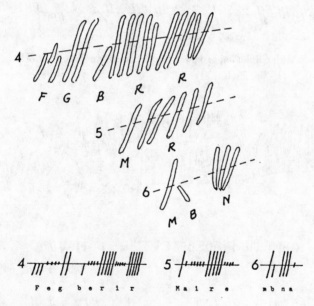

4. Behold, He is born of Mary, a woman.

1

MGN   TLGMIATGEA N BT

Am a-i-g   N-o-t-1-e-g, Am ait g-ea n   b-1-t.

A happy season is Christmas, a time of joy and goodwill to all people

2

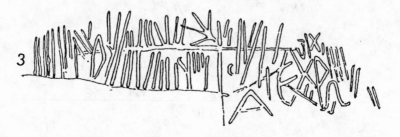

BHGTOI R G   L   G   GBM OIT   C DIA   H FC IO N D

Ba hog·   t-oi—r.a-g   l—e-g   gab m-oi-t-a—c   D ia   ha f—e—c, io-n-ad !

A virgin was with child; God ordained her to conceive and be fruitful. Ah, Behold, a miracle!

3

R GHMC UIHMNMCS BDLCS TUIG   N M OIDIA

A IOS XP Ω AMFL L

R-u-g   h-i m-a-c uihm, a-i- n - m c-o-i-s   B-e-d- 1-1   C-o-s. T-ui-g a-i- n- m oi-d-ea

Alpha Iosa Criosd Omega; am fel e(1)le.

She gave birth to a son in a cave, the name of the cave was the Cave of Bethlehem. His foster-father gave him the name Jesus, the Christ, Alpha and Omega. Festive season of prayer.

of America, climbed to the site in order to study the inscription and, while he and a colleague were there, a television crew from West Virginia Public TV of Morgantown also arrived, so an impromptu interview was broadcast, in which Dr. Meyer confirmed the Ogam and expressed the opinion that it was the work of Irish monks of the sixth century A.D. In subsequent statements and comment in ESOP Dr. Meyer expanded on his confirmation (see ESOP vols. 14 and 15, 1985–6). Professor Linus Brunner of the Chair of Classics at Sankt Gallen also added his confirmation, disputing the claims of others that the markings were marks made by Indians sharpening their spears.

While these events were in progress in West Virginia, there had been more developments at Gloria Farley's 1979 site find in Oklahoma (page 322). She and Jon Polansky had by now been joined by the NASA astronomer Rollin Gillespie and by two other members of the Epigraphic Society, William McGlone and Phillip M. Leonard. In February 1983 I received from Bill McGlone a set of excellent photographs of various other inscriptions in the cave, now known as Anubis Cave from the occurrence there of an Anubis petroglyph recognized as such by Gloria and Dr. Clyde Keeler (ESOP vol. 7, 1979). Gloria herself also sent me latex peels of some of these inscriptions. I was asked to provide whatever decipherments I could make in time for the approaching equinox of that spring, and asked also to send copies for each of about a dozen expected participants in observing the equinoctial phenomena. By March 14, a week before the event, I was able to send the requested translations, the most significant of which appeared to be a text that I translated as "In shade 12 intervals until the day after Balance Day," which I supposed to mean that "In shadow remain the 12 scale divisions until the second day of the March Equinox." On the day after the equinox a telephone call from Oklahoma informed me that six of the group of 12 parallel lines on the cave wall were illuminated on the day before the actual equinox, and that all 12 were illuminated on the following day. It was evident once again that the Ogam text had essentially forecast correctly the astronomical events connected with the equinox, and that here again we had an actual calendar-regulating site from ancient time, still function-ing many centuries later. The various members of the observing team combined to make reports on the circumstances and these, together with my decipherments, were published in ESOP vol. 14 (1985). A film of this subject was later made by Scott Monahan and it has been shown on public television, yet few archeologists appear to be aware of the implications.

North America's oldest towns still occupied are Oraibi, Arizona, and Acoma in New Mexico, built around 1100 A.D. and now the seat of a

OPPOSITE PAGE: Decipherment of the Horse Creek Ogam inscription in West Virginia.

fine pottery tradition maintained by the artist-descendants of the original founders. But equally old is the Viking church tower in Newport, Rhode Island, nowadays misattributed to Governor Benedict Arnold, whereas it is shown on Verrazano's map of 1524, and it was cited by would-be colonists in the time of Queen Elizabeth I as a good reason for settling that district, since the English troops would have an instant refuge should they be attacked. Belief in the authenticity of the Kensington runestone should no longer be withheld, following the extremely detailed analysis of the numerals, the letter forms, and the grammar by the most meticulous Norse scholar yet to have studied it, Dr. Richard Nielsen. Nielsen finds that all the previous objections were based on error and an inadequate knowledge of the rune variants and their occurrence in old Norse manuscripts in Scandinavia. Nielsen's comprehensive studies are to be found in ESOP vols. 15, 16, 17 and are still continuing.

And now, in the closing pages, I should like to address a few words to my readers. Over the past dozen years since *America B.C.* first appeared, there have been, I believe, about eighteen reprints of the book, and I have been honored to receive about twenty thousand letters. The book was also honored by the American Booksellers Association as one of the best books published, 1976, and a copy was presented to the White House library. For these kindnesses I am deeply grateful. But they do not reflect the attitudes and reactions of many professional archeologists. To them the book has apparently been anathema. Students tell me that they are warned not to read it, and they are punished if they cite it in exam papers or theses. Why, one asks, is this so?

Part of the answer may be found in a recent comment by Dr. Catherine Hills, who teaches archeology at Oxford University. "Professional archeologists," she points out, "have been very suspicious of astronomical interpretations, equating an interest in the moon with lunacy." Advocates of ancient astronomy are usually astronomers and mathematicians, and their writings appear obscure to innumerate archeologists who think that whatever they cannot understand must likewise have been incomprehensible to stone-age people. Dr. Hills cites the increasing attention now being given to the work of Alexander Thom and his family which, she says, "has begun to make the subject more respectable." As we have seen (page 323) Professor Thom has

OPPOSITE: Viking church tower at Newport, Rhode Island; although observed and mapped by the Italian navigator Giovanni Verrazano in 1524, modern tradition mistakenly attributes it to Governor Benedict Arnold. Below: Portion of the inscription in Norse runes on the so-called Kensington stone of Minnesota. It reports the misadventures of a party of Norse explorers in the year 1362. Recent studies by Dr. Richard Nielsen completely vindicate the authenticity of this historic document, and dispel charges of fraud raised by earlier writers.

considerably stronger language for describing his experiences at the hands of archeologists.

Another pretended reason offered by archeologists for rejecting belief in ancient visitors to America from the Old World is the alleged total lack of introduced artifacts. In actual fact, not only are the inscriptions in Old World alphabets and languages artifacts (for certainly nature does not produce them) but there are numerous discoveries of man-made objects from abroad: coins, amphorae, lamps, et cetera. And whenever an inscription is incontestably an inscription, then the archeologist in America almost instantly will declare it to be a fraud.

Perhaps the most fundamental reason for the reaction of many archeologists is the widespread human attitude of resistance to change. When the British archeologist Glyn Daniel declared *America B.C.* to be a "rubbish book" he was really saying that the ideas in it did not coincide with his own. This attitude in which ridicule and even personal abuse are employed to reject a new view of American prehistory often redounds to the advantage of the theory that is under attack, for the American reader and television viewer quickly detects when criticism oversteps reason, and he is then more likely to examine the book that is being condemned.

In notable contrast has been the favorable reception given the book by native Amerindian scholars. The Abenaki lexicographer Atian Lolo (Stephen Laurent) has spared no effort to assist in research. Chief Shup She of the Miami-Potawatomi contributes articles and vocabulary to ESOP. Several officers of the Epigraphic Society are affiliated with Indian tribes. Overseas archeologists and linguists have written articles in support of these researches, and the Portuguese Anthropological Society has published translations.

Columbus himself never claimed to be the first to sail across the Atlantic and, were he alive today, he would surely acknowledge the fact that there were also navigators and trailblazers before him. And so, as we approach the five hundredth anniversary of his memorable voyage, it will lend added luster to his name if we remember also the many lesser voyages that occurred through pre-Columbian times, some of them contributing Old World genes and skills to the Amerindian peoples who welcomed them. The latest finds imply that these voyages began over seven thousand years ago when ancient adventurers first explored the sea roads from Norway to Labrador. What new achievements of Stone Age man will the coming years reveal?

Bibliography

General Works

Cook, Warren L. 1987. Epigraphic Society Occasional Publications (ESOP)—A Guide to Volumes 1–15. Epigraphic Society, San Diego.

Fell, Barry (Howard Barraclough). 1976. America B.C. First edition. Quadrangle, New York Times Books, New York.

Fell, Barry. 1981. Kigen Zen no Amerika. So Shi Sha, Tokyo.

Gordon Harold S. 1947. Men Out of Asia. McGraw-Hill, New York.

Gordon, Cyrus H. 1971. Before Columbus: Links Between the Old World and Ancient America. Crown, New York.

Mahan, Joseph B. 1983. The Secret: America in World History Before Columbus. Mahan, Columbus, Georgia.

Schoolcraft, Henry R. 1851. Archaeological evidences that the continent had been visited by people having letters prior to the era of Columbus. Indian Tribes of the United States. Bureau of Indian Affairs, Part 1, pp. 106–08.

Totten, Norman 1981. Archaeology and Epigraphy—Confrontation in America. ESOP vol. 9, part 1, pp. 15–115. Includes comments by opponents and proponents of the epigraphic interpretation of American prehistory. Epigraphic Society, San Diego.

Trento, Salvatore Michael 1978. The Search for Lost America: Mysteries of the Stone Ruins in the United States. Penguin Books, New York.

Earliest Voyages and Transatlantic Contacts ca. B.C. 5000–3000

Morris, Ronald W. B. 1979. The Prehistoric Rock Art of Galloway and the Isle of Man. Blandford, Poole, Dorset.

Morris, Ronald W. B. 1988. The Cup-and-Ring motif in the rock art of the British Isles and in America. ESOP vol. 17, pp. 19–30. Epigraphic Society, San Diego.

Timreck, T. W. 1987. Search for the lost Red Paint People. *Nova* TV program and transcript. WGBH Educational Foundation, Boston.

Megaliths and Stone Circles

Clark, Evelyn 1961. Cornish Fogous. Methuen, London. Deals with subterranean stone chambers.

Dix, Byron E. 1975. An early calendar site in central Vermont. Occasional Publications of the Epigraphic Society, vol. 3, no. 51.

Goodwin, William B. 1946. The remains of greater Ireland in New England. Meador, Boston (attributes Mystery Hill to Culdee monks).

Hencken, Hugh O'Neill 1939. The "Irish Monastery" at North Salem. New England Quarterly, vol. 12 (attributes Mystery Hill structures in part to 19th-century colonial farmer).

Service, Alastair and Jean Bradbery 1981. A Guide to the Megaliths of Europe. Granada, London and New York.

Stone, Robert E. 1975. Mystery Hill Bibliography. NEARA report (unnumbered). Lists 80 references antedating December 1974.

Vincent, Brad 1989. Beaver Island Stone Circle. ESOP vol. 18 (recording data obtained from), Beaver Island Historical Society, St. James, Michigan.

Whittall, James P. II 1975. Precolumbian parallels between Mediterranean and New England archeology. Occasional Publications of the Epigraphic Society, vol. 3, no. 52.

Sumerian Settlers ca. B.C. 2000

Marini, Alberto 1985–1989. A Sumerian Inscription of the Fuente Magna, La Paz, Bolivia. ESOP vols. 13, pp. 9–13; 15, pp. 117–18 (continuing in later volumes). Epigraphic Society, San Diego.

Nordic Bronze Age Traders ca. B.C. 1700

Drier, Roy Ward and Octave Joseph Du Temple 1961, 1965. Prehistoric Copper Mining in the Lake Superior Region. Drier and Du Temple, Calumet, Michigan.

Fell, Barry 1982. Bronze Age America. Little, Brown and Company, Boston and Toronto.

Fell, Barry 1982. The Bohuslän Culture (Bronze Age Norse) in North America. ESOP vol. 10, pp. 17–29. Epigraphic Society, San Diego.

Galster, Jon 1987. Helleristningernes Tale—i Norden og Amerika. Dansk Historisk Håndbogsforlag, Copenhagen.

Rausing, Gad 1977. Bronzealderens Columbus. Skalk no. 1, pp. 9–10. Copenhagen.

Whittall, James P. II 1970. An Unique Dagger. NEARA Newsletter, Dec. 1970.

Wiene, Stig 1989. Did Denmark import Bronze-age copper from North America? ESOP vol. 18 (paper seen in proof). Epigraphic Society, San Diego.

Iberians and Iberic Scripts

Agire, Imanol 1986. La Escritura Vasca. ESOP vol. 15, pp. 206–18. Epigraphic Society, San Diego.

Cardozo, Mario 1965. Citania e Sabroso. Guimaraes, Minho (Excavations in northern Portugal).

Carmody, Francis J. 1969. Iberic Morphology. Carmody, Berkeley, California.

Cejador, Julio 1926. Iberica 2: Alfabeto e inscripciones Iberica. Barcelona.
Cejador, Julio 1928. Iberica 2. Hernando, Madrid (posthumous collection).
de Erro, Juan Bautista 1829. Alphabet of the primitive language of Spain, Butts, Boston. Considers Basque to be the original language of Europe, and gives partly correct key to Iberian script.
Diringer, D. 1968. The Alphabet (distinguishes the Punic, Iberian, and Libyan scripts, hitherto confused by most American collectors).
dos Santos, J. R. 1935. As pinturas pre-historica de Cachao da Rapa. Trans. Soc. Portug. Archeol. vol. 16. Records, but does not recognize bilingual Phoenician-Ogam inscriptions.
dos Santos Junior, Joaquim Rodrigues 1985. Animal Images and Zoolotry. ESOP vol. 13, pp. 109–15. Epigraphic Society, San Diego.
dos Santos Junior, Joaquim Rodrigues 1986. Prehistoric Zoolotry; the Berroes Culture of Tras-os-Montes, Portugal. ESOP vol. 15, pp. 109–12. Epigraphic Society, San Diego.
Fell, Barry 1975. Epigraphy of the Susquehanna steles. Occasional Publications of the Epigraphic Society, vol. 2, no. 43. Basque inscriptions identified by comparison with similar inscriptions in the Tras-os-Montes, Portugal.
Rodriguez, Adriano Vasco 1961. Arqueologia da Peninsula Hispanica. Grafico, Porto, Portugal (deals with Portuguese aspects).

Celts and Celtic Ogam Inscriptions

Anonymous author ca. 1380. Book of Ballymote (in library of Irish Academy).
Barron, David P. 1985. An Ogam Stone from Connecticut, Bulletin vol. 12, no. 1, Early Sites Research Society, Rowley, Massachusetts.
Brash, Richard Rolt 1879. The Ogam Inscribed Monuments of the Gaidhil. Bell and Sons, London.
Caesar, Julius 51 B.C. De Bello Gallico (especially Books III and VI, composed ca. 55–54 B.C.).
Calder, George (editor) 1917. Auraicept na n-eces. Grant, Edinburgh, Scotland.
Casey, Albert E. and Eleanor L. Downey-Prince 1978. Odyssey of the Irish; documented by blood group and craniometric analysis. Alabama Journal of Medical Science, vol. 15, no. 1; reprinted in ESOP vol. 6, Epigraphic Society.
Dawson, Burrell C. 1987—A Gadelic-English Dictionary. ESOP vol. 16, pp. 205–74. 1988—An English-Gadelic Dictionary (part 1) ESOP vol. 17, pp. 220–25. 1989—An English-Gadelic Dictionary (part 2) ESOP vol. 18 continuing).
Fell, Barry 1975. Celtic Iberian inscriptions of New England. Occasional Publications of the Epigraphic Society, vol. 3, no. 50.
Fell, Barry 1976. Takhelne—A Living Celtiberian language of North America. ESOP vol. 4, pp. 168–95; and Part 2—The Radicals. ESOP vol. 7, 1979, pp. 21–42. Epigraphic Society, San Diego.
Fell, Barry 1985. An Ogam bricren inscription to the Horse-Goddess. ESOP vol. 14, pp. 142–47. Epigraphic Society, San Diego.

Fell, Barry 1987. An Ogam Stone from Massachusetts. ESOP vol. 16, pp. 18–19. Epigraphic Society, San Diego.

Fell, Barry and Gloria Farley 1987. First American Poem in Ogam Script. ESOP vol. 16, pp. 96–97. Epigraphic Society, San Diego.

Fell, Barry and John Williams 1975. Inscribed sarsen stones in Vermont. Occasional Publications of the Epigraphic Society, vol. 3, no. 53.

Fell, Barry and James Whittall, Warren W. Dexter 1987. Ogam Consaine in County Tyrone, Castlederg Cromlech revisited. ESOP vol. 16, pp. 301–03. Epigraphic Society, San Diego.

Finn mac Gorman d. 1160. Book of Leinster (in library of University of Dublin).

Gilla-Isa-Mor mac Firbis 1416. Book of Lecan (in library of Irish Academy).

MacAlister, R. A. S. 1972, 1977. The Archaeology of Ireland. pp. 84–88, Beaker Folk considered to be the last invaders of Ireland, hence Celtic, bringing the Gaelic language. Arno Press, New York.

MacAlpine, Neil 1934. Briathradair Gaidhlig gu Beurla, Beurla gu Gaidhlig. Maclaren, Glasgow (Gaelic-English dictionary).

MacBain, Alexander 1911. Etymological Dictionary of the Gaelic Language. MacKay, Stirling, Scotland. Gives Old Gaulish roots.

Meyer, Robert T. 1985–6. West Virginia Inscriptions, ESOP vol. 14, 15. Epigraphic Society, San Diego.

O Conchuir, Doncha 1977. Corca Dhuibhne a Muintir agus a Seadchomharthai (A guide to the prehistory of the Dingle Peninsula). C.FC.D., Tra Li, Ireland.

Rhys, John 1877. Welsh Philology (first distinguishes Q-Celts and P-Celts).

Royal Irish Academy 1983. Compact edition of the Dictionary of the Irish Language based mainly on Old and Middle Irish Materials (numerous contributors); published by the Academy, Dublin.

Rule, Margaret 1985–1986. Media reports on discovery of sunken Celtic trading ship of ca. A.D. 125. Guernsey Archaeological Trust, Guernsey.

Sampson, John and R. A. Stewart MacAlister 1937. The Secret Languages of Ireland. Cambridge University Press.

Phoenician, Hebrew, and Punic Voyages

Bloom, Ernest and Jon Polansky 1979. Translation of the Decalogue Tablet from Ohio. ESOP vol. 8, pp. 15–20. Epigraphic Society, San Diego.

Cline, Donald 1982. The Los Lunas Stone. ESOP vol. 10, pp. 68–73. Epigraphic Society, San Diego.

Cross, F. M. 1968. The Phoenician inscription from Brazil, a 19th century forgery. Orientalia 37 (so claims, but Gordon refutes this in Orientalia, 37).

Fell, Barry 1975. An Iberian-Punic stele of Hanno. Occasional Publications of the Epigraphic Society, vol. 2, no. 44.

Fell, Barry 1985. Ancient Punctuation and the Los Lunas Text. ESOP vol. 13, pp. 35–41. Epigraphic Society, San Diego.

Fell, Barry and Erik Reinert 1975. Iberian Inscriptions in Paraguay. Occasional Publications of the Epigraphic Society, vol. 2, no. 43.

Gordon, Cyrus 1968. The Canaanite text from Brazil. Orientalia, 37.

Gordon, Cyrus 1971. Before Columbus. Crown, New York.

Gordon, Cyrus 1974. Riddles in History. Crown, New York.

Hoffman, Curtiss 1988. Dating of Bat Creek Burial leads to Surprising Conclusion. Newsletter, vol. 14, no. 2. Massachusetts Archaeological Society, Attleboro, Massachusetts.

Leonard, Phillip M. and William R. McGlone 1988. An epigraphic hoax on trial in New Mexico. ESOP vol. 17, pp. 206–19. Epigraphic Society, San Diego.

Mahan, Joseph B. 1988. Bat Creek Stone Dated. ISAC Report vol. 2, no. 3. Institute for the Study of American Cultures, Columbus, Georgia.

McCulloch, J. Huston 1989. The Bat Creek Inscription: Cherokee or Hebrew? Tennessee Anthropologist, Fall 1988. Tennessee Anthropological Association, Knoxville, Tennessee.

Morehouse, George E. 1985. The Los Lunas Inscriptions—A Geological Study. ESOP vol. 13, pp. 44–49. Epigraphic Society, San Diego.

Moscati, Sabatino 1965. The world of the Phoenicians. Praeger, New York.

O'Leary, de Lacy 1923. Comparative Grammar of the Semitic languages. Kegan Paul, London.

Peckham, Brian J. 1968. The development of the late Phoenician scripts. Harvard University Press, Cambridge, Mass.

Ramos, B. H. da Silva 1939. Inscripciones da America prehistorica. Amazonas, Manaos, Brazil (includes Paraiba decipherment).

Russell, Frank 1908. The Pima Indians. Ann. Rpt. Bureau American Ethnology, 26, Washington, D.C. (includes creation chant).

Stieglitz, Robert 1974. An ancient Judaean inscription from Tennessee. New World Antiquity, vol. 21, Brighton, England.

Stieglitz, Robert R. 1976. An Ancient Judean Inscription from Tennessee. ESOP vol. 3, no. 65. Epigraphic Society, Arlington, Massachusetts, and San Diego.

Stonebraker, Jay 1982. A Decipherment of the Los Lunas Decalogue Inscription. ESOP vol. 10, pp. 74–81. Epigraphic Society, San Diego.

Underwood, L. Lyle 1982. The Los Lunas Inscription. ESOP vol. 10, pp. 57–67. Epigraphic Society, San Diego.

Wehr, Hans 1971. Dictionary of written Arabic. Spoken Languages, Ithaca, New York.

Roman Voyages and Shipwrecks A.D. 225–375

Edgerton, Harold E. and Robert F. Marx 1982. Roman Amphoras discovered near Rio de Janeiro (*The New York Times,* cited in ESOP vol. 10, pp. 30–31).

Marx, Robert F. 1983. Did a Roman Ship Reach Brazil in Antiquity? ESOP vol. 11, pp. 14–21. Epigraphic Society, San Diego.

Marx, Robert F. 1984. Ancient Amphorae found in Brazil. Oceans, vol. 17, pp. 18–21. Oceanic Society, San Francisco.

Marx, Robert F. and Harold Edgerton 1985. Amphoras on the Brazilian Continental Shelf. ESOP vol. 14, pp. 132–33. Epigraphic Society, San Diego.

Comalcalco ca. A.D. 250

Fell, Barry 1984. Inscribed Bricks from Comalcalco, Mexico. ESOP vol. 14, pp. 118–25. Epigraphic Society, San Diego.

Fell, Barry 1988. A Christian North African Inscription from Comalcalco. ESOP vol. 17, pp. 283–84. Epigraphic Society, San Diego.

Fell, Barry 1988. A Punic Calendar from Comalcalco. ESOP vol. 17, pp. 284–86. Epigraphic Society, San Diego.

Steede, Neil 1984. Catalogo Preliminar de los tabiques de Comalcalco. Centro de Investigacion precolombina, Cardenas, Tabasco, Mexico.

Steede, Neil 1985. Comalcalco, the Brick City of the Mayas; Excavating the Inscribed Bricks. ESOP vol. 14, pp. 116–18. Epigraphic Society, San Diego.

Steede, Neil 1988. Inscribed Bricks from Comalcalco. ESOP vol. 17, pp. 276–82. Epigraphic Society, San Diego.

Christian Celtic Voyages to America A.D. 565–1170

Chapman, Paul H. 1973. The Man Who Led Columbus to America (Saint Brendan). Judson, Atlanta, Georgia.

Evans, Estyn 1966. Prehistoric and Early Christian Ireland. Batsford, London.

Fell, Barry, Arnout Hyde, Jr., Robert L. Pyle and Ida Jane Gallagher 1983. Wyoming and Boone County Petroglyphs Translated. Wonderful West Virginia, vol. 47, no. 1, pp. 2–19. Department of Natural Resources, Charleston, West Virginia. Same article also appears in ESOP vol. 11, part 1, pp. 23–53, 1983. Epigraphic Society, San Diego.

Jones, Tristan 1979. Madoc—A persistent legend. ESOP vol. 6, no. 132. Epigraphic Society (believed to have landed at Mobile Bay, Alabama, A.D. 1170).

Meyer, Robert T. 1985–1986. West Virginia petroglyphs are genuine archaic Old Irish. ESOP vols. 14, p. 108; 15, pp. 44–45. Epigraphic Society, San Diego.

Arab and Libyan Contacts in the Southwest ca. A.D. 800–1200

Fell, Barry 1976. A Triangular Stele from Cuenca. NEARA, vol. 10, no. 3.

Fell, Barry 1979. The Islamic Inscriptions of America. ESOP vol. 8, pp. 57–76. Epigraphic Society, San Diego.

Gladwin, Harold S. 1957. A history of the ancient southwest. Wheelwright, Portland, Maine.

Norman, Stanley 1958. Zuni Dictionary. International Journal of American Linguistics, vol. 24, no. 1. Bloomington, Indiana (omits sacred words, and comparative etymology).

Rickey, Don J., Jr. 1978. Potential relationship of two Southwestern pre-Columbian inscription petroglyph sites with some Bronze Age fertility concepts. Ed. Warren L. Cook. Ancient Vermont, pp. 50–56. Castleton State College, Vermont.

Rickey, Don J., Jr. 1979. Two Southwestern Petroglyph Sites. ESOP vol. 6, no. 138. Epigraphic Society, San Diego.

Norse Voyages and Settlements A.D. 982–1448

Anderson, Rasmus Bjørn 1906. The Vatican Manuscripts concerning the Church in America before the time of Columbus. Norroena Society, New York.

Anderson, W. R. 1989. Pre-Columbian Greenland Settlements. ESOP vol. 18.

Chapman, Paul H. 1981. The Norse Discovery of America. One Candle Press, Atlanta, Georgia.

Heywood, J. C. 1893. Documenta Selecta. Vatican Press; very rare, but reproduced in the Catholic Historical Review, 1917–1918, pp. 210–27, as "almost a complete series of authenticated sources for the history of Norse christianity in America before Columbus." See Anderson, W. R. 1989, ESOP, Epigraphic Society, San Diego.

Holand, Hjalmar R. 1940, 1968. Norse Discoveries and Explorations in America 982–1362. Dover, New York.

Keeler, Clyde 1985. The Newport Round Church. ESOP vol. 13, pp. 175–79. Epigraphic Society, San Diego.

Nicholas V, Pope 1448. Venerabilibus fratribus Shaoltensi et Olensi. Letter in the Latin tongue addressed to the Bishops of Norway, concerning the reported destruction of Greenland Christian churches by the attacks of pagan invaders from the neighboring shores (of Labrador). Vatican Archives.

Nielsen, Richard 1986–1988. The Kensington Runestone. ESOP vols. 15, 16, 17. Epigraphic Society, San Diego.

Pohl, Frederick J. 1974. Prince Henry Sinclair. Davis-Poynter, London.

Strandwold, Olaf 1948. Norse inscriptions on American stones. Björndal, Weehawken, New Jersey (attributes all American inscriptions to Norse visitors).

West African Voyages A.D. 1250–1311

Van Sertima, Ivan 1976. They Came Before Columbus: The African Presence in Ancient America. Random House, New York.

Van Sertima, Ivan (editor) 1987. African Presence in Early America. Journal of African Civilizations, vol. 8, no. 2. Africana Studies Department, Rutgers University, New Brunswick, New Jersey.

Archeoastronomy

Farley, Gloria 1985. The Anubis Caves. ESOP vol. 14. Epigraphic Society, San Diego.

Farley, Gloria 1985. Mythology of the Petroglyphs of the Anubis Caves. ESOP vol. 14. Epigraphic Society, San Diego.

Farley, Gloria 1985. The Anubis Caves: Oklahoma's ancient equinox site. ESOP vol. 14. Epigraphic Society, San Diego.

Farley, Gloria and Clyde Keeler 1979. Anubis in Oklahoma. ESOP vol. 7, pp. 225–31. Epigraphic Society, San Diego.

Fell, Barry 1979. A cartouche of Shishonq from Almunecar, Southern Spain. ESOP vol. 7, p. 233, and Libyan Anubis in Southern Spain, *ibid.* p. 235. Epigraphic Society, San Diego.

Fell, Barry 1979. An ancient Zodiac from Inyo, California. ESOP vol. 8, pp. 9–14. Epigraphic Society, San Diego.

Fell, Barry 1986. Parietal Inscriptions of the Anubis Caves. ESOP vol. 14. Epigraphic Society, San Diego.

Hills, Catherine 1986. The Blood of the British. George Philip, London.

Keeler, Clyde 1985. The Anubis Panel—Mythological Themes and Considerations. ESOP vol. 14. Epigraphic Society, San Diego.

McGlone, William R. and Phillip M. Leonard 1986. Ancient Celtic America. Panorama West Books, Fresno, California.

Monahan, Scott 1985. History on the Rocks. Video cassette dealing with Anubis Cave (see page 329) originally made for Public Television. ESOP vol. 14, p. 91.

Rommel, Sentiel 1975. Maui's Tanawa—a Torquetum of 232 B.C. Occasional Publications of the Epigraphic Society, vol. 2, no. 29.

Micmac, Abenaki, and Egyptian

Fell, Barry 1979. The Micmac Manuscripts. ESOP vol. 7, pp. 146–50. Epigraphic Society, San Diego.

Fell, Barry 1979. The Micmac Manuscripts—2. ESOP vol. 7, pp. 167–81. Epigraphic Society, San Diego.

Fell, Barry 1985. Ogam-inscribed stone pendants from Nova Scotia. ESOP vol. 14, pp. 140–41. Epigraphic Society, San Diego.

Gardner, Alan 1973. Egyptian Grammar. Oxford University Press.

Kauder, Christian (Rev.) 1866. Sapeoig Oigatigen tan tetli Gomgoetjoigasigel etc. Vienna (in hieroglyphs).

Kauder, Christian (Rev.) circa 1866. Letter to Eugene Vitromile. Cited by Vitromile, *vide infra.*

Lolo, Sozep (Joseph Laurent, Chief of the Abenakis). 1884. Abenakis and English Dialogues. Quebec.

Maillard, Pierre, l'Abbé (b. 1735–d. 1762). Collected hieroglyphic manuscripts, edited by Kauder as so-called *Vienna Plates.* Vienna, Austria.

Maillard, Pierre, l'Abbé (1921). Second (Ristigouche) edition of his hieroglyphic text, issued as Sapeoig Oigategen tan tetli Gomgoetjoigasigel.

Pacifique, F. (O. M. Cap.) 1921. Avant-propos (to previous item). Ristigouche, P. Q.

Rand, Silas T. 1902. Micmac Dictionary. Charlottetown, P.E.I.

Rasles, (Father) Sebastien S.J. (d. 1724). Manuscript of *Dictionnaire,* begun in the year 1691, for the language of the Abenakis of the Kennebec River area, Maine. Now in Harvard University Library.

Rasles, Sebastian (sic). 1834. A Dictionary of the Abnaki Language in North America. Ed. John Pickering. Mem. Amer. Acad. Arts Sci., XV, pp. 370–594.

Trumbull, James H. 1903. Natick Dictionary. Bulletin no. 25, Bureau of American Ethnology. Washington, D.C. (reconstructs pre-colonial Algonquian dialect, largely from John Eliot's Bible).

Vetromile, Eugene (Rev). 1866. The Lord's Prayer in Micmac Hieroglyphs. 1 sheet included in next item at p. 43.

Vetromile, Eugene (Rev). 1866. The Abnakis. New York.

Unpublished Letters and Manuscripts

Copies of these documents have been deposited in the Archives Section of the Widener Library, Harvard University, under reference Fell, H. B.

Brunner, Linus II Sept. 1975. Letter to Fell on New England's Celtic Bronze Age. also 24 Jul. 1975. Letter to Norman Totten.

Goodwin, William B. 16 Jan. 1937. Letter to Hencken on Upton beehive structure.

Goodwin, William B. 18 Jan. 1937. Postscript to prec., on Cornish aspects.

Hencken, H. O'Neill 13 Jan. 1937. Letter to Goodwin on Upton beehive structure.

Lethbridge, Thomas C. 8 May 1954. Letter to Vilhjalmur Stefansson on Celtic stone houses and related matters.

Lethbridge, Thomas C. 5 Jun. 1954. Letter to Vilhjalmur Stefansson reporting that British farmers do not store root crops in stone chambers.

Morrison, Hugh 30 Apr. 1954. Letter to Malcolm Pearson reporting that, in his capacity as professor of architecture, and specialist on Colonial architecture, he is about 95% certain that the North Salem stone structures cannot be the work of Colonial or 19th-century builders.

Movius, Hallam L. Jr. 15 Jul. 1937. Letter to Goodwin on proposed role of Peabody Museum, Harvard, in financing excavations at Mystery Hill.

Stefansson, Vilhjalmur 15 Feb. 1954. Letter to J. H. Beardsley on stone houses in Canadian Arctic, resembling New England archeological ruins, which he thinks may be Celtic.

Stefansson, Vilhjalmur 6 Mar. 1954. Paper circulated to Early Sites Research Society members on early Scandinavian settlements in Arctic.

Stefansson, Vilhjalmur 19 Apr. 1954. Letter to Robert A. McKennan on possible Phoenician provenance of the North Salem–Upton stone structures.

Stone, Robert E. and Krueger, Harold W. 1967–1971. File of 12 documents reporting carbon-dates for samples from Mystery Hill excavations at North Salem, New Hampshire.

Strong, W. A. and W. W. Strong n.d. Glossary of American Phoenician. A 10-page holograph manuscript on lettering found on Susquehanna stones.

Index